Illuminating the
NEW TESTAMENT

Illuminating the NEW TESTAMENT

THE Gospels, Acts, AND Paul

GERALD O'COLLINS, SJ

Paulist Press
New York / Mahwah, NJ

Unless noted otherwise, the Scripture quotations contained herein are from the New Revised Standard Version: Catholic Edition, Copyright © 1989 and 1993, by the Division of Christian Education of the National Council of the Churches of Christ in the United States of America. Used by permission. All rights reserved.

Cover image by Netfalls Remy Musser / Shutterstock.com
Cover and book design by Lynn Else

Copyright © 2022 by Gerald O'Collins

All rights reserved. No part of this publication may be reproduced, stored in a retrieval system, or transmitted in any form or by any means, electronic, mechanical, photocopying, recording, scanning, or otherwise, without either the prior written permission of the Publisher, or authorization through payment of the appropriate per-copy fee to the Copyright Clearance Center, Inc., www.copyright.com. Requests to the Publisher for permission should be addressed to the Permissions Department, Paulist Press, permissions@paulistpress.com.

Library of Congress Cataloging-in-Publication Data
Names: O'Collins, Gerald, author.
Title: Illuminating the New Testament : the Gospels, Acts, and Paul / Gerald O'Collins, SJ.
Description: New York / Mahwah, NJ : Paulist Press, [2022] | Includes bibliographical references and index. | Summary: "A collection of eighteen essays on the Gospels, Acts, and the letters of Paul, written throughout Gerald O'Collins' distinguished career"—Provided by publisher.
Identifiers: LCCN 2021023948 (print) | LCCN 2021023949 (ebook) | ISBN 9780809155835 (paperback) | ISBN 9781587689840 (ebook)
Subjects: LCSH: Bible. Gospels—Criticism, interpretation, etc. | Bible. Acts—Criticism, interpretation, etc. | Bible. Epistles of Paul—Criticism, interpretation, etc. | LCGFT: Essays.
Classification: LCC BS2361.3 .O26 2022 (print) | LCC BS2361.3 (ebook) | DDC 225.6—dc23
LC record available at https://lccn.loc.gov/2021023948
LC ebook record available at https://lccn.loc.gov/2021023949

ISBN 978-0-8091-5583-5 (paperback)
ISBN 978-1-58768-984-0 (e-book)

Published by Paulist Press
997 Macarthur Boulevard
Mahwah, New Jersey 07430
www.paulistpress.com

Printed and bound in the
United States of America

CONTENTS

Preface vii

Acknowledgments and Further Essays xiii

I. THE GOSPELS 1

1. From the Weather to Mustard Seeds: Jesus's Farming Images (Matt 10:29–31; 12:11; 13:31–32; 16:1–4) 3

2. Peter's Mother-in-Law: More to Be Said (Mark 1:29–31) 10

3. Unshrunk Cloth and New Wineskins (Mark 2:21–22 parr.) 18

4. Did Joseph of Arimathea Exist and Bury Jesus? (Mark 15:42–47) 26

5. The Terrified Silence of Three Women (Mark 16:8) 35

6. Thomas Torrance and Mark 16:19–20: The Ascended Christ's Prophetic Role 44

7. Mary and Simeon (Luke 1:38; 2:29) 54

8. The Nativity in View of the Cross and Resurrection (Luke 2:1–20) 61

9. Peter as Neglected Witness to Easter (Luke 24:34; 1 Cor 15:5) 73

10. Did Jesus Eat the Fish? (Luke 24:42–43) 94

11. Mary Magdalene as Major Witness to Jesus's Resurrection (John 20:11–18) 106

12. "His Life Rose with Him": John 21 and the Resurrection of Jesus ... 119

Contents

II. ACTS OF THE APOSTLES 137

13. Buried by His Enemies? (Acts 13:28–31) 139

III. PAUL'S LETTERS 147

14. The Language of Reconciliation (Rom 5:8–11; 2 Cor 5:18–21) .. 149
15. Love as a Verb (1 Cor 13:4–8a) 159
16. The Appearances of the Risen Christ (1 Cor 15:5–8) 165
17. "Power Made Perfect in Weakness" (2 Cor 12:9–10) 181
18. Power in Weakness: The Fate of a First Love (2 Cor 12:9–10) 191

Epilogue 203

Notes 205

Index of Names 259

Biblical Index 265

PREFACE

After receiving a PhD at the University of Cambridge in 1968, for five years I expounded the letters of St. Paul and taught fundamental theology as well. From 1973, departmental requirements meant confining myself to lectures in fundamental and systematic theology. Nevertheless, both those disciplines call for serious engagement with the Bible. There can be no genuine theological understanding where there is no love for the Scriptures. Moreover, dealing as it does with foundational issues, fundamental theology calls for an examination of the inspiration, truth, authority, and interpretation of the Bible. That resulted in my writing book chapters on those themes and, eventually, *Inspiration: Towards a Christian Interpretation of Biblical Inspiration* (Oxford: Oxford University Press, 2018).

Moreover, along the way I coauthored with my deceased friend, Daniel Kendall, SJ, *The Bible for Theology* (Mahwah, NJ: Paulist Press, 1997) and some articles for *Biblica, Catholic Biblical Quarterly, Gregorianum*, and other scholarly journals. After retiring from full-time teaching in 2001, I enjoyed more freedom to return, every now and then, to my first love, the inspired Scriptures. As the Italian proverb states, "*Il primo amore non si scorda mai*" (One's first love never comes apart).

This book gathers together eighteen articles I have written (and mostly published) on the four Gospels, the Acts of the Apostles, and the letters of St. Paul. Two of them (chs. 4 and 11) were originally coauthored with Daniel Kendall, SJ, and one (ch. 14) with T. Michael McNulty, SJ. In bringing the discussion up to date, the articles have been at least retouched and sometimes substantially rewritten.

Chapter 1 examines four farming images drawn by Jesus from forecasting the weather, selling sparrows, caring for animals (or a child), and cultivating mustard seeds (Matt 10:29–31; 12:11; 13:31–32; 16:1–4; parallels in other Gospels; hereafter parr.). Jesus proclaimed the divine kingdom through images coming from the natural world and the experience of farmers and much less through images coming from what he apparently did as a carpenter and builder (*tektōn*).

Chapter 2 moves to the cure of Peter's mother-in-law (Mark 1:29–31 parr.) and illustrates how commentaries at times miss some of its theological and spiritual richness. She is the first woman to be mentioned by Mark; she stands out as the only person in that Gospel who is cured by Jesus and then does something for him. The language of raising and serving used in the account of the cure will be taken up again in Mark's closing verses—an inclusion that also involves her. Thus with Peter (Mark 1:16–18; 16:7), she holds the narrative together. The service that women offer Jesus brackets the entire Gospel (Mark 1:31; 15:40–41).

Chapter 3 takes up two miniparables found in Mark 2:21–22 parr. and drawn from practices for mending torn clothes and storing new wine. The images derive from Jesus's own experience of life in ancient Galilee. They suggest how, in the light of God's kingdom, he appreciated such experiences and gave them a place in his teaching.

Chapter 4 tackles the historicity of the story of Jesus's burial (Mark 15:42–47 parr.) and its rejection by John Dominic Crossan. The chapter concludes that Crossan did nothing to undermine the story's credibility, which remains accepted by very many biblical scholars from Rudolf Bultmann to Joseph A. Fitzmyer and beyond to Joel Marcus.

Chapter 5 aims at reinstating an older interpretation (offered, e.g., by R. H. Lightfoot) of the astonishment, fear, and silent flight with which three women responded to the angel's message of Jesus's resurrection (Mark 16:8). Far from being a failure on their part, the response reacted appropriately to the astonishing revelation of the resurrection. Mary Magdalene and her two companions remained silent until they could deliver news of the resurrection to the right audience, the male disciples.

Chapter 6 retrieves the account of the ascension developed by Thomas F. Torrance—a picture of Christ as king/shepherd, priest, and *prophet* enthroned "at the right hand of God." To illuminate the prophetic activity of the risen and ascended Christ, Torrance appealed, in particular, to Mark 16:19–20. Unlike some exegetes who tend to water down the meaning of these verses, Torrance had a clear sense of Christ prophetically "working with" his missionaries and "confirming with signs" their proclamation.

Preface

Chapter 7 documents how Raymond Brown, François Bovon, Robert Tannehill, and other scholars have thrown light on the annunciation to Mary (Luke 1:26–38) by linking it back to Gabriel's announcement to Zechariah. But the meeting between Mary and Gabriel, above all her response (Luke 1:38), can also be fruitfully compared to details in her meeting with Simeon (e.g., Luke 2:29). Multiple associations between Mary and Simeon enrich the narrative and hold it together.

Chapter 8 notes how, in Luke's Gospel, the Last Supper closed a life that had begun with a birth outside the shelter of a public *kataluma* (2:7) and moved through a ministry that included a story involving a good Samaritan, an inn, and a good innkeeper (10:25–37). Jesus's life ended with a celebration in a Jerusalem guest room (called a *kataluma* in 22:11). "Doing this in memory of me" can also be understood as an invitation to show the hospitality that had failed at the birth of Jesus, was inculcated by the parable of the Good Samaritan, and supremely exemplified by Jesus the Good Innkeeper in an upper room of Jerusalem.

"The Lord has risen indeed, and he has appeared to Simon" (Luke 24:34). Chapter 9 illustrates how the role of Simon Peter as the official witness to the resurrection of Jesus Christ has been neglected even by such scholars as Martin Hengel, Christian Grappe, and Rudolf Pesch. Luke (in both his Gospel and Acts), Mark, John, and Paul offer grounds for interpreting Peter's primary (but not exclusive) role in emerging Christianity as that of spreading and gathering the Christian community through the power of his Easter message.

Chapter 10 argues that the fish-eating motif (Luke 24:42–43) expresses three things: the bodily reality of the risen Jesus; the qualifications of the apostles as witnesses; and the ongoing liturgical presence of the Lord. Possibly the passage is also intended to communicate a sense of forgiveness and reconciliation. The main thrusts of the motif are apologetic (concerning the living Jesus himself), apostolic (concerning the normative witnesses to the resurrection), and sacramental (concerning the eucharistic life of the community). Luke does not want his readers to imagine that the risen Lord quite literally consumed (and digested) some fish before the astonished eyes of his disciples. The Christ who had already entered into his glory (Luke 24:26) was beyond all that.

Chapter 11 recognizes that the postresurrection appearances of the risen Christ are not as such the *object* of Easter faith but rather the primary historical *catalyst* of such faith. Nevertheless, 1 Corinthians 15:5–8 illustrates the importance of the appearance tradition. In this tradition women, especially Mary Magdalene, have a lead role. Above all in John 20, Mary Magdalene is the human figure who holds the events together.

Chapter 12 illustrates how, in the final Easter episode (John 21), the history of Jesus as portrayed in the Fourth Gospel—not least his relationship with Peter and with the Beloved Disciple and his role as the Light and Life of the world—rose with him. The questioning style of Jesus and the love exhibited and inculcated by him also rose again in that resurrection narrative. Further themes from the history of Jesus, such as meals, the Eucharist, martyrdom, testimony, and truth find their risen place in John 21.

Chapter 13 moves from the Gospels to the Acts of the Apostles. Paul's address in Pisidian Antioch, as presented by Luke (Acts 13:28-31), seems at odds with what the evangelist has already written in Luke 23:50-56. It attributes to those responsible for Jesus's crucifixion his deposition from the cross and burial in a tomb. François Bovon has argued that "Jews hostile to Jesus and not a friendly Joseph of Arimathea buried the crucified one. The tradition [in Acts 13] must be older and historically more reliable than the data of the Gospels."[1] Pace Bovon, his comment ignores the generalizing usage of the plural. Concerned more with actions than with the precise agents, Acts attributes to a vague "they" not only Jesus's condemnation and crucifixion but also his deposition from the cross and burial. These four actions correspond exactly to actions found in Luke's passion narrative. Rather than recalling an older, historical tradition, the verses in Acts form a Lukan, kerygmatic summary. It contrasts the divine reversal of resurrection with the human condemnation that brought Jesus to his death and burial.

Chapter 14 examines the concept of reconciliation (*katallagē*) that Paul introduced to describe God's work of salvation in Christ (Rom 5:8-11 and 2 Cor 5:18-21). Translating these and further passages into English and commenting on them call for sensitivity to nuances and possibilities in the extended use of language. "Reconcile" and "reconciliation" have to do with (a) the acceptance of situations and facts; (b) the removal of contradictions and incompatibilities; and (c) putting aside enmity and conflict.

Chapter 15, the first of four chapters that focus more exclusively on Paul's Corinthian correspondence, examines sixteen verbs (active in meaning and in the present tense) used in 1 Corinthians 13:4-8a to express positive and negative characteristics of *agapē* (love). This choice of verbs contrasts Paul's hymn to love with other passages where he

Preface

describes love but not through an exclusive use of verbs (e.g., Rom 12:9–21). Some commentators note the apostle's use of verbs in 1 Corinthians 13, but without discussing reasons for the choice. Other commentators, including Wolfgang Schrage, do not even observe the presence of the sixteen verbs. I argue that, for Paul, love consists not so much in a set of habitual characteristics but in doing (or refraining from doing) certain things. One might even say that love exists in action or it does not exist at all.

Chapter 16 tackles the challenge of translating the language for the Easter appearances found in 1 Corinthians 15:5–8 and elsewhere in the New Testament. It then examines what can be said about the nature of these Christophanies. It proposes that the language used by the New Testament witnesses suggests some perception with the eyes, albeit a "graced" seeing on the part of those witnesses.

Chapter 17, originally published in 1971, expounded the heart of 2 Corinthians 12:9–10: the risen Christ reassures Paul that his power reaches its perfection right in the apostle's experience of weakness, even when a mysterious thorn in the flesh has affected Paul's situation. The divine coming with power brings an epiphany of this powerful presence. The apostle's "boasting" discloses to others what is victoriously at work in his sufferings. Christ's grace, defined here as power, is effective in Paul's "weakness" and hence can be revealed.

Chapter 18 examines the ways in which my exposition of 2 Corinthians 12:9–10 was endorsed by later scholars or else rejected or misunderstood. In particular, the chapter attends to major commentaries on 2 Corinthians. As well as updating scholarly discussion of these verses, the chapter illustrates the effective history and reception of my article.

An epilogue retrieves and classifies themes expounded by my chapters on Matthew (ch. 1), Mark (chs. 2—6), Luke (chs. 7—10), John (chs. 11—12), Acts (ch. 13), and Paul (chs. 14—18).

When quoting the Bible, I normally follow the New Revised Standard Version (NRSV) but occasionally prefer my own translation. I use the terminology of the Old Testament, rather than the Tanakh or Hebrew Bible. Here "old" is understood as good and does not imply "supersessionism," the view that the New Testament has simply rendered obsolete the Old Testament and so superseded it.

This book is dedicated to the memory of Professor Charles Moule. His New Testament seminar at the University of Cambridge trained and nurtured a love of the Scriptures in me and my fellow research students

Illuminating the NEW TESTAMENT

(David Catchpole, James Dunn, Harold W. Hoehner, Graham Stanton, Frances Young, and many others). For help in writing and publishing this book, my warm thanks go to Brendan Byrne, Daniel Kendall, Sean Kenny, T. Michael McNulty, and an anonymous friend at the University of Stanford, as well as to Enrique Aguilar, Donna Crilly, and others at Paulist Press.

Jesuit Theological College,
175 Royal Parade, Parkville, Victoria 3052, Australia

ACKNOWLEDGMENTS AND FURTHER ESSAYS

While recognizing that many texts that fed into the chapters in this book have now been altered, sometimes quite substantially, I wish to acknowledge and thank the journals in which they originally appeared: chapter 2 (*Australian Biblical Review*, 2020), chapter 3 (*Expository Times*, 2020), chapter 4 (*Biblica*, 1994), chapter 5 (*Gregorianum*, 1988), chapter 6 (*Scottish Journal of Theology*, 2021), chapter 7 (*Expository Times*, 2020), chapter 8 (*The Way*, 2020), chapter 9 (*Theological Studies*, 2012), chapter 10 (*Gregorianum*, 1988), chapter 11 (*Theological Studies*, 1987), chapter 12 (*Irish Theological Quarterly*, 2019), chapter 13 (*Expository Times*, 2019), chapter 14 (*Colloquium*, 1972), chapter 15 (*Expository Times*, 2020), chapter 16 (*Irish Theological Quarterly*, 2014), and chapter 17 (*Catholic Biblical Quarterly*, 1971). For articles that originally appeared in the *Expository Times*, *Irish Theological Quarterly*, and *Theological Studies*, I want to thank Sage Publications.

Chapters 4 and 11 were originally coauthored with Daniel Kendall, while chapter 14 was originally coauthored with T. Michael McNulty.

Further Essays

"Anti-Semitism in the Gospel," *Theological Studies* 26 (1965): 663–66.

"Is the Resurrection an Historical Event?" *Heythrop Journal* 8 (1967): 381–87.

"Jesus the Martyr," *New Blackfriars* 56 (1975): 373–75.

"Jesus between Poetry and Philosophy," *New Blackfriars* 57 (1976): 53–62.

"The Crucifixion," *Doctrine and Life* 26 (1976): 247–63.

"Jesus' Concept of His Own Death," *The Way* 18 (1978): 212–23.

"Peter as Easter Witness," *Heythrop Journal* 20 (1981): 1–18.

"Christ's Resurrection as Mystery of Love," *Heythrop Journal* 25 (1984): 39–50.

"Luminous Appearances of the Risen Christ," *Catholic Biblical Quarterly* 46 (1984): 247–54.

"Jesus," in *The Encyclopedia of Religion*, vol. 8, ed. Mircea Eliade (New York: Macmillan, 1987), 15–28.

With Daniel Kendall, "The Uniqueness of the Easter Appearances," *Catholic Biblical Quarterly* 54 (1992): 287–307.

"Crucifixion," in *Anchor Bible Dictionary*, vol. 1, ed. David N. Freedman (New York: Doubleday, 1992), 1207–10.

"Salvation," in Freedman, *Anchor Bible Dictionary*, vol. 5, 907–14.

With Daniel Kendall, "The Faith of Jesus," *Theological Studies* 53 (1992): 402–23.

With Daniel Kendall, "Christ's Resurrection and the Aorist Passive of *egeirō*," *Gregorianum* 74 (1993): 725–35.

"Luke on the Closing of the Easter Appearances," in *Luke and Acts*, ed. G. O'Collins and Gilberto Marconi, trans. Matthew J. O'Connell (Mahwah, NJ: Paulist Press, 1993), 161–66.

With Daniel Kendall, "On Reissuing Venturini," *Gregorianum* 75 (1994): 153–75.

"Did Apostolic Continuity Ever Start? Origins of Apostolic Continuity in the New Testament," *Louvain Studies* 21 (1996): 138–52.

"Images of Jesus and Modern Theology," in *Images of Christ Ancient and Modern*, ed. Stanley E. Porter et al. (Sheffield, UK: Sheffield Academic Press, 1997), 128–43.

Acknowledgments and Further Essays

"Jesus Christ the Liberator: In the Context of Human Progress," *Studia Missionalia* 47 (1998): 21–35.

Review of Larry W. Hurtado, *Lord Jesus Christ: Devotion to Jesus in Early Christianity* (Grand Rapids: Eerdmans, 2003) in *Biblica* 86 (2005): 283–87.

"The Virginal Conception and Its Meanings," *New Blackfriars* 89 (2008): 431–40.

"The Hidden Story of Jesus," *New Blackfriars* 89 (2008): 710–14.

"In Praise of Paul," in *In Praise of Paul*, ed. Michael A. Hayes (London: St. Paul's Publications, 2008), 17–26.

"The Origins and Scope of Biblical Spirituality," in *The Bloomsbury Guide to Christian Spirituality*, ed. Richard Woods and Peter Tyler (London: Bloomsbury, 2012), 20–29.

"Word, Spirit, and Wisdom in the Universe: A Biblical and Theological Reflection," in *Incarnation: On the Scope and Depth of Christology*, ed. Niels Gregersen (Minneapolis: Fortress Press, 2015), 59–77.

"Collaborators of the Apostles and the Reform of the Roman Curia," *Irish Theological Quarterly* 82 (2017): 185–96.

"The Church in the General Epistles," in *The Oxford Handbook of Ecclesiology*, ed. Paul Avis (Oxford: Oxford University Press, 2018), 147–60.

Review of Enrique Aguilar, ed., *The Paulist Biblical Commentary* (Mahwah, NJ: Paulist Press, 2018) in *Theological Studies* 80 (2019): 214–16.

"The Faith of Jesus: Translating Hebrews 12:2a," *Expository Times* 132 (2021): 387–93.

I
THE GOSPELS

1

FROM THE WEATHER TO MUSTARD SEEDS

Jesus's Farming Images
(Matt 10:29-31; 12:11; 13:31-32; 16:1-4)

The Gospel of Mark recalls the people of Nazareth identifying Jesus as "the carpenter/builder [*tektōn*]" (6:3 au. trans.). Matthew repeats but modifies this identification by having Jesus called "the son of the *tektōn*" (13:55 au. trans.).[1] Yet the pictures that Jesus used in his preaching hardly suggest an imagination shaped by the activity of contemporary carpenters and builders. The Gospels contain, to be sure, a few items concerned with building practices that may derive from Jesus: for instance, safe foundations for constructing houses (Matt 7:24–27 parr.), and correct calculations about the cost of erecting a tower (Luke 14:28–30). Q, a source of Jesus's sayings shared by Matthew and Luke, refers to a *zugos* (Matt 11:29–30 parr.) or "frame used to control working animals or, in the case of humans, to expedite the bearing of burdens."[2] Presumably carpenters had a hand in fashioning such frames. We might have expected more of such images associated with carpentry and building from a first-century Galilean *tektōn*, but they remain largely absent in Jesus's preaching.

Sean Freyne wrote of the parables of Jesus (and further gospel material) as both "the product of a religious imagination that is deeply grounded in the world of nature and the human struggle with it, and at the same time deeply rooted in the traditions of Israel which speak of God as creator of heaven and earth and all that is in them."³ "Deeply grounded in the world of nature and the human struggle with it" might be summarized as "shaped by farming."

Both in his parables and elsewhere, agriculture and the care of cattle seem to have entered the imagination of Jesus and helped to shape the flow of his preaching.

This chapter samples farming images used by Jesus, examining, in particular, forecasting the weather, the sale of sparrows, the care of animals, and the planting of mustard seeds. A longer account could take up, for example, what Jesus said about figs and fertilizers, hens with their chickens, wild birds, foxes, snakes, scorpions, goats, camels, fruit trees and their produce, cultivating and harvesting vines, fishing, caring for sheep, Gentiles feeding pigs on carob pods, testing up to five yoke of oxen, using sickles for harvesting grain, the challenges to crops posed by weeds, thorns, rocky soil and birds, and bumper harvests that could result from good seed, well-prepared soil, and the right weather. But let us limit ourselves to four examples to (a) see whether and how they justify Freyne's statement about the religious imagination of Jesus, and (b) suggest a reason for Jesus's preference in images.

Forecasting the Weather

In the ancient world, as also today, travelers and farmers rely on ways of forecasting the weather. Farmers, in particular, want to know what the weather will be like when they cultivate the soil and plant or harvest barley, wheat, and other crops—not to mention harvesting (or planting) olives, grapes, figs, and other fruit trees. Agricultural societies are deeply affected by the weather and are constantly concerned with predicting what it will be like.

Luke reports Jesus to have said to the crowds, "When you see a cloud rising in the west, you immediately say, 'It is going to rain hard [*ombros*],' and so it happens. And when you see the south wind [*notos*] blowing, you say: 'There will be scorching heat [*kausōn*],' and so it happens. You hypocrites! You know how to interpret the appearance of earth and sky, but why do you not know how to interpret the present time?" (12:54–56; NRSV corrected).⁴

Matthew has Pharisees and Sadducees testing Jesus by asking him "to show them a sign from heaven." Jesus answered them by saying,

"[When it is evening, you say, 'It will be fair weather, for the sky is red.' And in the morning, 'It will be stormy today, for the sky is red and threatening.' You know how to interpret the appearance of the sky, but you cannot interpret the signs of the times.] An evil and adulterous generation asks for a sign, but no sign will be given to it except the sign of Jonah" (16:1–4).[5]

Both evangelists probably draw on Q, their common source for the sayings of Jesus. Matthew, as François Bovon points out, "contrasts the evening with the morning, fair weather with stormy weather, and one red sky with another.[6] Luke, on the other hand, makes a distinction between clouds coming from the west and the hot wind from the south, and between [heavy] rain and scorching heat."[7] Matthew denounces "an evil and adulterous generation," whereas Luke speaks of "hypocrites."

Nevertheless, despite the different meteorological descriptions and differences in form, the lessons drawn in both cases converge.[8] Everyone can predict the future, if they attend to and discern the meaning of what faces them. Without using the language of "creation" (or "nature") and "history," Jesus called on his audience to look at and discern not only creation but also the events of history—specifically what was happening through his mission. They should open their eyes to "the present time" or "the signs of the time"; in his ministry, the final rule of God was breaking into our world. If they were so good at predicting the weather, why did they remain blind to their own time and its history?

The Sale of Sparrows

A second image, which likewise had a particular resonance for those who lived on the land or in country villages, concerned the sale of sparrows, "the poultry of the poor" and "by far the cheapest birds" on the market.[9] In Matthew's version, "are not two sparrows sold for a penny [*assarion*]? Yet not one of them will fall to the ground apart from your Father. And even the hairs of your head are all counted. So do not be afraid; you are of more value than many sparrows" (10:29–31). Luke has five sparrows for two *assaria* in his version of what he also draws from the common source of Jesus's sayings: "Are not five sparrows sold for two pennies? Yet not one of them is forgotten in God's sight. But even the hairs of your head are all counted. Do not be afraid; you are of more value than many sparrows" (12:6–7).

THE GOSPELS

Despite the difference of price between Matthew and Luke, the central idea remains the same. Many sparrows could be bought with not too much money. "Although the sparrow is cheap, 'you,' by contrast, are worth a [very] great deal."[10] Matthew's version (when it speaks about not "falling to the ground apart from your Father") hints at God being all-powerful and exercising the divine power for creatures that are utterly small and cheap. Luke's version (when it speaks about not being "forgotten in God's sight") uses a typical anthropomorphism that turns up in the Psalms (e.g., 9:12; 74:19, 23) and pictures God as being all-knowing, always "in the know."[11] In reconstructing the saying's original form in Q, Bovon suggests trusting "Luke's figures" but following "Matthew's wording (with hesitation concerning the word 'Father,' which is so Matthean)."[12]

If the Matthean version represents more accurately Q and behind it the original saying from Jesus, the power of God is to the fore. Apart from the divine will, not even "a single sparrow" would "become a hunter's prey."[13] A fortiori, the providential care of God extends to human beings, who—as is humorously stated—are more valuable than innumerable sparrows.

A similar sense of the divine providence that cares for the slightest details of human life is also evoked through the brief, parenthetic example: God even cares about a single hair on our heads, something that forms "a very insignificant part of the entire person."[14] This parenthetic image also seems to derive ultimately from Jesus himself. The whole saying in both Matthew and Luke, by returning at the end to trade in sparrows, points once again to the outdoor setting of hunting and marketing: "do not be afraid; you are of more value than many sparrows."

Caring for Animals and a Child

Ancient disputes over Sabbath observance are reflected by Jesus's words in Luke 14:5: "If one of you has a son or an ox that has fallen into a well, will you not immediately pull it out on a sabbath day?" (NRSV corrected).[15] While he refrains from pronouncing on the question of the sparrows saying deriving from Jesus himself, Bovon is quite assured when he comes to Luke 14:5: "In this verse we have the oldest saying preserved in Luke, one known to Matthew as well, one that must have been pronounced by the historical Jesus." Matthew 12:11 reads, "Suppose one of you has only one sheep and it falls into a pit on the sabbath; will you not lay hold of it and lift it out?" Bovon argues that "while Matthew 12:11 and Luke 14:5 transmit the same saying of Jesus, they do not rely on the same Greek source, since the wording is divergent throughout. Instead, they furnish us with two independent translations of the same saying." He lists the stylistic and narrative divergences that support this judgment. But the saying from Jesus, albeit in two forms, has the same message: on the Sabbath's day a human being and even an animal should be saved.[16] Jesus fashioned this image of rescuing animals (and also human beings) on the Sabbath from what he had experienced in a rural environment.

Luke draws on Jesus to offer two cases, a son or an ox who has fallen into a well. By "mentioning a father who rushes to help his son, Luke makes a particularly intense relationship come alive before our eyes." As "the one who gave life to his son," the father would now "do everything in his power to pull his son out of the well….In that respect he resembles both God the Creator, who gives life to his children, and God the Redeemer, who preserves them."[17]

Instead of picturing an emergency situation that could occur on the Sabbath—an animal or even a young boy falling into a well or a pit—in Luke 13:15 Jesus speaks rather of livestock being regularly untied and led out of their stalls every day (including the Sabbath) to be given water. In ancient Galilee that was the daily practice of peasant farmers, and Jesus held that they were perfectly justified in doing so, even on the Sabbath.[18]

The Parable of the Mustard Seed

Recalling the modern history of interpretation, Bovon judges that most commentators have considered the parable of the mustard seed (Luke 13:18–19), along with that of a woman mixing leaven in flour (Luke 13:20–21), "to be authentic and to provide access to the Master's thought."[19] The version in Mark (which stands alone and is not paired with the parable of the leaven) brings out a contrast left unstated in Luke: "with what can we compare the kingdom of God, or what parable will we use for it? It is like a mustard seed, which, when sown upon the ground, is the smallest of all the seeds on earth; yet when it is sown it grows up and becomes the greatest of all shrubs, and puts forth large branches, so that the birds of the air can take shelter [*kataskēnoun*] in its shade" (Mark 4:30–32; NRSV corrected).[20] It is from Mark that Matthew takes and includes "the smallest of all seeds" growing to become "the greatest of shrubs": "the kingdom of heaven is a like a mustard seed that someone took and sowed in his field; it is the smallest of all the seeds, but when it has grown, it is the greatest of shrubs and becomes a tree, so that the birds of the air come and take shelter in its branches" (Matt 13:31–32; NRSV corrected).

Jesus used parables to announce and explain his message and activity in the service of the kingdom of God. Elsewhere he introduced mustard seed to encourage at least a minimum of faith: "If you have faith the size of a mustard seed, you will say to this mountain, 'Move from here to there,' and it will move; and nothing will be impossible for you" (Matt 17:20). In the parable of the mustard seed, Jesus directed attention to something he had seen in the world of nature. The proverbially tiny mustard seed can grow into "one of the largest vegetable plants,"[21] a small tree in which birds shelter. Very modest beginnings can be followed by extraordinary outcomes; the mysterious but active presence of the kingdom of God will bring marvelous growth. To quote Bovon, "in a small but nevertheless real fashion, [Jesus] introduced into our world and our history the reign of God, which…by a miracle of God alone, was going to be transformed into a glorious, powerful, and universal reign."[22]

Ezekiel had used the image of a cosmic tree, specified as a lofty and beautiful cedar of Lebanon in which birds made their nests, to depict Assyria's original greatness and power. Assyria was destroyed in several battles between 614 and 609, like such a mighty tree being cut down and the life it once sheltered being scattered (Ezek 31:1–18; see Dan 4:10–15). Earlier in Ezekiel "the proud cedar is used as an image for the future restoration of the kingdom of Israel" (Ezek 17:22–24). Thus "the real surprise of the parable" is that Jesus took his image "not from the mountains of Lebanon but from the vegetable garden" and that he spoke "not of the largest tree but of the smallest seed." An inconspicuous beginning will have unexpected results.[23] From his rural environment Jesus used his experience of mustard trees to convey the message of a divine kingdom: it will grow from tiny beginnings to a nesting place for innumerable people.

Conclusion

The four examples of images chosen by Jesus leave us with this question: When proclaiming the kingdom of God, why did he prefer to draw his images, not from his own activity as carpenter and builder, but from the natural world of his rural environment? The former source highlighted what human beings do (in building houses, constructing towers, and fashioning yokes); the latter source highlighted the mysterious but very real, creative, and re-creative power of God.

Jesus's proclamation of God's present and coming kingdom stressed the priority of the divine action. Jesus could convey that message more effectively through images drawn from the natural world and the experience of the farming community rather than through images that came from his own work as a carpenter and builder.

Hence Jesus chose to take his language from the rural environment and speak of God at work in the weather of "the present time," of the divine providence that extends even to the smallest creatures, of the divine love that does not exclude the real needs of human beings and livestock even on the Sabbath day, and of the extraordinary activity of God that produces astonishing outcomes even from the most inconspicuous beginnings.

Some scholars decline to make any such claims about the experiences and choices of the historical Jesus. But this is to ignore the way in which the Gospels, by preserving some authentic sayings of Jesus, do allow us to draw some modest, yet important, conclusions about how Jesus thought and decided. Not knowing much about his mindset is not the equivalent of knowing nothing at all.

2

PETER'S MOTHER-IN-LAW

More to Be Said (Mark 1:29-31)

The Gospel of Mark dedicates only three verses to the healing of Peter's mother-in-law, but these verses have much to say and imply. Examining, comparing, and contrasting some commentaries on Mark can bring out the theological and spiritual richness to be found here. But it may also reveal how experts sometimes pass over significant items. Let me sample works by M. Eugene Boring, John R. Donahue (with Daniel J. Harrington), Camille Foçant, Morna Hooker, Joel Marcus, Francis J. Moloney, and Dennis Nineham.

Dennis Nineham

When commenting on Peter's mother-in-law being cured from fever, Nineham has much to say, albeit in less than two pages. He opens by remarking that immediately prior to this cure, "the messianic power of Jesus" dealt with "a case of demonic possession. Now we learn that it can also deal with other forms of sickness."[1] To deliver from possession, "the power of Jesus worked through a word; here there is an action—*he took her by the hand and lifted her up*—but no word is reported."

Nineham moves on to discuss whether Mark received the story of her healing directly from Peter, points out the "impression of a cure performed effortlessly," and suggests that the reference to her serving

Peter's Mother-In-Law

"them" (Jesus, Peter, and three other disciples) presumably means at table. The immediate service illustrates "the completeness of the cure" and "its miraculous speed." Apropos of the last comment, Nineham cites an apposite remark from St. Jerome: "The human constitution is such that after fever our bodies are rather tired, but when the Lord bestows health, restoration is immediate and complete."[2]

Like other commentators I have consulted, Nineham fails to say that Peter's mother-in-law is the first woman mentioned in Mark. Two other Gospels also report her cure (Matt 8:14–15; Luke 4:38–39), but, by that stage, they have recalled numerous women, notably Mary in their infancy narratives. But it is the mother-in-law of Peter, not Tamar (Matt 1:3), Elizabeth (Luke 1:5), or anyone else who is the first woman to appear in Mark's Gospel. Mark will refer later to other women: Jesus's mother Mary (3:31–35; 6:3); Jairus's daughter and the woman who touches Jesus's garment (5:21–43); a Syro-Phoenician woman (7:24–30); a widow who makes an offering in the temple (12:41–44); another woman left anonymous who anoints the feet of Jesus in the house of Simon the leper (14:3–9); and then numerous women, both named and anonymous, who attend Jesus's death and burial and were the first to learn of his resurrection (15:40—16:8)—not to mention Herodias and her daughter, who are directly responsible for the murder of John the Baptist (6:14–29) and the anonymous "servant-girl of the high priest" who identifies Peter as a follower of Jesus (14:66–69).[3] The mother-in-law of Peter enjoys particular significance through being the first woman to make an appearance in Mark's narrative.[4] While observing that the healing of Peter's mother-in-law "is the first account of the healing of a woman by Jesus in Mark," Susan Miller neglects to mention that she is the first woman *tout court* to be mentioned by Mark.[5]

Nineham and other commentators also fail to note that Peter's mother-in-law stands out as the *only person* in Mark's Gospel who, after being cured by Jesus, does something for Jesus.[6] At table she serves him and others (specifically, her son-in-law and three other disciples), with her service apparently mentioned as an appropriate response to being healed by Jesus. There may also be overtones of "victory over evil" being celebrated with messianic feasting (see Isa 35:6–8). In Mark 2:18–20, Jesus will "describe his mission as a time of feasting."[7]

Nineham also remains silent about the significance and associations of the precise verb used of Peter's mother-in-law: "*diēkonei autois* (she began to serve them)." The same verb has already appeared when, in his brief account of Jesus's temptation, the evangelist ends by saying that "the angels served him" (Mark 1:12–13 au. trans.).[8] It will recur when Jesus declares that "the Son of Man has come not to be served but to serve, and to give his life as a ransom for many" (Mark 10:45). After Jesus has given his life on Calvary, we read of the presence at the crucifixion of Mary Magdalene and two other named women who "used to follow him and serve him when he was in Galilee; and there were many other women who had come up with him to Jerusalem" (Mark 15:40–41 au. trans.). Nineham has nothing to say about the use of "serve" in these other contexts.[9]

Yet, as Donahue and Harrington observe, "Peter's mother-in-law embodies and foreshadows the ideal of discipleship as service of others which Jesus will address to all the disciples." Through their ambitious request, James and John (Mark 10:35, 41), who have been present at the healing of Peter's mother-in-law (Mark 1:29), prompt Jesus into insisting that "the greatest among them should be their servant (*diakonos* [10:35–45, at 43])—an ideal Jesus himself incarnates (10:45)."[10]

Boring points out how "serve" resonates with "overtones of Christian ministry." The same verb will be used of Paul's "co-ministers, Timothy and Erastus" (Acts 19:22) and in Romans 15:25 of "Paul's own ministry." Thus "in ministering to Jesus and the disciples, this woman who has been healed and raised by Jesus performs a ministry" that anticipates and is "analogous to later pastoral ministry."[11]

Before leaving Nineham, we should observe that he does not comment on the verb *egeirō* (raise up), which will be used of the resurrection of people (12:26) and of Jesus (14:28; 16:6; see also, apropos of John the Baptist, 6:14, 16). The same verb will appear in the healing of a paralytic (2:9, 11) and of a man with a withered hand (3:3); in the resuscitation of Jairus's daughter (5:41); in the cure of an epileptic boy who had "become like a corpse" and seemed dead (9:26–27); and in the healing of blind Bartimaeus (10:49). Nineham does mention that, in speaking of Jesus's raising up Peter's mother-in-law, the Gospel introduces "a conventional Talmudic expression" meaning to "cure" or "heal." Hence the action of Jesus can make us think of "various healings by rabbis in the Talmudic literature."[12] But this historical, extratextual comment neglects the subsequent and richly suggestive usage of *egeirō* within the narrative of Mark's Gospel itself.

Camille Foçant

In *The Gospel according to Mark: A Commentary*, Foçant notices the rich cargo of meaning carried by the verbs "serve" and "raise up." At the first level, the service of Peter's mother-in-law agrees quite simply "with the rules of hospitality." But her service not only recalls the angels serving Jesus in the wilderness but also anticipates "a rare but important theme" that turns up later in Mark.[13] Foçant refers to the service of female disciples in Galilee (Mark 15:41), and leaves it at that.

After citing all the verses in Mark that feature "raise up" (listed above), Foçant describes the action of Jesus in raising up Peter's mother-in-law as "a symbolic theme whose harmonies will be developed in what follows." He does not press on to describe these "harmonies" that are to be developed. He does, however, dwell on a significant word order when, in the original Greek, Mark says that Jesus "raised her up, seizing her by the hand" (*ēgeiren* [main verb] *autēn kratēsas* [aorist participle] *tēs cheiros*). Nineham has played down this significance by reversing the order of the two verbs found in the Greek text. He produces a translation that respects the normal chronological order we might expect: "he took her by the hand and lifted her up."[14] Foçant notes, however, "In adopting the reverse presentation, Mark emphasizes the verb *egeirō*."[15] That lends, subsequently, more emphasis to the ways in which the evangelist will later use "raise up." We return below to that subsequent usage.

Francis Moloney

Francis Moloney does not seem alert to this "reverse presentation" when he observes that "the miracle unfolds as a classical healing narrative: problem, request,[16] touch, miracle, demonstration."[17] In the text itself the sequence is rather problem, (implicit) request, miracle, touch, and demonstration. But the heading Moloney provides for Mark 1:29–31 ("Jesus vanquishes sickness and taboo") shows that he is interested rather in Jesus seeming to break taboos by touching a woman and letting her serve him, as well as violating the Sabbath by performing a healing. He "could well be accused of contracting uncleanness and violating the Sabbath."[18]

But breaking such taboos seems more to the fore when Jesus touches a leper (Mark 1:41) and when a woman with permanent hemorrhages touches Jesus's clothing (Mark 5:25–34). The healing of Peter's mother-in-law takes place not in the public setting of these two miracles but in the home of two friends, Peter and Andrew, to which Jesus will return (Mark 2:1). As for violating the Sabbath, that issue moves center stage later: in the healing of a disabled person on the Sabbath and in a very public place, a synagogue (Mark 3:1–6). Apropos of Jesus taking the hand of Peter's mother-in-law, Moloney's doctoral supervisor, Morna Hooker, far from thinking of a taboo being broken, remarks that "as so often in healings of this kind in Mark, he [Jesus] heals through physical contact with the patient." Jesus touches "patients" (Mark 1:41; 5:41; 6:5; 7:32–33; 8:22–25) or is touched by them (Mark 3:10; 5:27–31; 6:56). Hooker thus connects the healing of Peter's mother-in-law with other such miracles in Mark's Gospel and introduces it with the title "Jesus heals a friend."[19]

Some may consider it slightly optimistic to call Peter's mother-in-law "a friend," at least at this point in the narrative. But certainly she is related to disciples who are already Jesus's close friends, Simon Peter and his brother Andrew. Hooker's choice of title implicitly recalls that, in Mark's Gospel, Peter's mother-in-law is the only person healed by Jesus with whom he already has or will come to have a personal relationship. All the others cured by him are strangers, who are brought to him (e.g., the paralytic in Mark 2:1–12), who have sought him out (e.g., the woman in Mark 5:24–34), who find themselves in his presence (e.g., the epileptic boy in Mark 9:14–29), or whose cure is requested by someone who went looking for Jesus (the daughter of the Syro-Phoenician woman in Mark 7:24–30). The only, partial exception is Bartimaeus, who after being cured becomes a follower of Jesus "on the way" (Mark 10:46–52). Prior to being healed, Bartimaeus does not enjoy a personal relationship to Jesus. He has evidently heard about Jesus, but that is all.

Judgments vary. But it seems to me that the healing of Peter's mother-in-law enjoys richer and clearer significance in ways not mentioned by Moloney (or Hooker). The first woman to be mentioned in Mark's Gospel and the only person healed by Jesus who then "serves" him, she helps produce an *inclusio*, as we shall see, with Mark 15:40—16:8.[20] The story of her healing uses the language of "raising up" and "serving," which play important roles in Mark's narrative. Moloney says nothing about the verb *egeirō*, which makes its first appearance in Mark through the healing of Peter's mother-in-law, and refers only briefly in a footnote to a "discipleship of service."[21]

Joel Marcus

When expounding "the symbolic significance for Mark's readers," Joel Marcus appreciates the relevance of the phrase in Greek "about Jesus grasping the woman's hand" coming "*after* 'he raised her.'" "This unusual position may be designed to concentrate attention" not on a taboo being broken (Moloney), but "on the charismatic power of Jesus' touch, which Mark elsewhere emphasizes" (see also Hooker[22]). But Marcus considers "even more significant the verb used to describe Jesus lifting the woman from her sickbed, *ēgeiren* ('he raised'); the same verb is used in the story of the resuscitation of a dead girl in 5:41–42." This verb, Marcus believes, "would probably also have reminded Mark's readers of the general resurrection of the dead (12:26) and of Jesus' resurrection in particular." Thus Mark "probably wishes to imply" that the "raising power" revealed "in Jesus' healing miracles was the same eschatological power by which God later resurrected him from death."[23] Thus Marcus spells out what Foçant merely refers to as "a symbolic theme whose harmonies will be developed in what follows."

Marcus also goes beyond Foçant by commenting that the verb employed to report the service at table offered by the healed woman "was used to describe the angels' support of Jesus during his testing by Satan" (Mark 1:13). The "ministry of Peter's mother-in-law" "literally mirrors that of the angels and anticipates that of Jesus himself (Mark 10:45)."[24] Marcus might have added that her "serving" Jesus also anticipates what three named women and, seemingly, also "many [other] women" do in Galilee before they go up to Jerusalem and witness the crucifixion (Mark 15:40–41).

Presenting Mark's place "in Christian life and thought," Marcus includes a discussion of links between Mark and Paul.[25] Tentatively one might add to those links Peter's mother-in-law prefiguring Christian baptism. After being raised from a life-threatening sickness, she at once dedicates herself to serving Christ and others. Paul describes baptism as sharing in Christ's death and resurrection, so that we might "walk in newness of life" (Rom 6:3–4; see 6:1–23).[26] The account of the healing of Peter's mother-in-law as "being raised" and then "serving" seems analogous to the vision of baptism presented by Paul. With the baptized she shares a death/life experience and then behaves like a baptized person committed to a discipleship of service.

Sensitive to hints of "women's domestic servitude,"[27] Deborah Krause challenges those—including such feminists as Luise Schottroff, Elisabeth Schüssler Fiorenza, and Mary Ann Tolbert—who understand Peter's mother-in-law to exemplify early Christian discipleship. I believe the majority to be correct here. Without entering into the full debate, I find various items in Krause's argument less than convincing. Let me mention one detail; she states that "the references to *diakoneō* in Mark 1:31 and 15:41 are different."[28] Of course, they are partly different in their contexts: the verb refers in the first context to what an individual did at a specific family meal in Galilee and in the second context to what a large group, now present at a crucifixion, had been doing (also in Galilee) over a period of time prior to this tragic execution. But it would be quite gratuitous to allege that "these and other references" to this verb—it would be preferable to speak of usages of this verb—are totally different in meaning. Schüssler Fiorenza and others correctly hold some consistency and overlap in the usage and meaning of *diakonein* in Mark.[29]

Summing Up

This sampling of comments by eight biblical scholars on the story of the healing of Peter's mother-in-law pays respect, I hope, to their valuable observations, as well as introducing some additions and corrections that appear necessary.

What seems a little surprising is, first, that none of the eight alerts readers to the fact that, in Mark's Gospel, Peter's mother-in-law is the first woman to make an appearance and the only person cured by Jesus who then does something for him.[30] One might have expected Adela Yarbro Collins to have noted these two points but she fails to do so. All she does is refer to Krause's chapter as "a nuanced feminist reading" of the cure of Peter's mother-in-law.[31] Second, the language of "raising" and "serving," used in the account of the mother-in-law's healing and then, in a reverse order, of "serving" and "raising," at the close of this Gospel (15:41 and 16:6), encourages us—along with other data—to recognize a certain *inclusio* between the opening and ending of Mark.[32] At the outset in Galilee, a woman who is Peter's mother-in-law and lives in (and

Peter's Mother-In-Law

presides over?) his house is "raised" and then begins to "serve" Jesus and four of his male disciples. At the end, her action is recalled by the women who, after following and "serving" Jesus in Galilee, then came to Jerusalem and were present at his crucifixion; three of them were the first to know of his being raised. Peter's mother-in-law may even have been one of those women courageously there on Calvary (among the "many other women" of Mark 15:41). Peter failed to turn up at Calvary. It would be supremely ironical if his mother-in-law was there.

Many commentators rightly recognize how Peter, the leading disciple, who is called in Galilee (Mark 1:18–19), features in an *inclusio*. Richard Bauckham has recognized that, and gone further by presenting, albeit not exclusively, "the Petrine perspective" of the entire Gospel of Mark. Peter's call is quickly followed by the healing of his mother-in-law in the very house in Galilee where he lives and over which she seems to preside. The main eyewitness in Mark's Gospel, he is then the last disciple to be named and, in fact, named in connection with Galilee (Mark 16:7).[33]

But along with an *inclusio* in which Peter is central, we can also recognize an enlarged *inclusio* in which his mother-in-law also figures. This accentuates rather than reduces the rich significance of the healing narrative in which we meet her (Mark 1:29–31). The enlarged *inclusio* (between Mark 1 and 16) includes Jesus, Peter, an act of "raising" from a deadly situation, an anonymous mother-in-law/other anonymous women, the context of Galilee, and the service of Jesus (and others).

What then should be added to all that we might glean from existing commentaries on Mark's account of the healing of Peter's mother-in-law? First, her significance is announced through being the *first woman* mentioned by Mark, who identifies her not by name but through her relationship to the leading disciple, her son-in-law Simon Peter. Second, she stands out as the *only person* in that Gospel (with the possible exception of Bartimaeus), who is cured by Jesus and then does something for him. The unnamed woman in Mark 14:3–9 performs a very significant action for Jesus, by anointing him in advance of his burial. But she does this without his having healed her.[34] Third, the language of "raising" and "serving" used in the account of the cure of Peter's mother-in-law, along with its location (in the Galilean house of Peter and Andrew, who have just been called to become disciples), locates her in the initial material that will be taken up again in Mark's closing verses. Any *inclusio* involving Peter brings in, rather than excludes, his mother-in-law.

3

UNSHRUNK CLOTH AND NEW WINESKINS

(Mark 2:21-22 parr.)

No one sews a piece of unshrunk cloth on an old [*palaion*] cloth; otherwise, the patch pulls away from it, the new [*kainon*] from the old, and a worse tear is made. And no one puts new [*neon*] wine into old [*palaious*] wineskins; otherwise the wine will burst the skins, and the wine is lost, and so are the skins, but one puts new [*neon*] wine into new [*kainous*] wineskins. (Mark 2:21-22)[1]

After a conflict story that turns on the forgiveness of sins (Mark 2:1-12) and a second conflict story involving eating with sinners (Mark 2:13-17), Mark's Gospel reaches a further conflict story concerned with different practices of fasting that distinguish the Pharisees, the followers of John the Baptist, and the disciples of Jesus (Mark 2:18-22). Whatever the provenance of the first three verses (vv. 18-20), the two verses that follow (vv. 21-22) seem to have circulated independently in the early Christian tradition.

Eugene Boring recognizes two parables in Mark 2:21-22; Dennis Nineham calls them "little parables."[2] We might add that, together with the brief parables about Jesus as the physician come to heal sinners (Mark 2:17) and as the bridegroom at his wedding (Mark 2:19-20), these are the first parables in Mark's Gospel. They introduce language about familiar figures (a physician or a bridegroom) or activities (involving new and old cloth and new and old wineskins) to evoke insight into realities that go beyond the literal level (the identity of Jesus and the new power of God's final kingdom). These parables use common experiences (of medical visits, weddings, mending torn clothes, and storing wine that is still fermenting) as analogies with something uniquely new: the coming of the divine kingdom in and through Jesus. Apropos of the parallel passage about torn cloth and new wine in Matthew 9:16–17, Ulrich Luz writes, "Jesus speaks in two basic parabolic sayings of the incompatibility of the old and the new."[3]

As does Luke 5:36 in a parallel version of the cloth and wine sayings ("he spoke a parable to them"), Francis Moloney acknowledges in Mark 2:21–22 only one parable, albeit one featuring "a gradual progression." Moloney comments, "The image of unshrunk cloth being used to patch an old garment focuses upon the subsequent damage done to the old garment if the newer cloth is sown to it. The patch tears away, and the old garment is left in an even more damaged state." It is "the [partial surely?] destruction of the older garment that is the point." With the image of the new wine, however, the focus is "upon the need to preserve the new wine. Such new wine poured into less pliant, old wineskins will destroy" *the wineskins and the wine*. An image of further damage leads on to an image of total destruction (of the wineskins) and complete loss (of the wine).[4]

Exegetes tend to agree with Moloney that the language about the cloth and wineskins "existed independently in the pre-Markan tradition."[5] Eduard Schweizer allows that Mark 2:21–22 "may be words of Jesus."[6] Marcus considers this attribution to Jesus "plausible."[7] Yarbro Collins holds that at least the "metaphorical warning," involving the image of the new wine, "could well have been issued by the historical Jesus."[8] Usually such scholars concern themselves more with reflecting on what meaning(s) the two parables convey within Mark's narrative, and do not explore their probable origin in the preaching of Jesus himself. Let me indicate some of these reflections, before taking up the question of origins.

The Context: A Question of Fasting

As Schweizer remarks, Mark did not suppose that verses 21–22 "applied only during the time of Jesus' earthly life." These words of Jesus "formed a *general warning* against any compromise which would unite the old and the new." That is to say, "we cannot use the new for repairing the old or pour the new into old forms."[9] Both brief parables "point to the impossibility of mixing old and new."[10] Newness is stressed, especially in the first parable. Camille Foçant writes, "The unshrunk cloth is a raw cloth that no one has yet prepared. It is impossible for cloth to be newer. The image therefore insists on the most total newness."[11]

This warning does not call for the old to be abandoned. To be sure, the new is understood to be more powerful than the old, but the two parables "show a concern lest the old be lost. While the new is stronger than the old, it "neither replaces it," as if the old cloth and old wineskins were to be thrown away, "nor merely supplements" the old.[12]

The evangelist applies this warning to the particular question of fasting for the disciples of Jesus—both during the ministry of Jesus (when they did not fast but anticipated with him the messianic banquet) and in the post-Pentecost situation. In that later time, Christians fasted,[13] and did so confronted with different fasting practices of Jews and those followers of John the Baptist who failed to enter the Christian community (see Luke 7:18; 11:1; Acts 19:1–7). For Christians, the space between Christ's postresurrection departure and final return was a time of absence (his being "taken away"). Those early believers obviously anticipated his return very keenly and longed for it—their true redemption—even though they were conscious of a relationship with God that was already that of the kingdom. Yet they were in a sense "back" in the premessianic situation when fasting was appropriate. They longed for full redemption when Jesus would complete his messianic work.[14]

More broadly, the parables protest, Boring writes, "against seeing the eschatological newness that came into the world with Jesus as merely a supplement to Judaism, a repairing of the deficiencies of the old." The new does not so much "replace the old but fulfil it eschatologically."[15]

By privileging the language of *final fulfillment* (over replacement, supplement, and repair), Boring is preferable to Nineham, who speaks rather of difference and incompatibility: "The state of affairs he [Jesus] has inaugurated is quite different from what went on before, and the conduct appropriate to it is as incompatible with the practices of Judaism as a new patch on an old garment or new wine in old wineskins." Yet Nineham also writes of "the eschatological character of his [Jesus's] coming," which calls for "new and eschatological fasting."[16]

Moloney stresses the radical nature of what is at stake. "The eschatological event of Jesus's death [and resurrection] cannot be contained within the closed religious system of Israel. The new wine, a symbol of the time of salvation, must be preserved, and this calls for new wineskins. The coming of the kingdom introduces a new time into the relationship between God and the human condition [surely and human beings?]." As much as any commentator, Moloney highlights the discontinuity between the new and old ways of doing things: "Israel's tradition" has "done its task as garment and wineskin, but something radically new is present and cannot be contained in the old."[17] We might add that being content with the old should not be allowed to prevent openness to the new.

The Background and Possible Origins

As we saw above, such commentators as Marcus, Schweizer, and Yarbro Collins explicitly allow for Jesus being the source of one or even both of the two parables (or metaphors, as Yarbro Collins and others call Mark 2:21–22). Moloney does not rule this out. When speaking of new wine as symbolizing "the time of salvation," Moloney might have suggested a specific origin for this symbolic language but does not do so.[18] Like other commentators on Mark, he refrains from exploring possible sources for Jesus's brief parables involving cloth and wine.

At least four words come under scrutiny here: *himation* (clothing, garment), *agnaphos* (unshrunken, unbleached), *oinos* (wine), and *askos* (wineskin). In the Greek version of the Jewish Scriptures (LXX), *himation* is a widely used noun. The adjective *agnaphos* never occurs, but we do find numerous instances of the related verb, *hagnizein* (to cleanse). In a literal, metaphorical, or symbolic sense, *oinos* turns up abundantly. There are also some examples of *askos*, but seemingly used always in the literal sense. These are the headlines; let us examine the small print.

Right from the Book of Genesis, *himation* turns up abundantly in the literal sense of clothing or garment (e.g., Gen 27:27; 28:20; 37:29, 34; 38:14, 19; 44:13). There are references to "worn out" clothing or garments (Gen 9:5, 13). With its codes of cleanliness, Leviticus contains references to washing clothes (e.g., Lev 13:6, 17, 22, 27, 34; 14:8, 9, 14,

47; 15:5, 6). Clothes are to be washed, for instance, as part of the ritual on the Day of the Atonement (Lev 16:26, 28). Various laws apply to wearing garments made of different materials (Lev 19:19) and to the wearing and tearing of ritual garments or vestments (Lev 21:10).

Sometimes prophets speak of filthy clothing. Isaiah uses that as an analogy for describing human alienation from God:

> We have all become like one who is unclean,
>   and all our righteous deeds are like a filthy cloth.
> We all fade like a leaf,
>   and our iniquities, like the wind, take us away. (Isa 64:6)

Ezekiel speaks of the way God has enhanced the beauty of Jerusalem: "Your clothing was of fine linen, rich fabric, and embroidered cloth" (Ezek 16:13). But Jerusalem would turn out to be an unfaithful wife, stripped of her beautiful clothes and jewels (16:39).

To express the mortality of human beings and contrast it with divine eternity, the Psalmist introduces an analogy with wearing out and changing clothing:

> They will perish, but you endure;
>   they will all wear out like a garment.
> You change them like clothing, and they pass away. (Ps 102:26)

In particular, this analogy applies to those who refuse to follow a prophet's teaching: "all of them will wear out like a garment; the moth will eat them up" (Isa 50:9; see 51:8).

Clothing is used metaphorically of God—for example, in his punishing and redeeming activity: "he put on garments of vengeance for clothing, and wrapped himself in fury as in a mantle" (Isa 59:17). Vengeance on Edom is described through vivid pictures of blood-stained garments (Isa 63:1–6). A passage in the Psalms, attributed to the people of Judah, uses clothing as a metaphor for salvation and righteousness:

> I will greatly rejoice in the LORD,
>   my whole being shall exult in my God;
> for he has clothed me with the garments of salvation,
>   he has covered me with the robe of righteousness. (Isa 61:10)

Sometimes reference is made to *tearing* clothes (Lev 13:45), as happens when during a siege by the Assyrians, King Hezekiah tore his clothes and covered himself with sackcloth (Isa 37:1). Earlier a king of Israel tore his clothes, on receiving a letter from the king of Aram-Damascus who asked that his army commander, Naaman, be cured from his leprosy. Only God who "gives death or life" could effect such a healing (2 Kgs 5:7).

This image of tearing clothes is a striking one that will occur in Mark's Gospel itself when we are told that the high priest "tore his clothes" because he rejected Jesus as uttering blasphemy (Mark 14:63). But in the Scriptures that Jesus inherited for use in the synagogue and beyond, I have been unable to find any cases of torn clothes being mended, let alone warnings against such a misguided practice as using new, unshrunk cloth to repair some old garment.

In a story about Noah and his sons, we read of Noah being the first to plant a vineyard, produce wine (*oinos*), and get drunk from drinking it (Gen 9:18–27). God gifts human beings with wine, as well as with oil and bread:

> [You] bring forth food from the earth,
>   and wine to gladden the human hearts,
> oil to make the face shine,
>   and bread to strengthen the human heart. (Ps 104:14–15)

Wine, along with other blessings of fertility, comes from God and fidelity to the divine covenant: "the LORD your God…will bless the fruit of your womb and the fruit of your ground, your grain and your wine and your oil, the increase of your cattle and the issue of your flock" (Deut 7:12–13).

The Scriptures also use "wine" metaphorically. It enters, for example, a picture of the future messianic banquet to be celebrated on Mount Zion:

> On this mountain the LORD of hosts will make for all peoples
>   a feast of rich food, a feast of well-aged wines,
>   of rich food filled with marrow, of well-aged wines strained
>   clear. (Isa 25:6)

The wines that portray and evoke this eschatological banquet are "well-aged," rather than "new," as in Jesus's parable of the new wine being poured into new wineskins.

Wineskins (*askoi*), when they are mentioned in the Scriptures, seem to be understood literally, rather than as symbolizing "new" or "old" stages in salvation history, as in Jesus's parable. The Gibeonites, for instance, bring "worn out, torn, and mended" wineskins, along with "worn out and patched sandals on their feet" and "worn out clothes," when they go to persuade Joshua of their poverty and seek a peaceful settlement with him. On meeting him, they say, "These wineskins were new when we filled them, and see, they are burst; and these garments and sandals of ours are worn out from the very long journey" (Josh 9:4–5, 13). The story that is being told here requires that the wineskins, no less than the clothes (and the sandals), are interpreted in a normal, literal sense.

To sum up. Unquestionably, in his parables and other sayings, Jesus could use (and adapt) language and imagery that others had used before him, notably those who composed and put together the Scriptures with which he was familiar. But he could also be original and draw in his own way on such ordinary human activities as mending clothes and storing wine to proclaim the appropriate reaction to the kingdom of God that he was bringing through his own person and activity. Those responsible for the inspired Scriptures of his people wrote often of clothing and wine, and sometimes employed this language metaphorically. But none of them anticipated the way Jesus used language in his miniparables about storing new wine and mending torn clothes.

The Experience of Jesus

Van Iersel, as we saw above, remarks laconically that the destructive result of unwise attempts to combine the new and the old is "a common, empirical fact."[19] This remark raises this question: Are we meant to think of common, empirical facts about mending torn clothes and storing wine that Jesus himself experienced in the daily life of ancient Galilee? If so, his two miniparables about clothes and wine derive from his own experience.[20] They witness to what he has learned. They reveal an imagination and religious sensibility that are sensitively aware both of what is going on in his world and how common activities can match and illuminate the divine rule and the appropriate human reaction to it.[21]

Unshrunk Cloth and New Wineskins

We can conclude that the brief parables about mending torn clothes and storing new wine, since they have no plausible origin elsewhere, derive from Jesus's own experience of life in ancient Galilee. They reflect how his religious imagination took up such experiences and gave them a place in his teaching. These miniparables tell us how Jesus thought of himself and the dawning reign of God. As always with parables, the context in which hearers and readers find themselves and the questions they bring to the parables will partly shape the meaning they proceed to construct.

4

DID JOSEPH OF ARIMATHEA EXIST AND BURY JESUS?

(Mark 15:42-47)

To assess critically the New Testament accounts about the discovery of Jesus's empty tomb, we need to evaluate the prior burial story, as found in its first intracanonical form (Mark 15:42–47).[1] But, in approaching that story, we may not overlook a reference made to Jesus's burial in the early kerygma quoted by Paul (1 Cor 15:4a). Ulrich Luz argues that "the primitive kerygma of 1 Corinthians 15:3–5…presupposes that there was a special tradition about Jesus' burial—also that the location of Jesus' tomb was known."[2]

Around fifteen years after Paul wrote 1 Corinthians and cited that kerygma, Mark completed his Gospel. It included a passion narrative that finished with the episode about Joseph of Arimathea following the prescriptions of Deuteronomy 21:22–23 and burying Jesus's body before sunset on the day of the crucifixion. Obviously if we deny any historical reliability in this burial story and dismiss it as a legend created either by the evangelist or one of his sources, we would have to pass the same negative judgement on the subsequent narrative of the tomb being discovered to be open and empty (Mark 16:1–8 in its earliest intracanonical form).

Did Joseph of Arimathea Exist and Bury Jesus?

Among the pioneers of form criticism, Rudolf Bultmann accepted the substantial credibility of the burial narrative. He described the basic story (Mark 15:44–45, 47) as "an historical account which creates no impression of being a legend."[3] Sometime later Joseph A. Fitzmyer wrote, "Joseph of Arimathea is otherwise unknown, but in all four Gospels he is linked to the burial of Jesus; clearly a historical reminiscence is being used. Who would invent him?"[4] In his *Anchor Bible Dictionary* article "Joseph of Arimathea," Stanley E. Porter followed Bultmann, Fitzmyer, Joachim Gnilka, Morna Hooker, and other biblical scholars who recognized a historically reliable nucleus in the story of Joseph of Arimathea burying Jesus's body after the crucifixion.[5]

Raymond E. Brown agreed "that the burial was done by Joseph from Arimathea is very probable, since a Christian fictional creation from nothing of a Jewish Sanhedrist who does what is right is almost inexplicable, granted the hostility in early Christian writings towards the Jewish authorities responsible for the death of Jesus." Brown added, "Moreover, the fixed designation of such a character as 'from Arimathea,' a town very difficult to identify and reminiscent of no scriptural symbolism, makes a thesis of invention even more implausible." Brown concluded, "While high probability is not certitude, there is nothing in the preGospel account of Jesus' burial by Joseph that could not plausibly be deemed historical."[6]

Commentators on the Gospels have continued to accept, with varying degrees of emphasis, the historicity of the Joseph of Arimathea story: for instance, James R. Edwards, *The Gospel according to Mark*.[7] One can cite other New Testament scholars, such as Luz: "I think it more likely that the story of Joseph of Arimathea has a historical core."[8] Nevertheless, every now and then the burial story has been dismissed as completely nonhistorical, a narrative created by the evangelist Mark. In three books, John Dominic Crossan argued that the tradition about Joseph of Arimathea originated with Mark and was then passed from him to the other Gospels.[9] Essentially four arguments come into play to support Crossan's position: three are general presuppositions (about the original source for Mark's passion narrative that, though no longer extant, is embedded in the Gospel of Peter; the tendency to historicize Old Testament prophecies; and Mark's extraordinary creativity), and one argument dealing with a specific point (Joseph of Arimathea as an "in-between" figure). Let us look at them in turn.

THE GOSPELS

First Presupposition: The Original Source

From the first of his trilogy, *Four Other Gospels*, Crossan argued that much of the apocryphal Gospel of St. Peter antedated Mark, Matthew, Luke, and John, and provided the narrative from which their passion (and resurrection) stories derive. In particular, the passion narratives in the four canonical Gospels can "all be adequately and plausibly explained as layers of redactional expansion on that single primary source."[10] In *Four Other Gospels* Crossan calls this source, allegedly a major part of the Gospel of Peter, "the original Passion-Resurrection Source."[11] In *The Cross that Spoke* it becomes the "Cross Gospel, a document presently embedded in the Gospel of Peter, just as Q is in Matthew and Luke."[12] According to "the original Passion-Resurrection Source" (soon to be called "the Cross Gospel"), Jesus's burial was completely under the motivation and control of his enemies. Crossan refers his readers to the Gospel of Peter 2:15; 5:15; and 6:21—verses that belong, he claims, to the original Passion-Resurrection Source or Cross Gospel.[13]

Denying without evidence the presence of any female disciples at Jesus's burial, Crossan associates a shocking assertion with his view that Jesus's enemies were totally in charge not only of his execution but also of his burial: "Those closest to Jesus had fled his crucifixion and had no idea how or where he was buried."[14] In *The Historical Jesus* he makes the same claim, but more rhetorically: "With regard to the body of Jesus, by Easter Sunday morning, those who cared did not know where it was, and those who knew did not care."[15]

In his 1986 presidential address to the Society of New Testament Studies, Raymond E. Brown exposed the weakness of Crossan's first general presupposition: the dependence of the canonical Gospels on the Gospel of Peter (or rather the first half of it, 1:1—6:22, but without 2:3–5a) for their passion narratives.[16] Brown rejected all such literary dependence: there are noticeable inconsistencies in the narrative of the Gospel of Peter that cannot be explained by Crossan's thesis of an earlier self-coherent passion story (= his "Passion-Resurrection Source," also called the "Cross Gospel") and a later redaction under the influence of the canonical Gospels. Brown then pointed to examples of a massive transferal or switching of details affecting the dramatis personae when incidents in the Gospel of Peter are compared to similar incidents in the canonical Gospels. All this tells against Crossan's thesis. Brown concluded that the Gospel of Peter "does not constitute or give the earliest Christian account or thoughts about the passion."[17]

One might have expected Crossan to have answered this very public challenge to his thesis that the sole source for the passion narrative in all four canonical Gospels was embedded in the Gospel of Peter. Instead, he made no reference to Brown's 1986 address when developing at length the same thesis in his 1988 *The Cross that Spoke* and using it in his 1991 *The Historical Jesus*. As much as anything, this silence about Brown's elaborate critique gave substance to John Meier's remark in *America* magazine about "Crossan's refusal to debate other scholars who hold alternate views."[18]

Apart from one or two sympathetic reactions,[19] scholars have generally remained unconvinced by Crossan's 1988 lengthy and tortuous attempt to rehabilitate the Gospel of Peter and claim that its postulated mid–first-century core (his "Cross Gospel") served as the sole source for Mark's story of the passion (and resurrection). The reviews of *The Cross that Spoke* demolished Crossan's case for attributing an early date to a supposed core of the Gospel of Peter and for inventing a literary dependence from it on the part of Mark and other canonical Gospels.[20] In a later commentary on Mark, Joel Marcus would say, "It seems intrinsically unlikely that the fantastic account in the *Gospel of Peter*, which is after all a second-century document, should be the source for Mark's sober, first-century narrative."[21]

As regards the passion narrative, our earliest source remains Mark's Gospel. Most scholars, Marcus remarks, "think that in composing his passion story Mark is dependent on a pre-Markan passion account that had been passed down in the church, either in oral or in written form."[22] Luz likewise accepts that there were oral and written traditions behind the passion narratives in the four Gospels. But one of these sources is not to be found embedded in the Gospel of Peter; that text was composed after the four Gospels and has "points of contact" with them.[23]

Second Presupposition: Historicizing Prophecies

A second presupposition that underpins Crossan's rejection of the historicity of the Markan burial narrative is his conviction that historicized prophecy rather than historical memory "ruled the creation of the passion narrative," particularly the earliest such narrative (according to him, imbedded in the Gospel of Peter).[24] Such historicizing of Old Testament "prophecies," so *Four Gospels* assures its readers, was a "pervasive process"; right from the original passion narrative, biblical prophecy dictated "the very details" in the formation of the story. Historical memory could hardly play any role, as the followers of Jesus knew "absolutely little" about the events of his passion, crucifixion, and burial.[25] (So much for any information coming from faithful women followers of Jesus, the Beloved Disciple, and others!)

The burial tradition, the Passion-Resurrection Source identified by Crossan in the Gospel of Peter, was simply derived from Old Testament texts, especially from Deuteronomy 21:22–23 and its legal injunction about burying executed persons on the same day. "It is because of respect for this law," Crossan maintains, "that the [earliest Christian] tradition presumed the Jewish authorities would have buried Jesus themselves. Since they were in total charge of the crucifixion, they were in total control of the burial as well."[26] Right through to the final work of his trilogy, *The Historical Jesus*, Crossan claims the Old Testament origins for the Passion-Resurrection Source or Cross Gospel. His hypothetical Cross Gospel is supposed to have created from different prophetic allusions "a narrative passion" in "a coherent and sequential story."[27] In short, Crossan presumes the highly influential contribution of Old Testament texts to a passion narrative that lacked almost all historical memory.

In their reviews of *The Cross that Spoke*, C. Clifton Black, Reginald Fuller, and Joel Green challenged this presupposition. Green, for instance, wrote,

> Crossan here walks along what has become a well-trodden path opened earlier in this century by Martin Dibelius (though Dibelius was much less skeptical about the possibility of historical information for the passion than Crossan). In opting for this route, Crossan failed to consider substantial works of the last decade on the hermeneutics of late Judaism, especially on the question whether the creation of current history from Old Testament texts was an accepted and widely-practiced phenomenon. In fact, while more work needs to be done, study of *pesharim* texts from Qumran,

postbiblical historiography, and selected apocalyptic writing is already suggesting that the direction of influence was *from event to biblical texts*.[28]

What Green names as influence from text to event, Fitzmyer calls "literary embellishment." The Old Testament references and resonances help to tell the story, not to create it.[29] Hence Fitzmyer insists that the Gospel passion stories contain historical narrative: "If there were ever a part of the gospel tradition which must be so characterized, this is it."[30] Specifically apropos of the story of Jesus's burial, Hooker finds "nothing to commend" the suggestion that "the incident was created" to "fulfil" Old Testament texts.[31]

Marcus places the question in the full context of Mark's Gospel: "The Markan passion narrative, like the Markan Gospel in general, is a mixture of memory and theological insight." While "the Markan passion narrative preserves remembered events," it is "also probable that Mark, like the other Gospel writers, has fleshed out his passion narrative in order to bring its significance home to his readers."[32] Recognizing the "both/and" quality of the passion story, Marcus states firmly that "Crossan's dichotomy between 'history remembered' and 'prophecy historicized' is a false one."[33]

Third Presupposition: Mark's Extraordinary Creativity

Crossan's third presupposition concerns Mark's creativity, allegedly of quite an extraordinary kind. In *The Historical Jesus* Crossan speaks of the evangelist's "consummate theological fiction" and informs his readers, "It is impossible, in my mind, to overestimate the creativity of Mark."[34]

Many New Testament scholars would dispute this remarkable view of Mark's creativity. Marcus speaks for many when he warns against tipping "the balance too far either toward the 'creative theologian' or toward the 'conservative redactor' side of the evaluation of Markan literary activity."[35]

Two obvious problems and a question emerge from Crossan's third presupposition. First, if Mark's creativity is "impossible to overestimate," why did he bother to make use of any written passion narrative? Such an exceptionally creative author would not have needed to adjust and enlarge Crossan's hypothetical Cross Gospel when composing his own story of Jesus's death and its aftermath. Second, if one credits Mark with extraordinary, impossible-to-overestimate creativity, how can we know that the evangelist made the three "profound changes" in the passion narrative of the Cross Gospel that Crossan alleges?[36] The formation of a text by any author of such theological and literary creativity would be very difficult indeed to track. In other words, the more Crossan emphasizes Mark's creativity, the more precarious become any hypotheses about the sources and composition of the second Gospel.

The question I have in mind is prompted by an observation made by Albert Schweitzer (1875–1965) on those who contributed to the classic, nineteenth-century quest of the historical Jesus: "It was not only each epoch that found its reflection in Jesus; each individual created Him in accordance with his own character. There is no historical task which so reveals a man's true self as the writing of a Life of Jesus."[37] George Tyrrell (1861–1909) put the same point more vividly when commenting on Adolf von Harnack (1851–1930): "The Christ that Harnack sees, looking back through nineteen centuries of Catholic darkness, is only the reflection of a Liberal Protestant face, seen at the bottom of a deep well."[38] When Crossan credits Mark with "impossible-to-overestimate creativity" and "consummate theological fictions," is he revealing himself and creating the evangelist in accordance with his own character and intentions? Has Crossan been looking down the well of history in search of Mark but in fact seeing his own image at the bottom? Does Tyrrell's remark also apply to Crossan, his fellow Irishman?

Did Mark Invent Joseph of Arimathea and the Burial Story?

We come at last to Crossan's central claim: the story of Jesus's burial by Joseph of Arimathea originated with Mark, who "began the process of taking Jesus's burial away from his enemies and giving it to his friends." The evangelist did so by inventing the in-between figure, Joseph of Arimathea, who mediates "between enemies and friends."[39]

Did Joseph of Arimathea Exist and Bury Jesus?

According to Crossan, this "limbo" character is described in Mark 15:43 with two carefully balanced qualities:

> First, he is "a respectable member of the council" but, second, he is "one who was also looking for the kingdom of God." This locates him somewhere in between the "Jewish" and the "Christian" side. Still one recognizes a problem in that description. If he was a member of the Sanhedrin, where was his voice when Jesus needed him earlier during the trial? The rest of the intra-canonical tradition would solve, each in its own way, the problem created by Joseph's ambiguous position and Mark's difficult description.[40]

Three questions show up the weakness in this explaining away of the burial story as simply originating with Mark. First, was he ready to create an entire episode, very closely connected to what precedes (Jesus's crucifixion) and what follows (the news of his resurrection), invent its central protagonist, give him a name, and assign him an origin from a relatively obscure town? Crossan obviously sets no limits to what the evangelist might do "creatively."

Second, do the redactional changes introduced by Matthew and Luke indicate that these two evangelists found some special problem in the story of Joseph of Arimathea? Matthew's antipathy to the Sanhedrin, interest in discipleship, and (apologetical?) desire to explain why Joseph easily secured the body from Pilate may account, respectively, for Joseph no longer being named as "a respectable member of the council," but being called "a disciple of Jesus" and "a rich man" (Matt 27:57–58).[41] Luke 23:50–56 uses various redactional omissions and additions to shape the Markan burial narrative. For instance, he names Joseph as "a good and upright man" who is not a party to the Sanhedrin's decision against Jesus—thus stressing his "moral character,"[42] and perhaps also, indirectly, the innocence of Jesus and his followers. The redactional changes Matthew and Luke introduce in the burial story reflect their normal theological interests rather than show them grappling with some difficult problem created for them by Mark.[43]

"The rest of the intra-canonical tradition," which had to solve the problem (that Crossan believes was left by Mark's creation of Joseph of Arimathea), amounts simply to the Gospel of John. This Gospel depends, he claims, on the Synoptics, at least for the passion narrative.[44] Beyond question, there is considerable overlap between the Johannine passion story and the passion stories found in the Synoptic Gospels. But, far from John depending here on the Synoptics, this overlap, as Marcus points out, "may be explained by a common dependence of John and the Synoptics on a pre-existent passion narrative," oral or written.

Third, is there anything historically suspicious about Mark's burial story centering on an "in-between figure," someone "within the Jewish leadership elite" and "connected with Jesus"?[45] By the end of Jesus's ministry we would expect the presence of at least a few "in-between" figures, devout and leading Jews who were attracted to his message of the kingdom but had not (yet) become his disciples. Crossan's suspicions here fly in the face of antecedent historical probability.

The core historicity of the burial story in Mark cannot be demonstrated as absolutely certain. But we may conclude at least that Crossan did nothing to undermine its historical credibility. That has remained accepted by very many biblical scholars: for instance, from (a) Brown, Bultmann, Josef Ernst,[46] Fitzmyer, Gnilka, Hooker, Dennis Nineham,[47] Rudolf Pesch,[48] Porter, Eduard Schweizer,[49] Vincent Taylor,[50] down to (b) Dale C. Allison,[51] James R. Edwards,[52] Camille Foçant,[53] Marcus, and Robert H. Stein.[54] In varying degrees and over different issues, they have recognized the redactional contribution of Mark. But they do not invest him with the "creativity" needed to have invented tout court the burial story, as asserted by Crossan.

Coda

Years before he rejected the historicity of Mark's narrative about Joseph of Arimathea burying Jesus, Crossan published an article, "Anti-Semitism and the Gospel."[55] In a subsequent note I examined a number of questionable, historical features in his argument.[56] Revisiting in 2020 his rejection of Joseph of Arimathea's intervention after the death of Jesus, I must ask myself, Did Crossan ever learn to assess in a satisfactory manner the historical evidence available to take a reasoned stand on a variety of New Testament questions?

5

THE TERRIFIED SILENCE OF THREE WOMEN

(Mark 16:8)

The Gospel of Mark, as we have it, ends in a disturbing way.[1] Mary Magdalene, Mary the mother of James, and Salome have discovered the tomb of Jesus to be open and empty. Inside the tomb they meet an angelic figure who announces the resurrection and gives them the instruction: "Tell his disciples and Peter that he is going ahead of you to Galilee; there you will see him, just as he told you" (16:7). But "they went out of the tomb and fled; for trembling [*tromos*] and bewilderment [*ekstasis*] took hold of them. And they said nothing to anyone, for they were afraid [*ephobounto*]" (16:8 au. trans.). How are we to understand this flight and fearful silence of the three women?

Earlier commentators such as Robert Henry Lightfoot, Dennis Nineham, and Rudolf Pesch offered a positive interpretation of this terrified (temporary) silence of the women. It was an appropriate reaction to the revelation of Jesus's resurrection from the dead. Then scholars like Norman Perrin, Morna Hooker, Francis J. Moloney, and Joel Marcus proposed understanding the women's reaction negatively. At the end the women, like the male disciples, failed. But is this view of total failure on the part of all disciples, men *and women*, truly convincing? Should a positive view of the women's fearful silence be reinstated?

THE GOSPELS
Lightfoot, Nineham, and Pesch

Robert Henry Lightfoot

Robert Henry Lightfoot argued that "the whole tenor" of Mark 16:5–8 suggests "a fear or dread of God," a fear caused by "revelation" that produces the women's amazement, fear, and silent flight. In accounting for the women's emotions and reactions, Lightfoot pointed to the stilling of the storm (Mark 4:35–41): the "physical alarm" of the disciples was "replaced by a much deeper fear." He noted the parallel between the silence of the three women in Mark 16:8 and the "bewildered utterance" of the male disciples in Mark 4:41. These reactions "arise from the same cause, namely, an increasing and involuntary realization of the nature and being of Him with whom they have to do."[2]

Lightfoot went on to recall how various episodes of revelation in Mark's Gospel regularly produce in the disciples or others "fear or astonishment or both together."[3] In a climactic way the reaction of the women at the tomb—their amazement, trembling, fear, and silence—gathers up the emotions caused earlier by the revealing presence of God conveyed through Jesus's actions and teaching.

Dennis Nineham

With considerable attention to Lightfoot's comments, Dennis Nineham interprets the fearful silence and flight of the women as expressing "the overwhelming and sheerly supernatural character of that to which" they were responding. Nineham attends not only to protagonists in the narrative but also to the response that could be expected from readers. If they even begin to "understand the full significance of what had occurred," they "too will be bound to respond with amazement and godly fear."[4]

Rudolf Pesch

In his own way and without reference to Lightfoot or Nineham, Rudolf Pesch detected in the women's fearful silence "a motif of reaction to the reception of revelation" found in "the [Old Testament] accounts of epiphanies." He referred to such texts as Daniel 7:28.[5] (Lightfoot had exemplified the connection between some revealing message from God and human silence by citing passages such as Luke 1:20 and 2 Cor 12:4.[6]) Pesch noted that the fear, trembling, and silence of the three women are apocalyptic themes—he cited Daniel 7:15, 28; 8:17, 27; and 10:7—that "underline the meaning of the angel's *revelatory* message."[7]

The "overwhelming secret" communicated by the angel's announcement of Jesus's resurrection produced trembling, ecstatic amazement, and silence. Such a response emphasized "the *mysterium tremendum* of the divine revelation." The women have planned to anoint the corpse of the crucified Jesus. Instead, they are "confronted with the message of his resurrection and are torn away from" their normal ways of thinking.[8] Pesch might have used the full account of the holy coined by Rudolf Otto: *mysterium tremendum et fascinans*.[9] The women go to the tomb drawn unconsciously by the fascinating mystery of God about to be disclosed to them. They flee from the tomb shocked by the awe-inspiring message of Jesus's resurrection. The contrasting activity of the women exemplifies Otto's classic thesis about the twofold human reaction to God and the revelation of the divine mystery.

Pesch commented that the readers of the Gospel, confronted with the women's response to the "epiphany of God" that has taken place in Jesus's resurrection, are invited to let themselves "be *fascinated* into faith."[10] Here Pesch recalled—for the sake of the Gospel *readers*—the *fascinans* from Otto's phrase but ignored the *tremendum*. Surely readers are invited to imitate the women by being both fascinated *and* awe-inspired, and so come to faith (or be strengthened in an Easter faith that already exists)? While profitably introducing Otto to illuminate Mark 16:8, Pesch could have deployed more fully the language of *mysterium tremendum et fascinans*.

Perrin, Hooker, and Moloney

Norman Perrin

Norman Perrin was among the first to interpret Mark 16:8 as disobedience and failure on the part of the three women. Perrin rightly connected the story of the women at Jesus's tomb (Mark 16:1–8) with two other narratives (Mark 15:40–41, 42–47). These three narratives (which deal, respectively, with women at the cross, at the burial of Jesus, and at his tomb) are closely related—not least by the fact that two of the three women named in 15:40 turn up again in 15:47 and all three are named again in 16:1. Perrin also noted the progressive failure of Jesus's male disciples that begins at Mark 6:52 and reaches its highpoint in the passion story with Judas's betrayal, Peter's denial of Jesus, and their total absence at the crucifixion. Meanwhile women enter Mark's story (from 14:3-9) and "take over the role" one "might have expected to be played" by the male disciples. They remain faithfully present at Jesus's death and burial and are "prepared to play their role in anointing him." It is "their great honor to discover the empty tomb and the fact of the resurrection."[11]

Then, like the male disciples before them, "the women also fail their trust" by not delivering "the message entrusted to them." Mark's Gospel ends with total "discipleship failure," as "every disciple fails the master." Perrin admits that this is a "grim picture" and a "dark" and "stark" vision of what Mark intends by the frightened silence of the three women.[12] But is this picture of total failure on the part of all the disciples, both male and female, the right vision to be drawn from Mark 16:8?

Morna Hooker

In her commentary on Mark's Gospel, Morna Hooker agrees with Perrin. She explains the reaction of the women as a final act of disobedience and failure: Mark ends with "the statement that the women disobeyed the divine command because they were afraid"; "their silence is culpable."[13] The male disciples have failed to understand the message and identity of Jesus, who denounces their "hardened" hearts (8:14–21). At the end, one of the Twelve betrays Jesus to his enemies, Peter denies him three times, and none of the others have the courage to support him at his death on the cross. The young man who flees naked into the night (14:51–52) symbolizes the way all the male disciples fail Jesus. Having persistently misunderstood and failed Jesus, not surprisingly they all abandon him at the end. Hooker acknowledges that the record of women in Mark's Gospel has been different: "individual women have been commended for their faith and their actions (5:34; 7:29; 12:41–44; 14:5–9); and the women who follow Jesus from Galilee stand by him at his crucifixion; they alone witness his death (15:40–41) and burial (15:47). But, surprisingly, at this point even they fail." Their fear and failure to deliver the message "demonstrate their inability to believe the good news" of the resurrection of the crucified Jesus.[14] Hooker considers it "ironic that on Easter morning those who had faithfully followed

Jesus to his crucifixion should flee from his tomb—just as the [male] disciples fled from arrest (14:50, 52): this stupendous act is too great even for their [the three women's] loyalty."[15]

Hooker's list of references to the faithful activity of women needs to be enlarged by adding details from 1:29-31, the account of Peter's mother-in-law being cured and then "serving" Jesus—the only example from the many people cured in Mark's Gospel who does just that. The full account of what female followers of Jesus did in Mark 1—15 remains totally positive. Not a single misstep prepares readers for an abrupt failure at the end. Such failure would be totally out of character with all that the women associated with Jesus have done since the start of Mark's Gospel.

Francis J. Moloney

Nevertheless, Hooker's interpretation has been followed by her former doctoral student, Francis J. Moloney: "The women, who had overcome the scandal of the cross by looking on from afar as Jesus died (15:40-41) and watched where he was buried (15:47), have not been able to overcome the scandal of the empty tomb and the Easter proclamation. They have joined the [male] disciples in flight and fear."[16] Hence Moloney discusses Mark 16:1-8 under the title "the Failure of the Women."[17] Mark, he insists, proposes that, just as the male disciples failed, "so also the women failed (16:8). In the end, *all human beings fail*...but God succeeds. God has raised Jesus from the dead (16:6)."[18]

Moloney's totally negative interpretation of "they were afraid [*ephobounto*]" (Mark 16:8) is central to his argument. Already used eleven times in Mark's Gospel, the verb is "regularly associated," he rightly insists, "with the fragility of the disciples and others."[19] But it is a fragility, we should add, that reacts appropriately to the epiphany of Jesus's power over the created world when he calms a storm (Mark 4:40-41) and walks on the sea (6:50), to the exercise of his authority over evil spirits (5:15), and to the bewildering announcement of his coming death and resurrection (9:32; 10:33).

The women's reaction to the discovery of the empty tomb and the message of the angel strikingly parallels the way in which Peter, James, and John "became terrified [*ekphoboi*]" (Mark 9:6). They experience the transfiguration, which the evangelist connects with Jesus's coming death and resurrection (Mark 9:9-13). Both in the case of the three women and that of the three men, it was the experience of the transcendent that inspired human fear—not any fragile and cowardly failure. Moloney does not take into account the experience of Peter, James, and John at the transfiguration. It helps us correctly read the experience of Mary Magdalene and her two companions on the first Easter Sunday.

Nowadays scholars seem increasingly inclined to recognize links between Mark's Gospel and Paul's letters.[20] Just as Paul had earlier quoted the kerygmatic announcement of Jesus's death, burial, resurrection, and appearances "to Cephas and the Twelve" (1 Cor 15:3–5), so Mark tells the story of Jesus's crucifixion and burial, followed by the announcement "he has been raised" and a promise: "tell his disciples and Peter that he is going before you into Galilee; there you will see him" (Mark 16:6–7). Mark describes the state of the three women in terms of trembling (*tromos*), bewilderment (*ecstasis*), and fear (*ephobounto*). Paul exhorts his beloved community in Philippi to "work out your own salvation with fear and trembling" (Phil 2:12; see Eph 6:5). Here fear and trembling appear to be suitable and even requisite feelings for the followers of Jesus. Why should they be stigmatized as signs of failure in Mark 16:8, especially since "for they were afraid [*ephobounto gar*]" stands in apposition to "they were seized by trembling and bewilderment [*eichen gar autas tromos kai ecstasis*]"?

Joel Marcus

Joel Marcus recognizes how the women's fear is "a typical biblical reaction to a theophany or angelophany." He points out how Abraham "responds to a covenant-inaugurating theophany" with *ecstasis* (astonishment) and *phobos* (fear) (Gen 15:12). Moreover, "when God or an angel appears in the Bible, the recipient of the appearance sometimes becomes mute," for instance, "because of shock" (Dan 10:15). Nevertheless, Marcus claims that the women in Mark 16:8 remain deliberately silent: "they choose not to" speak.[21] He finds their fear and flight "easy to understand: the women have just encountered an angel, and they have seen a rolled away rock and an empty tomb where they expected a sealed and full one. The sheer unexpectedness of these events and the impression of supernatural power at work help explain their trembling and astonishment."[22]

Marcus suggests that "the muteness of the women in our story seems to arise not from inability to speak but from unwillingness to do

The Terrified Silence of Three Women

so." The "resurrection kerygma" must "now be proclaimed to the whole world," but the women react to the angel's instruction with "fearful silence and flight."[23] "The fleeing [and silent] women provide an image of what not to do, as they run away in fear and squelch the marvelous tidings of the resurrection."[24]

Marcus, nevertheless, goes on to qualify his conclusion about the women's allegedly deliberate and disobedient failure to deliver the message. He raises "the question whether the women eventually overcame their fear and told the disciples about the meeting in Galilee, to which they then went and were restored to fellowship with Jesus. The mere existence of the narrative suggests a positive answer."[25] The narrative, I would argue, not only suggests but also requires such a positive answer. If the women never delivered to anyone whatsoever the message about a rendezvous in Galilee and, indeed, about their own experience at the tomb of Jesus, how has Mark come to know about these matters? Apropos of the key instruction of the angel, M. Eugene Boring points out how, "at the narrative level of presenting past events, the reader is aware that the disciples did somehow get the message."[26]

A provisional silence on the part of the women is accounted for by the various astonishing elements they experienced at the empty tomb— elements acknowledged by Marcus and just listed above as typical of theophanies and angelophanies. Their silence was not a deliberate act of disobedience, but a stunned, temporary silence produced by their unexpected discovery and bewildering encounter at the tomb of Jesus. Like Pesch (see above), Timothy Dwyer illustrates how in biblical stories silence, at least for a time, can "result from a divine encounter."[27] The silence of the women, he proposes, is best understood as provisional: in due course they spoke to the male disciples.[28] The women remained silent with inappropriate persons, until their message could be passed on "to the appropriate audience, the disciples."[29]

Early in Mark's Gospel, Jesus cured a leper and instructed him to "say nothing to any one" as he went off to show himself to a representative of the priestly establishment (1:44). He was to remain silent until he reached the appropriate person, a priest in Jerusalem. Now the three women, although not explicitly so instructed, "said nothing to any one" as they ran to bring the angel's message to the appropriate persons, the male disciples.

The temporary silence of the women belongs to three dramatic contrasts that heighten the numinous nature of the revelation expressed by Mark 16:1–8. A first contrast pits not only the *darkness* of the night (between the Saturday and the Sunday of the resurrection) but also the darkness that enveloped the earth at the crucifixion (15:33) against the *light* of the sun that has just risen when the women go to visit the tomb (16:2). The second contrast emerges once the women enter the tomb itself. The *absence* of Jesus's body is set over against the *presence* of Jesus mediated through an interpreting angel in the form of a well-dressed "young man." A third contrast pits the confident *words* of the heavenly figure ("he has been raised; he is not here; see the place where they laid him"; and the instruction about the rendezvous in Galilee) against the *silence* of the women when they flee from the tomb.[30] Their provisional silence belongs to an appropriately dramatic way of using contrasts to narrate the revelation of Jesus's resurrection from the dead, and should not be taken to be a disobedient refusal to pass on the angelic message.

Some readers may wonder why I have not discussed the hypothesis that explains the women's silence as "a later-first-century attempt to explain why no one had previously heard the story about the empty tomb, which according to this theory had recently been concocted, either by Mark or by a predecessor."[31] Marcus did not find those who argue for the later invention of an empty tomb story to be convincing. Neither have I. Both before and after his 2009 commentary appeared, I have argued against those who hold such a later invention view.[32]

Camille Foçant

Besides respecting the narrative of Mark 16:1–8, we should also note what it can require of its readers and hearers—something that J. Lee Magness called "the completion of the story by the readers and their dramatic participation in its conclusion."[33] We also saw above how Nineham and Pesch introduced the role of readers into their interpretation of Mark 16:1–8.

Like other commentators, Camille Foçant recognizes how the "the mention of Galilee" in Mark 16:7 recalls "the start of the gospel narrative that begins with the preaching in Galilee." This carries momentous implications for readers of the Gospel. In a striking reversal and extension, "the epilogue of the gospel [16:1–8] thus constitutes a prologue to the work of the reader" (reversal). Moreover, "where the work of the narrator ends, that of the reader begins" (extension). Readers are invited to complete the story. They are led to register themselves "personally in the evangelical drama and assume it."[34]

Thus the (provisional) silence of the three women becomes an invitation to speak. Readers can become "voices crying out in the wilderness" (Mark 1:3) and play their part "in the history of the gospel kerygma."[35]

A positive interpretation of the women's fearful silence in Mark 16:8 should be reinstated. That silence embodies an appropriate reaction to the unique divine revelation conveyed in the resurrection of the crucified Jesus. The comments of Nineham, Pesch, Magness, and Foçant add to this, by calling on us to acknowledge in the enigmatic final verse of Mark an invitation to complete what we read by speaking up and proclaiming in life and word the resurrection.

A Chiasm?

Let me conclude this chapter with a suggestion about a possible chiastic structure that can be detected in Mark 16:6–8 (au. trans.):

 a. He has been raised; he is not here; see the place where they laid him.
   b. But go, tell his disciples and Peter that he is going before you to Galilee; there you will see him, just as he told you.
     c. So they went out and fled from the tomb,
     cc. for fear and amazement had seized them
   bb. and they said nothing to anyone;
 aa. for they were afraid.

Such a chiastic arrangement throws up interesting and illuminating links—not least between "he has been raised" and "they were afraid." Confronted with the unique and uniquely disturbing act of God that is the resurrection, human beings respond appropriately with a deeply reverential fear. This reaction is called forth and justified by the revelation of Jesus's risen life and final glory.

6

THOMAS TORRANCE AND MARK 16:19–20

The Ascended Christ's Prophetic Role

Despite the ascension of the risen Christ being confessed in both the Nicene-Constantinopolitan Creed and the Apostles' Creed and celebrated from early centuries in Christian liturgy and iconography, the mystery of the ascension has not always attracted theological attention.[1] In modern times, Thomas Forsyth Torrance (1913–2007) was a shining exception. He attended to the christological implications of the ascension and did so in the light of the threefold office of Christ as king/shepherd, priest, and prophet.[2] The ascension brought Christ to a new stage in his exercise of this triple office, and not least in his prophetic role attested by Mark 16:9–20. It is to Torrance's understanding of this postascension prophetic role that this chapter attends.

Christ's Postascension Prophetic Activity

Torrance understood Christ's postascension prophetic activity to be manifested and effective in the church's ministry of the word. When the church proclaims, it is Christ who proclaims: "It is Christ's own *kerygma*, his self-proclamation, which through the Spirit he allows to be echoed and heard through the preaching of the Church, so that their *kerygma* about Jesus Christ is made one with his own *kerygma*." Torrance distinguished (but did not separate) the apostolic and subsequent proclamation: "It was the special function of the Apostles to translate the self-witness of Christ into witness to Christ, the self-proclamation of Christ into proclamation of Christ by the Church." Both then and later, "in and through the preaching and teaching of that Word, it is Christ himself, the incarnate and risen Lord, who is *mightily at work*, confronting men and women with himself and summoning them to believe and follow him." In the ministry of the word, "Christ effectively ministers himself to us."[3]

In this context Torrance appealed to Mark 16:19–20: "The Lord Jesus, after he had spoken to them [the eleven], was taken up into heaven [*anelēmphthē*] and sat down at the right hand of God. And they went out and proclaimed [*ekēruxan*] everywhere, while the Lord worked with [*sunergountos*] them, and confirmed [*bebaiountos*] the word [*logon*] by the signs that accompanied it" (NRSV, corrected).[4] These verses round off the "longer ending of Mark" (16:9–20), which the majority of biblical scholars understand to be a later addition to the Gospel. While possibly written in the early second century, these verses belong to canonical Scripture and express the faith of the first generations of Christians.[5]

In Mark 16:20, the risen and ascended Jesus is recognized as the primary coagent of Christian proclamation, working with the visible proclaimers and confirming with signs their proclamation. By calling their message "the word," the author of the Markan addition used a term that, as the Acts of the Apostles and, above all, John's Gospel, First Epistle, and Revelation witness, was already fairly widely used to identify the incarnate Word of God. Being the object of the postascension proclamation, the Lord Jesus confirmed himself, the Word of God, through the signs that accompanied the proclamation.[6]

Torrance's principle, when the church proclaims it is Christ who proclaims, finds a contemporary counterpart in the Second Vatican Council's 1963 Constitution on the Sacred Liturgy (*Sacrosanctum Concilium*), even though the document does not cite Mark 16:19–20: "He is present in his word since it is he himself who speaks when the holy Scriptures are read in church" (art. 7). A later paragraph of *Sacrosanctum Concilium* taught, without citing any scriptural authority, that "in the liturgy God speaks to his people and Christ is still proclaiming his Gospel" (art. 33). Yet this constitution went on to weaken a sense of

Christ being present not only through the reading of the Scriptures *but also through the word of preaching*. It explained the purpose of the homily as drawing on "the sacred text" to "expound" the "mysteries of faith and the norms of Christian life" (art. 52). This was to understand the homily as primarily an *instruction about the revealed mysteries* and *moral norms* rather than as an encounter with Christ, *the mystery of God* (Eph 3:4), *the living Word of God*, and the supreme *moral norm*.[7]

Mark 16:9–20 and Recommissioning for Proclamation

Like the majority of commentators on Mark 16:9–20, Joel Marcus questions the provenance of this longer ending to the Gospel. He concludes with others that "overall, 16:9–20 gives the impression of being a compressed digest of resurrection appearances narrated in other Gospels." He sums up the thrust of this second-century addition as the eleven (male) disciples now being "rehabilitated" and "recommissioned."[8]

Let me set out what this recommissioning involves. The disciples are to "go into all the world and proclaim [*kēruxate*] the good news [*euaggelion*] to the whole creation. The one who believes and is baptized will be saved; but the one who does not believe will be condemned" (Mark 16:15–16). The risen Jesus then promises, not his powerful presence with the missionaries, but that healing the sick, speaking "in new tongues," and other "signs" will "accompany those who believe" and use "my name" (16:15–18).

The Markan ending goes on to note the aftermath. The eleven "went out [from Jerusalem or Galilee?] and proclaimed [*ekēruxan*][9] everywhere [*pantachou*], while the Lord worked with them and confirmed the word with the signs that accompanied it" (16:20).

A mission to "the whole world" and "the whole creation" becomes a mission "everywhere." The instruction to "proclaim the good news" is then followed simply by "proclaimed," with the object of the proclamation specified a few words later as "the message" or, better, "the word." Although the risen Jesus insists on baptism as the believing response to the proclamation (Mark 16:16), baptizing is not explicitly mentioned as an essential part of the mission with which the eleven engage themselves. Jesus describes his missionaries as "those who believe," and specifies five kinds of "signs" that using his name will effect. The final verse of the ending reports that "signs," without specifying their nature, accompany the proclamation of the word.

But that closing verse goes beyond Jesus's original commission to state that he "worked" with the missionaries and to specify that, through the signs that accompanied their proclamation, he himself "confirmed" this proclamation.[10] What happened when the word was proclaimed involved his active, personal presence, and not merely results (that also take the form of miraculous, visible signs) that believers should expect from using the name of Jesus or appealing to his authority. We can compare the longer commission and the briefer execution as follows:

COMMISSION (MARK 16:15–18)	EXECUTION (MARK 16:20)
"Go into all the world and proclaim the good news to the whole creation."	"They went out and proclaimed everywhere."
"The one who believes and is baptized will be saved."	----------------------
"These signs will accompany those who believe: by using my name they will cast out demons…they will lay hands on the sick, and they will recover."	"The Lord worked with them and confirmed the word by the signs that accompanied it."

While proclamation to the whole world figures in both the commission and its execution, the commission stresses more the universality of the mission by the repetition: "the whole world" and "the whole creation." Neither faith nor baptism are expressly mentioned as outcomes of the actual proclamation. Whereas the commission specifies five kinds of "signs," the execution merely speaks of "the signs" that accompanied the proclamation. The commission promises—to "those who believe" and use the Lord's name, rather than to those who proclaim and use his name—that they will bring about spectacular signs. This commission simply promises that these signs will accompany the mission and result from "using the name" of the Lord. The account of the execution goes further by stating that the Lord himself worked with the proclaimers and confirmed their message with signs that accompanied the proclamation.[11] He was effectively present in this universal, prophetic activity.

Morna Hooker, without entering into details, refers this summary of the mission to the Acts of the Apostles: "the picture of the disciples preaching everywhere and the Lord working with them is reminiscent of Acts."[12] This remark requires and deserves unpacking.

In the Lukan view of things, the risen Jesus needs to be withdrawn from the visible scheme of things before the Holy Spirit comes at Pentecost. The ascension does not, however, mean that Jesus has gone away, as it were, on an indefinitely long, sabbatical leave in another universe. He remains powerfully, if invisibly, present in and to the church and its missionaries. Here distinctions may seem to become a little blurred. Luke can move from cases of guidance by the risen and ascended Lord (Acts 9:10–16; 18:9–10; 22:17–21) to cases of guidance by the Holy Spirit (Acts 8:29; 10:19; 16:6) without distinguishing clearly between them. At least once he reports guidance by "the Spirit of Jesus" (Acts 16:7). Does Luke intend here the Spirit that comes from Jesus, the Spirit who is somehow identical with Jesus, or the Spirit who brings us to Jesus? Are the risen Jesus and the Holy Spirit interchangeable? As regards the initial coming of the Spirit, Luke distinguishes Jesus as the divine co-sender from the divine Spirit, who is sent or poured out (Luke 24:49; Acts 2:33). Although Luke, often in a seemingly undifferentiated manner, refers to the powerful guidance of Jesus and that of the Spirit in the spread and life of the Christian community, it is the risen Jesus who pours out the Spirit. As Peter says at the first Pentecost, "being exalted at the right hand of God, and having received from the Father the promise of the Holy Spirit, he [the risen and ascended Jesus] has poured out what you both see and hear [the effects of the Spirit]" (Acts 2:33).[13]

It is notable that in this passage from Acts, Peter goes on at once to quote a verse from Psalm 110:1:

> The Lord said to my Lord,
> "Sit at my right hand,
> until I make your enemies your footstool." (Acts 2:34–35)

Jesus himself may have quoted this verse (Mark 12:36; 14:62 parr.) and so encouraged the first Christians into making it a key text indicating his divine status (e.g., Heb 1:13). The sitting at God's right hand could be associated with Christ's assuming universal sovereignty and being enthroned as kingly ruler of the cosmos: he "has gone into heaven and is at the right hand of God, with angels, authorities, and powers made subject to him" (1 Pet 3:22). But Mark 16:19, without quoting Psalm 110:1, simply linked the sovereign *sessio ad dexteram Dei* with the ascended Christ's prophetic activity to the advantage of human beings.

At the Right Hand of God: Christ's Prophetic Activity

The ascension of the risen Christ is completed, as Vincent Taylor recalls,[14] with "sitting at the right hand of God." This *sessio ad dexteram Dei*, called in the Nicene Creed and the Apostles' Creed "sitting at the right hand of *the Father*," is associated with an active role of the ascended Christ. We may detect three ways the New Testament makes this connection—in relation to the *present*, *past*, and *future*.

First, the Letter to the Ephesians speaks of "the immeasurable greatness of his [God's] power [*dunameōs*] for us who believe, according to the working of his great power [*kata tēn energeian tou kratous tēs ischuos autou*]. God put this power to work [*hēn energēsen*] in Christ when he raised him from the dead and seated him at his right hand in the heavenly places" (Eph 1:19–20). This passage from Ephesians stresses the divine power (expressed through four nouns) working not only on the crucified Christ himself but also here and now exercised in and through the risen and ascended Christ "for us who believe." The passage understands Christian faith as resulting from the power at work in Christ sitting at God's right hand; it will cite other effects of this power, in particular, Christ's becoming "head over all things for the church" (Eph 1:21–22). *Kingly* power seems to be intended here; elsewhere Christ's priestly or prophetic activity is to the fore when the *sessio ad dexteram Dei* is invoked.

After speaking of the Holy Spirit interceding for us and "the saints" (Rom 8:26–27), Paul moves to speak of "Christ Jesus," after his death and resurrection interceding for us "at the right hand of God" (Rom 8:34). This continuing activity of the risen and ascended Christ *ad dexteram Dei* expresses the ongoing *priestly* mediation of Christ, expounded by Torrance in *Theology in Reconciliation*.[15] In particular, the Eucharist is "what it is" because of its grounding in "what God in Christ has done, does do, and will do for us in his Spirit."[16] We return below to this priestly mediation.

Both of the examples just cited from Ephesians and Romans, respectively, refer to the ascended Christ's activity seated *ad dexteram Dei* and benefiting "us who believe" (plural). The Acts of the Apostles pictures Christ "standing" at the right hand of God and doing so for an individual. As Stephen is about to be stoned to death, "he gazed into heaven and saw the glory of God and Jesus standing at the right hand of God. 'Look,' he said, 'I see the heavens opened and the Son of Man standing at the right hand of God'" (Acts 7:55–56). Four reasons show this passage to be unusual or even unique not only among those passages associating Christ's being at the right hand of God with the past but also among all passages "placing" the ascended Christ there.

(a) Apart from Revelation 1:13 and 14:14, this is the only time we find a New Testament reference to the Son of Man outside the four Gospels. (b) Nowhere else is the risen and ascended Jesus represented as standing rather than sitting *ad dexteram Dei*. (c) It is the only place that a New Testament author writes of *seeing* Christ sitting or standing at the right hand of God.[17] (d) Nowhere else is Christ *ad dexteram Dei* represented as his doing something for an individual. Here exegetes differ about details. It is either to speak (as judge or advocate) "forensically" for an individual believer facing martyrdom or to welcome him into heaven that the risen and ascended Christ "rose to his feet" at the right hand of God.[18] Either way, Christ *ad dexteram Dei* did something in the past, and did it for an individual believer.

Apart from the Stephen episode, several New Testament passages present the *sessio ad dexteram Dei* simply as the past outcome of Christ's previous activity: for instance, "when he had made purification for sins, he sat down at the right hand of the Majesty on high" (Heb 1:3; see 8:1; 10:12; 1 Pet 3:22). The *sessio* crowned and completed what Christ had already done.

Third, some passages, like Colossians 3:1, mention Christ's being "seated at the right hand of God" and link that to what he will do at the second coming. Thus, the Christians of Colossae are to maintain constantly a heavenly perspective until the end: "when Christ who is your life is revealed, then you also will be revealed with him in glory" (Col 3:4).

Mark 16:19–20 in a particular way associates the *sessio ad dexteram Dei* not so much with the past or future, but with Christ's present, ongoing activity, "mightily at work" in the preaching of the word (Torrance, see above). To illuminate further what is at stake in Torrance's appeal to the final verses of Mark to illuminate Christ's prophetic activity, let us examine comments from three exegetes.

Nineham, Schweizer, and Moloney on Mark 16:19–20

In the final verses of the ending added to Mark's Gospel, as in the whole of that addition,16:9–20, the Holy Spirit is not explicitly mentioned. Only the risen and ascended Jesus is named as "working with" the disciples and "confirming by signs" their proclamation of the word. The Spirit does, however, enter a passage in Hebrews to which Dennis Nineham refers: "How can we escape if we neglect so great a salvation? It was declared at first through the Lord, and it was attested [*ebebaiōthē*] to us by those who heard him, while God added his testimony [*sunepimarturountos*] by signs and wonders and various miracles, and by the gifts of the Holy Spirit distributed according to his will" (Heb 2:3–4).

This exhortation not to fall away, rather than being directly concerned with apostolic proclamation to the world, is addressed to an existing Christian community. They have previously accepted the witness of the apostolic generation ("attested to us by those who heard him"). Their acceptance of this witness was prompted by the divine testimony (expressed in "signs, wonders and various miracles") and by "gifts of the Holy Spirit" that have been distributed. God, rather than the ascended Christ, is named as having been present and actively witnessing when the gospel was proclaimed and received in faith.

To an extent this passage from Hebrews concurs with Mark 16:20. It does not, however, fully fit the observation Nineham makes when he brings together the two passages: "from his heavenly throne the risen Christ continues to guide and help his followers."[19] The risen and ascended Christ, who sits at God's right according to the closing verses of Mark 16, works with and confirms the *proclamation* of missionaries rather than guiding and helping them in general.

Nineham follows here what Vincent Taylor had earlier suggested about Mark 16:20: "The idea of the co-operation of the Exalted Christ with the disciples has a parallel in Hebrews 2:3–4."[20] The cooperation intended by the final verse of Mark does not point to a general "cooperation with the disciples" but is notably specific—working with and confirming missionary proclamation of the good news. And, unlike the passage from Hebrews, no mention is made of the Holy Spirit.

Commenting on Mark 16:20, Schweizer weakens the force of the Lord's "working with" the apostles in their proclamation: "The agents of the proclamation are the disciples whom the resurrected One receives back into his service." "His power, dominion, and victory are manifested in the proclamation."[21] Beyond question, the apostolic proclamation manifests his "power, dominion, and victory." But that manifestation takes place precisely because the risen and ascended Lord is "working with" the missionaries and "confirming" his active presence with various signs.

Francis J. Moloney tends to modify even more the full force of what Torrance correctly found in Mark 16:20. Moloney writes, "Fundamental to the missionary activity of the early church was the conviction that the missionaries were doing the work of the Lord."[22] True, but the Markan verse expresses a more startling conviction. It was in a strong sense that "the missionaries were doing the work of the Lord," since he was working with them. You can do the work of someone without that person working with you. Mark 16:20 represents the Lord being present, working with the apostles, and actively confirming their proclamation with various signs.

Moloney adds, "The author [of the Markan appendix] recalls the prodigious signs that the believers [and the proclaimers, please] were able to do, and indicates that the authority of the absent Lord [communicated] to his missionary church is certified by these and other signs." Jesus "is no longer present to them as he was during his days on earth," but, "despite his physical absence, they [the missionaries] are acting with his authority."[23]

Moloney speaks of a "physical absence" of the risen and ascended Lord. But does Christ's being invisible necessarily entail a physical absence? Modern science has established the physical presence of innumerable, invisible agents; they are actively present, despite their being physically invisible. What Moloney says about "the authority of the absent Lord" seems to suggest a situation in which others (the missionaries) act with this authority, while the Lord himself is simply absent. Unquestionably they do act with his authority, but Mark 16:20 goes beyond mere authorization: the Lord works with them and confirms with signs their message. This justifies Torrance in saying that, when they proclaim the message, it is Christ who actively proclaims the message. It is not merely the case of missionaries proclaiming the word because they have been authorized by Christ to do so.

Moloney describes the signs that accompany the proclamation as "evidence of the authority of the risen Lord, enabling them [the apostolic missionaries] to perform successfully what they have been commanded to do."[24] But surely Mark 16:20 claims something more? It is the power of the Lord *who works with them* that enables them to carry out their mission successfully. Torrance, rather than Moloney, respects the full force of what the Markan addition states about the prophetic activity of the risen and ascended Christ.

Conclusion

In *Space, Time and Resurrection* Torrance appeals to Mark 16:19–20 to present the ascended Christ *ad dexteram Dei* being actively and *prophetically* present when his apostles and other ministers proclaim the good news. "The Lord himself," he writes, "is immediately present with them in his Spirit, making the preaching of the Gospel effectual as Word and Power of God."[25]

Torrance at once attended to the closely related, active, *priestly* presence of the risen Christ in the liturgy of the Church: "Ministers [visibly] lead the worship of God's people, declare the forgiveness of sins, and celebrate Baptism and the Lord's Supper." But, invisibly, "through the power of his Spirit it is Christ himself who confers forgiveness, builds up his Church on earth, renews it in the power of his resurrection, and presents it as his own Body to the Father."[26] In *Theology in Reconciliation* and *The Mediation of Christ*,[27] Torrance developed at length the priestly function of Christ, the high priest who intercedes for us *ad dexteram Dei* (Rom 8:34; Heb 7:25).

Torrance rightly used Mark 16:19–20 to legitimate his view of the active presence of the ascended Christ in his prophetic role. That has been the main argument developed in this chapter. Yet Torrance championed this prophetic function not independently but within the full scheme of Christ as prophet, priest, and king/shepherd. Hence at appropriate points I have drawn attention to Torrance's concern with the kingly and priestly office of the risen and ascended Christ.

7

MARY AND SIMEON

(Luke 1:38; 2:29)

Luke, and not least in the infancy narratives, introduces parallels, which, featuring similarities and differences, enrich the story and its theological meaning. In a parallel not fully appreciated by François Bovon, Robert Tannehill, and other commentators, Luke links Mary and Simeon through the themes of "slave," "word," and in other ways. This article explores eight links that the evangelist makes between Mary and Simeon.

When reflecting on Simeon's words in Luke 2:29 ("now, Master, you release your slave according to your word in peace," au. trans.), Tannehill notes how Simeon "refers to himself as God's 'slave,' as Mary did previously (1:38)."[1] This is to connect two verses, which occur, respectively, in the annunciation to Mary (Luke 1:26–38) and in the presentation of the Christ child in the temple (Luke 2:22–38). Where Tannehill draws at least a minimal connection, Luke Timothy Johnson makes none at all. Instead of linking Luke 2:29 with what has already been found in Luke 1:38, he looks far ahead and associates the verse with Acts 4:24: "'Servant' (*doulos*) is correlative to 'master' (*despotēs*, here and Acts 4:24)."[2]

In his longer, now-classical commentary on Luke, Bovon likewise does not take up the rich connection that exists between the words of Mary and those of Simeon.[3] Nevertheless, as we shall see, he offers insights that serve to elaborate the connection. Let us examine seven features of what Mary says in Luke 1:38 (and related verses) before taking up Luke 2:29 (and related verses).

Mary and Simeon

The presence of two common items ("slave" and "according to your word") and two equivalent expressions (*kai idou* and *nun*, and *kurios* and *despotēs*) in both 1:38 (Mary's final words in her meeting with Gabriel) and 2:29 (the opening words of Simeon's canticle, the *Nunc Dimittis*), respectively, makes a prima facie case for connecting 1:38 and 2:29. While we are not discussing the provenance of the two verses, it seems more plausible to understand 1:38 as Luke's own composition. He may have taken from a tradition the opening and other verses of the *Nunc Dimittis*, but some scholars argue for Lukan authorship of the whole canticle.[4]

Seven Features of Mary's Words

The story of the angel Gabriel's prophecy of Jesus's conception and birth ends: "Then Mary said, 'Here am I, the slave of the Lord; let it be with me according to your word.' Then the angel departed from her" (Luke 1:38; NRSV corrected).

First, "here am I" (which translates *idou*) points to a graced moment, the historical moment in which "Mary places herself at God's behest…she does not merely submit herself but demonstrates her agreement." Bovon recognizes how "her human response appertains to history" (Bovon, 53) and the grace of the present moment.[5] Later in the Gospel of Luke, Jesus, when preparing to celebrate with the disciples his last Passover, tells Peter and John, "When you have entered the city [Jerusalem], look [*idou*], a man carrying a jar of water will meet you" (Luke 22:10; NRSV modified). "Look" signals in advance something of the significance of Jesus's last meal with his disciples and the institution of the Eucharist.

Just before Mary uses *idou* in 1:38, the angel Gabriel introduces a birth prophecy by using the same word: "And behold [*kai idou*], you will conceive in [your] womb and give birth to a son, and you will name him Jesus" (1:31 au. trans.). Gabriel moves on to introduce in the same way a sign, Mary's older relative Elizabeth now being pregnant: "And behold, your relative Elizabeth in her old age has also conceived a son" (1:36 au. trans.). The angel points successively to two decisive moments in salvation history, and so creates a link "between the two mothers" (Bovon, 52–53).

Second, in Luke's narrative after 1:38, Mary will name herself once again "slave": "God my Savior looked with favor on his slave, lowly as she is" (Luke 1:48 au. trans.). Many translations of 1:38 and 1:48, but not that in Tannehill's commentary, have, of course, softened the sense of *doule* and in both cases introduced "servant" or "handmaid."[6] This often happens when the apostle Paul calls himself "the slave of Christ Jesus" (e.g., Rom 1:1 au. trans.) but is translated as saying "servant." However, "servant" takes away something of the utter self-subjection conveyed by "slave." Normally, of course, people are made slaves against their will. In the case of Mary and Paul, however, a free, personal choice puts them totally at the disposition of "the Lord."

Third, Mary's response to the angel follows immediately on Gabriel's closing remark about Mary's cousin Elizabeth conceiving a son in her old age: "for nothing will be impossible with God" (Luke 1:37), or, in the rather free translation provided by the New English Bible, "God's promises can never fail." The key term in what both Gabriel and Mary say is *rēma*, literally "word" or "thing," which expresses here the sense of some remarkable thing (or event) being promised (the divine word). Neither Elizabeth's advanced years nor Mary's unmarried situation will stand in the way of what God promises—in Elizabeth's case the birth of John the Baptist and in Mary's case the birth of Jesus the Messiah. To the saying or "word" of the angel there corresponds a wonderful "thing," the promised deed of God.

Fourth, when the angel Gabriel conveys to Mary the divine promise, the event of her virginal conception and motherhood has not yet happened. It will happen when the Holy Spirit overshadows her (1:35). After the angel departs, "Mary awaits the fulfilment of God's will" (Bovon, 53), the unique highpoint in God's plan of salvation to be brought through the power of the Spirit. She expects that the divine fidelity will be revealed, and her son will be born.

Fifth, Bovon notes that what is happening to Mary illustrates once again the surprising choices God makes to fulfill the divine plan of salvation: "God chooses the humanly limited and overlooked, this time a girl of about twelve (Luke 1:27) and long ago the young man Gideon (Judg 6:15). The impossible, which for God is possible, becomes evident by a comparison of the feeble means with the greatness of the result" (Bovon, 53). The humble slave girl who has been chosen (Luke 1:48) contrasts with the great things that follow—not least for Israel, the servant of God (1:51–54).

Sixth, Bovon adds, what he calls "feebleness" is not "weakness, for Mary possesses inner strength and trusting faith" (Bovon, 53). Her "explicitly formulated assent" is remarkable; it presses beyond any of the supposed parallels to be found in the Hebrew Bible (Bovon, 53n96). Tannehill also signals the faith that Mary displays: "Mary's encounter with the angel ends with her submission to her appointed role as Mother of the Messiah (1:38), an act of acceptance which reveals her faith (1:45)."[7] It is a faith that responds to the divine word and evokes praise from Mary's cousin, Elizabeth: "blessed is she who believed that there would be a fulfilment of what was spoken to her by the Lord" (1:45).

Seventh, Tannehill notices how Gabriel's words to Mary associate the special pregnancy of Elizabeth (Luke 1:36) with that of Mary. These two pregnancies embody Israel's hopes that are beginning to be fulfilled. Tannehill observes, "Ancient hopes, treasured in the hearts of the Jewish people are coming to fulfilment."[8]

Lukan Parallelism

Before spelling out connections between Mary and Simeon, we need to follow Johnson (and others) in observing Luke's "extensive use of parallelism. He matches persons and events [and, we should add, language] in different parts of his narrative."[9] Similarities *and differences* characterize parallelisms found in Luke's narrative: for instance, that between John the Baptist and Jesus:

John will be great before the Lord (1:15).	Jesus will be great and Son of the Most High (1:32).
John will prepare a people (1:17).	Jesus will rule the people (1:33).
John's role is temporary (1:17).	Jesus's kingdom will never end (1:33).
John is to be a prophet (1:15).	Jesus [is] more than another prophet: he is Son of God (1:35).
John will be "filled with the Holy Spirit" as a prophet (1:15).	The overshadowing of the Spirit and Power will make Jesus "the Holy One" (1:35).

THE GOSPELS

Johnson comments also on "another obviously deliberate" linking and contrast: between Zechariah and Mary.[10] Bovon notes as well how there are obvious similarities and differences between the two annunciations (Bovon, 48).

Tannehill recognizes how "repetitive patterns" often "contribute to the forward movement" in the story Luke tells. The similarities and differences that characterize particular cases of repetition belong "to a single divine purpose."[11] Tannehill adds, "The parallels between John the Baptist and Jesus in Luke 1—2 have been widely recognized and discussed." For a summary of these parallels, he refers to what Raymond Brown and Joseph Fitzmyer have written.[12] Tannehill himself sketches the "most obvious" "parallels in the annunciations to Zechariah and Mary."[13] Brown provides a fuller vision of these parallel annunciations.[14]

Simeon and Mary

The presentation of Jesus in the temple (Luke 2:22-38) focuses primarily on Simeon (2:25-35). Just as Luke's narrative has connected Mary with an older man who had *already* appeared in the story, Zechariah, so it now connects her to an old man who appears *later*, Simeon. Luke's story writes large the link Mary/Zechariah/Simeon by assigning to each of them hymns of praise and blessing—respectively, the Magnificat, the Benedictus, and the *Nunc Dimittis*. Let us review eight aspects of the link between Mary and Simeon.

First, the evangelist introduces Simeon with a word (*nun*), similar to that used by Mary in responding to the divine invitation (*idou*): "here am I" (1:38). When introducing Simeon the word is better translated "now" (2:25). The term also signals a graced moment that will occur when two old and faithful Israelites, Simeon and Anna, meet in the holy temple three people: Mary, Joseph, and the Christ child.

Simeon's opening words take the form of blessing God: "now [*nun*], Master [*despotēs*], you release your slave [*doulon*] in peace according to your word [*rēma*] in peace" (2:29 au. trans.). Like *idou*, "now" alerts the reader to the blessed point in time that has arrived—for Simeon as well as for the Jewish people.[15] A little earlier in Luke's narrative, Mary's song of praise has already joined together the verb *idou* with the adverb *nun*: "behold [*idou*] from now on [*apo tou nun*] all generations will call me

Mary and Simeon

blessed" (1:48 au. trans.). Her language anticipates that used of Simeon (*idou* 2:25) and by Simeon (*nun* 2:29).

Second, like Mary, Simeon calls himself a "slave" of God. He too presents himself as totally submitted to God. Unlike Mary, he supplies the correlative of a "slave" by addressing the divine "Master."

Third, a submission that takes place "according to your word [of promise]" connects Mary with Simeon. The wonderful thing promised by God to Mary, the birth of her Son, has just taken place when she meets Simeon. In his case, years before it had been revealed to him that he would not die "before he had seen the Lord's Messiah" (2:26). That word of promise is now fulfilled when he receives Mary's child into his arms (2:28).

Fourth, just as the Holy Spirit proved central to what happened to Mary, so the Spirit who "was upon" Simeon "revealed" to him that he would see the Messiah, and "guided" him into the temple precinct for a rendezvous with the Christ child (2:25-27). The meeting between Simeon and the newborn Jesus is "a Spirit-caused event" (Bovon, 101). It was through the working of the Holy Spirit that, in their different ways, both Mary and Simeon experience the divine fidelity, embodied in the newborn Jesus.

Fifth, Simeon was "righteous" and "devout" (2:25), a man of prayer who frequented the temple. Like the young Mary, this old man seemed of no particular importance from a human and religious point of view.[16] Unlike Zechariah, for instance, he did not belong to the ranks of the priesthood. In the case of Simeon, God also made a surprising choice— this time for welcoming the Messiah, not into the world, as Mary did, but into the central place of divine worship, the temple in Jerusalem.

Sixth, after Mary reveals her faith in action when she encounters the angel Gabriel, so Simeon reveals his strong and trusting faith when he encounters Mary, Joseph, and the Christ child. Elizabeth's words could also be applied to him: "blessed is [he] who believed that there would be a fulfillment of what was spoken to [him] by the Lord" (1:45). A beatitude referred to Mary might appropriately be applied to Simeon.

Seventh, the ancient hopes of Israel find fulfillment in the pregnancy of Elizabeth and then, supremely, in the pregnancy of Mary. Simeon, like Anna (2:36-38), symbolizes eminently these hopes. While in his case they could not be fulfilled by a pregnancy, something analogous happens when he receives the newborn Jesus "into his arms" (2:28). Through a "maternal gesture" (Bovon, 101), which stands out as the only time that the four Gospels ever mention Jesus being taken into the arms of anyone, Simeon associates himself with Mary.

Eighth and finally, within the account itself of the presentation in the temple, Mary and Joseph (2:23–24, 27) are linked to Simeon (2:25) and Anna (2:37–38). They all belong among the devout Jews devoted to the law and cherishing hopes for Israel's redemption (see also 1:54–55).[17]

Conclusion

Unquestionably, Johnson, Tannehill, and others throw light on Luke's narrative by linking Mary back to Zechariah. The two "annunciations" mutually illuminate each other, both in their similarities and differences. But various details in the meeting between Mary and the angel Gabriel, above all in Mary's response, are echoed and interpreted also by what is to come at the presentation in the temple. The old man Simeon can be fruitfully compared and contrasted with Mary, so as to develop an even fuller picture of what Luke's narrative conveys. Multiple associations between Mary and Simeon enrich the narrative and hold it together. They guide the reader in exploring the symbolic and theological world of the narrator.[18]

8

THE NATIVITY IN VIEW OF THE CROSS AND RESURRECTION

(Luke 2:1-20)

In his commentary on the Gospel of Luke, François Bovon discusses the Roman census that brings Mary and Joseph to Bethlehem for the birth of Jesus (Luke 2:1-5). He draws attention to "the striking juxtaposition of [a] the emperor [Augustus, the ruler of the *imperium romanum*, which covered the *oikumenē*, or inhabited world] known to all, with [b] the hidden Messiah."[1] In the contemplation on the nativity to be made in the second week of the *Spiritual Exercises*, St. Ignatius Loyola hints at this juxtaposition. He mentions "the tribute which Caesar had imposed" (*SpEx* 111), and eventually describes it in terms of "Joseph acknowledging his subjection to Caesar" (*SpEx* 264).[2]

Elsewhere Ignatius alerts retreatants to the humility that Christ showed and the humiliations he suffered. In the Meditation on Two Standards, he imagines Christ our Lord, "the supreme and true commander" taking "his stand in a lowly place" (*SpEx* 143-44). Before proposing the Elections, Ignatius wants retreatants "to consider attentively" three kinds of humility, the third of which incorporates imitating Christ in his poverty and in "ignominy rather than fame" (*SpEx* 164, 167). For the contemplation on the nativity, Ignatius might have contrasted the humility and anonymity of Christ, born "in a lowly place," with the "fame" and earthly power of Augustus ruling his empire from his Roman palace. But it is a cross that takes the form of "extreme poverty" that Ignatius highlights.

The Extreme Poverty of the Nativity

For the contemplation on the nativity, Ignatius proposes watching and considering what they (Mary, Joseph, and a servant girl) are doing: "their travel and efforts, so that Christ comes to be born in extreme poverty and, after so many labors, after hunger, thirst, heat and cold, outrages and affronts, he dies on the cross" (*SpEx* 116). In his notes for "the mysteries of the life of Christ our Lord," Ignatius adds details from Luke 2:7: "she [Mary] bore her first-born son, and wrapped him in clothes, and placed him in the manger, [because there was no room for them in the inn]" (*SpEx* 264).

Summing up the circumstances of Jesus's birth as those of "extreme poverty," Ignatius anticipates the suffering that would ensue when Jesus grew to manhood: a ministry, characterized by "so many labors, hunger, thirst, heat and cold," the passion when Jesus faced "outrages and affronts," and, finally, death "on the cross." Being placed after birth in a feeding trough for animals is not the only detail explicitly cited to explain what constituted the extreme poverty that opened a life of suffering that would end in crucifixion. In the composition of place for the contemplation on the nativity, Ignatius speaks of "the grotto" in which Jesus was born (*SpEx* 112). "Because there was no place for them in the inn [*kataluma*]" (Luke 2:7), Jesus was born in a grotto or cave. Here Ignatius follows an early tradition about Jesus being born in a cave, which was derived from the Protoevangelium of James (18.1) and St. Justin Martyr (*Dialogue with Trypho*, 78) in the second century and Origen (*Contra Celsum*, 1.51) in the third century. On his own pilgrimage to the Holy Land, the cave of the nativity might have been one of the shrines Ignatius visited, even if he does not explicitly mention this.[3]

Modern biblical scholarship supports Ignatius's notion of "extreme poverty" through the various translations it endorses for "manger [*phatnē*]." While it probably means (a) a feeding trough for animals,[4] it could also mean (b) an indoor or outdoor "stable" or "stall" where animals were tied up or penned (as in Luke 13:15), or (c) "a feeding place under the open sky, in contrast to *kataluma*, a shelter where people stayed."[5] Any of these three meanings indicates the extreme poverty that characterized the place where Mary and Joseph stopped and where Jesus was born. He came into this world, not in a proper shelter for human beings nor in a proper place for a birth, but among the animals.

The text of Ignatius does not incorporate literally the early tradition of animals being present around the manger, a tradition inspired by words of Isaiah 1:3[6] and incorporated in the practice of Christmas cribs launched by St. Francis of Assisi (d. 1226). But Ignatius has already included, in the first preamble to the contemplation on the nativity, a donkey on which Mary rides from Nazareth to Bethlehem and an ox that Joseph and a servant girl bring along as well. Two animals have shared the journey from Nazareth and are presumably present to share also in the birth at Bethlehem (*SpEx* 111).

One modern interpretation of *phatnē* connects it with the entombment of Jesus. When born, he was placed in a manger, just as after his crucifixion he would be placed in a tomb (Luke 23:53).[7] This view, unintentionally, coincides with icons of the nativity created by Eastern Christians. They portray the newly born Christ child wrapped in what might pass as a shroud and lying in a kind of trough that has been cut in a large rock and could seem like a tiny tomb.

In Luke's nativity narrative, the swaddling clothes symbolize the ordinary, human condition of the newborn Christ child. Like any baby, he was wrapped in bands of cloth (see Wis 7:4–7). Mary "did for Jesus what any ancient Palestinian mother would have done for a newborn babe." What she did expressed her "maternal care."[8]

Some Western artists link the swaddling clothes of the Christ child with the loin cloth he will wear on the cross. Thus, on the Isenheimer altar painted by Matthew Grünewald (d. 1528), "in his portrayal of Christmas, Our Lady holds her child in the same cloth that Jesus will wear at the end of his life on the cross."[9] Sometimes, as in the case of Sandro Botticelli's *The Mystical Nativity* (see below), the swaddling clothes are associated with the shroud in which he will be buried.

Geertgen Tot Sint Jans (d. about 1490) does not make either of these links; he omits the swaddling clothes altogether. In his *The Nativity at Night*, found in the National Gallery, London, the child lies completely naked in a rough, hard container, more a tomb than a cradle. Christ's future suffering can also be detected in the way Geertgen encloses the composition within the wooden beams of a stable. On the one hand, the beams show us that the child, although naked, is protected by a roof. On the other hand, the way the beams extend into the sky hints at the wooden arms of the cross on which the child will die for us.

Sacred art, both East and West, converges with Ignatius in linking the birth of Christ with his crucifixion. But we should not neglect the way Ignatius and (before him) Luke introduce elements of cross *and resurrection* in presenting the story of the nativity. Both Ignatius and Luke do this through the angels who encounter the shepherds and send them to Bethlehem. Luke *also* includes, as we shall see, elements of cross and resurrection through the three "inns" that punctuate his narrative: Luke 2:7; 10:34; and 22:11.

The Shepherds

In his *notes on the mysteries* of Christ's life, Ignatius quotes from Luke's Gospel 2:13–14 to propose the third point for prayer inspired by "the Nativity of Christ Our Lord": "there came a multitude of the heavenly army, which said, 'glory to God in the heavens'" (*SpEx* 264). Following straight on from the second point for the contemplation on the nativity ("she bore her first-born son, and wrapped him in clothes, and placed him in the manger"), the third point implies that "a multitude of the heavenly army" came to the place of Christ's birth and there proclaimed "glory to God in the heavens." From their appearing to shepherds out in the countryside, Ignatius has moved the multitude of angels into Bethlehem, where they announce the glory of God revealed in the lowly birth of the Messiah. This does not correspond to Luke's narrative, in which the angels leave the shepherds and return "into heaven" (Luke 2:15). The "divine glory shines not around the manger but around the angels," appearing outside Bethlehem to shepherds. It is they alone who can then go into town and bear witness to a heavenly revelation (Bovon, 1:87).[10]

Ignatius belongs to a tradition, reflected in Christian art both before and after his time, which placed an angelic host proclaiming the nativity right there in the stable or grotto where Christ was born. This tradition, through the presence of angels in Bethlehem, associates heavenly glory, and not merely the cross, with the cave where Jesus was born and the manger in which he was laid. *The Mystical Nativity* (1500–1501) by Botticelli (now in the National Gallery, London) portrays an open cave where Jesus was born but includes twelve angels dancing under the golden dome of heaven right above the child, who lies on a sheet in his rustic manger. For good measure, at the bottom of the painting three further angels embrace three men. Botticelli's masterpiece blends earthly poverty and lowliness with heavenly joy and celebration, the cross with the glory of risen life.

Ignatius's *notes* for a contemplation "on the shepherds" (Luke 2:8-20) immediately follow those for a contemplation of the nativity and feature even more heavenly glory and corresponding human joy. According to the first point, "the nativity of Christ Our Lord is made known to the shepherds by the angel: 'I declare to you a great joy, because today the Savior of the world has been born.'" Ignatius closes his sketch for a contemplation on the shepherds with the third point: "the shepherds went back, glorifying and praising the Lord." The glory and joy of the resurrection pervade the first and third points. Poverty and the cross make their appearance in the second point. The shepherds "found the child laid in the manger" when they went to Bethlehem (*SpEx* 265).

In his contemporary biblical commentary, Bovon presents a vision of Jesus's birth that "intertwines glory and lowliness." A heavenly army of angels witnesses to the greatness of Jesus, who is Savior and Christ the Lord; the manger expresses the lowliness of his birth. The "humble birth" "stands under the sign of the cross" (Bovon, 1:93), conveyed specifically through the sign of the manger. Bovon notes "the thrice-repeated, refrain-like occurrence of 'child lying in a manger'" (1:90). Mary "laid" her newborn son "in a manger" (Luke 2:7); the sign the shepherds received from the angel of the Lord was that of "a child wrapped in bands of cloth and lying in a manger" (2:12); when the shepherds went to Bethlehem, they found "the child lying in a manger" (2:16). But heavenly glory was not absent.

Bovon uses two sermons by Martin Luther, a contemporary of Ignatius, to summarize the message of human misery and heavenly glory conveyed by the Lukan account of Jesus's birth. The Savior was born so wretchedly on earth, but there followed the happy song of the angels (Bovon, 1:93-94). The sign of the manger interpreted the birth of one who would die on a cross, but his birth was also the occasion of a revelation of divine glory (Luke 2:8-9) and of a heavenly liturgy led by an angelic choir (2:13-14). That revelation and liturgy acclaimed the "peace" that God conveys and the human "joy" it occasions (2:10, 14).

Bovon appropriately points to an *inclusio* that, through the presence of angels, binds together the humble "birth" of Christ and "his rebirth in the resurrection."[11] At the end angels will attest "the hand of God at work" in the resurrection (Luke 24:4), when "the people experience peace" (24:36) and "great joy" (24:52) (Bovon, 1:88). The *inclusio* joins cross and resurrection.

Three Inns as Scenes of Cross and Resurrection

Reflecting on the inn where Mary and Joseph found no room, Bovon notes how "the holy duty of hospitality" had waned somewhat since the days of tribal nomads (Bovon, 1:86). But the inn in Bethlehem is only the first of three inns in Luke's Gospel where such a place of hospitality is endowed with meaning drawn from the cross and resurrection.

Luke's story of Jesus's birth states that the baby was "laid…in a manger, because there was no place for them in the inn [*kataluma*]" (Luke 2:7). The New Revised Standard Version (NRSV) translates *kataluma* as "inn," as does the Revised English Bible (REB) and the Jerusalem Bible (JB). The King James Version (KJV) had called it "the village inn," unlike its influential predecessor, the Tyndale Bible, which translated the verse as Mary "layed him in a manger because ther was no roume for them in the ynne." Suggesting that "inn" (Bovon, 1:80) is probably intended "vaguely," Bovon thinks of "a room in a private house in which travelers could usually spend the night." But he also speaks of a roadhouse, "a place where one can stop and unharness a mount or draught animal…a provisional place to spend the night" (Bovon, 1:86).

The noun *kataluma* has a related verb *kataluō* ("to let/bring down"). The meanings of this verb vary widely but include to put down one's baggage, unharness an animal, unload its burden, stop doing what one is doing, and so halt, rest, find lodging (*kataluma*), and receive hospitality. We find the verb used with one or more of such meanings in Luke 9:12 and 19:7.

Almost halfway through Luke's Gospel, Jesus delivers his famous parable of the Good Samaritan (10:25–37). The Samaritan takes a wounded traveler to an "inn" (NRSV, REB, and JB), does his best for him, and leaves him next day in the care of the "innkeeper" (NRSV, REB, and JB). The two terms in Greek are, respectively, *pandocheion* and *pandocheus*; each term occurs only here in the entire New Testament. Etymology suggests their meaning: "*pan* (all) *docheion* (receiving)," that is to say, receiving/welcoming anyone and everyone.

Toward the end of Luke's Gospel, Jesus sends Peter and John into Jerusalem to prepare the Passover, where they are to say to the owner of a house, "The teacher asks you, 'Where is the guest room [*kataluma*], where I may eat the Passover with my disciples?' He will show you a large room upstairs [*anagaion*], already furnished. Make preparations for us there" (22:8–12; NRSV). In this passage from Luke, the REB translates *kataluma* simply as "the room" rather than as "the guest room," and continues, "he [the householder] will show you a large room upstairs all set out." The JB renders *kataluma* as "the dining room," and then by inserting "with couches" adds to what we find in the Greek text: "the man will show you a large upper room furnished with couches."[12] It is only in Luke 2:7; 22:11; and Mark 14:14 (on which Luke 22:11 draws) that we find *kataluma* in the whole of the New Testament.

The magisterial *Greek-English Lexicon of the New Testament and Other Early Christian Literature* (*BDAG*) judges "inn" to be only a possible translation in Luke 2:7, with *kataluma* being "best understood" here as "lodging" or "guest-room" as in Luke 22:11.[13] The context of Luke 22:11 (and Mark 14:14) would also permit "the sense [of] dining room." *Pandocheion* (Luke 10:34) is the more specific term for "inn," where a traveler could find lodging.[14] Thus *BDAG* prefers "lodging" or "guest-room" for Luke 2:7, "inn" for Luke 10:34, and "lodging," "guest-room," or "dining room" for Luke 22:11.

So much for the translation of three passages from Luke. How might this use of *kataluma* (twice) and *pandocheion* (once) be drawn together and nourish reflection on the cross and resurrection? Jesus came into this world, not in a *kataluma*, which offered a normal stopping place where people on a journey could shelter, but in some kind of stable where Mary placed her newborn child in a trough for feeding animals. That "there was no room for them in the inn" prompts prayerful thought about the presence of the cross right from the beginning of Jesus's story.[15] But we have also seen how this failure in hospitality was offset by the anticipation of resurrection conveyed by the heavenly glory and angelic message revealed to the shepherds. We find life, even heavenly life, as well as death in contemplating the story of Jesus's nativity.

THE GOSPELS

The Inn of the Good Samaritan

In Luke's Gospel after the nativity story, we hear no more of Bethlehem or mangers. But an inn (*pandocheion*) returns with the parable of the Good Samaritan (10:29–37). Even before that, the verb that corresponds to *kataluma* has turned up. At the end of a day on which Jesus had spoken in a deserted place to a crowd of five thousand "about the kingdom of God" and "healed those who needed to be cured," the twelve apostles came to him and said, "Send this crowd away, so that they may go into the surrounding villages and countryside, to find lodging [*katalusōsin*] and get provisions" (au. trans.). Instead, Jesus multiplied five loaves and two fish and fed the crowd (9:11–17). The apostles had presumed that, late in the day and even for such a large number of people, lodging and food would be available elsewhere.

Despite the differences between the miraculous feeding (concerning the needs of thousands) and a story involving only a handful of people, an "example story,"[16] as some call the parable of the Good Samaritan, a similar presumption shows up. The Samaritan seems to take it for granted that he will find shelter and care for a wounded man at a nearby "inn."

Unlike some parables that may feature only one or two characters—for instance, the sower and the seeds (Luke 8:4–15) and the lost sheep (15:3–7)—the parable of the Good Samaritan includes several *dramatis personae*: the man traveling to Jericho, the robbers, a priest, a Levite, a Samaritan, and an innkeeper. The hero who practices compassion toward someone in dreadful need is undoubtedly the Samaritan, described by Bovon as "a nondescript individual with a despised background," someone "usually associated with evil" (Bovon, 2:56, 57). The Samaritan's heart goes out to the wounded traveler. Through administering first aid and transporting him to a nearby inn, he establishes a "relationship" with him (58). "Having done his part, the Samaritan passed the torch to others"—in particular, to the innkeeper. He has "taken care" of the wounded man and asks the innkeeper to do the same (59).

Undoubtedly, it is the example of the Samaritan that provides the central answer to the question, "Who is my neighbor?" (Luke 10:29). But what of the innkeeper? Does his heart go out to the wounded traveler? We do not know, but we do know that he establishes a relationship with the man by agreeing at once to give him shelter and care. He does not object: "there is no room for badly wounded people in my inn." To be sure, he is given two denarii by the Samaritan who promises that, on his return, any further expenses will be repaid. The innkeeper does not supply lodging and help for nothing. But he lives up to the meaning of his name in Greek, someone who "receives everyone." His kind help may be less spectacular, but it does carry further the concern and care of the Good Samaritan. The innkeeper is also a true neighbor to someone in great distress. If this example story invites its readers to "be a Good Samaritan," it also invites them, albeit secondarily, to "be a good innkeeper."

Ancient Christianity provides examples of writers positively appreciating the inn and the innkeeper, and not merely the Good Samaritan. Bovon summarizes Origen's account of an earlier interpretation that understood the innkeeper to be "the head of the Church, in charge of administration." Bovon goes on to quote from Origen's *Homilies on Luke*, 34.7: "The Samaritan…carries the dying man and takes him to an inn, i.e., into the Church that welcomes everyone, does not refuse aid to anyone, and to which all are invited by Jesus" (Bovon, 2:60–61).

Bovon notes how "in the past the image of the Samaritan was often applied to Christ giving help to humanity, rather than to some charitable Christian."[17] Bovon has no quarrel with this christological application, provided that it is not "done at the expense of the ethical dimension." He explains that the "Christological structure is rooted in God, who is compassionate and active, and acts through the Church, whose members carry on their Lord's charitable acts by means of their faith and practice" (Bovon, 2:51; see 59).

Bovon also recalls how "Samaritan" in Hebrew means "watchman" or "shepherd" (Bovon, 2:58n38). Being a Good Samaritan hints at the Good/Beautiful Shepherd, who lays down his life for his sheep (see John 10:11, 14).

Cross and resurrection belong to the example story that Jesus told, in the sense that it turned on a traveler in great distress. He had been robbed, beaten, and left half dead, only to be rescued and nursed back to life in the shelter of an inn. But we should not ignore the personal loss and personal risk suffered by the Good Samaritan. His kindness cost him some oil, wine, clothing, and money—as well as the loss of time caused by an unforeseen break in his journey. We should also remember the element of danger: if one traveler had been robbed, bandits could still have been prowling around to attack and rob others. It was dangerous to stop at the side of the road and then move slowly ahead keeping a badly wounded man from falling off his seat on the pack animal.

The life of Jesus, as Christian preachers and others have appreciated, dramatized his role as the Good Samaritan (Bovon, 2:64n75). Luke encouraged them to do so by providing a link through a striking verb, "his heart went out [*esplanchnisthē*]" (au. trans.), with which he described not only the reaction of Jesus to the widow of Nain who had just lost her only son (7:13) but also the reaction of the Samaritan (10:33) to the half-dead traveler. At his own personal risk and cost, Jesus stopped to save wounded people who had been robbed and stripped. But in this case, however, compassionate love for his neighbors cost much more than possessions, money, and time. Jesus as the good Samaritan was stripped and wounded in his passion. He became the victimized traveler, not rescued but left to die on a cross.

To conclude, the parable of the Good Samaritan reflects its lights and shadows back over the earlier story of Christ's nativity. It does so not only (a) through the contrast between two inns, the first in which there was "no room" for the birth of the messianic shepherd (prophesied by Mic 5:2–5a) and the second in which a wounded traveler found unquestioning shelter and care, but also (b) through the figures of the Good Samaritan (or Good Shepherd) and the good innkeeper. The cross and the resurrection belong in both the parable and the story of the nativity.

The "Inn" of the Last Supper

Before we arrive at the *kataluma* where Jesus celebrated the Passover with his disciples on the night before he died (Luke 22:7–13), we should note the related verb used in the account of Jesus's visit to Zacchaeus in Jericho: Jesus went "to be the guest [*katalusai*]" (Luke 19:7) of a notorious sinner, a chief tax collector (19:1–10; see Bovon, 2:590–602).

The identity (as "Lord" and "the Son of Man") and mission of Jesus ("to seek out and save the lost") are prominent in this meeting between Zacchaeus and Jesus. Zacchaeus begins by "wanting to see" the traveler and ends by recognizing him at a meal as "Lord" and showing his repentance by what he does and promises to do. As with the Passover to come, Jesus initiates this meal: "Zacchaeus, hurry and come down; for I must stay at your house today" (Luke 19:5). But then a totally critical

The Nativity in View of the Cross and Resurrection

audience ("all who saw it") grumble (19:7) at Jesus agreeing to accept hospitality from a very disreputable man—unlike those involved in preparing the Passover, the last meal Jesus will eat with his disciples.

Jesus prepared to eat the Passover by sending Peter and John to the owner of a house in Jerusalem. They were to ask him what Jesus "the Master" told them: "Where is the guest room [*kataluma*], where I may eat the Passover with my disciples?" (Luke 22:11). The house owner at once showed Peter and John "a large room upstairs, already furnished"; there they prepared the Passover (22:12).[18] Jesus knew in advance who would offer hospitality to him and his apostles. To be sure, "the inhabitants of Jerusalem were prepared to make space available to the pilgrims" who wanted to celebrate the Passover. "They were even expected to perform this service free of charge" (Bovon, 3:143). Nevertheless, without hesitation the anonymous house owner did what Jesus asked through Peter and John. While Jesus was in command of the situation, the three of them collaborated to put his plan into action; Jesus and his apostles could all sit down to eat the Passover meal.

By being able to eat in the privacy of the guest room upstairs—a *kataluma* in that sense rather than in the sense of being a public shelter for a random group of travelers—celebrating the Passover provided Christ and his core group of followers with a "wonderful intimacy."[19] The Jewish feast served "as a framework for the Last Supper of Jesus. This will become the first example of a new Christian rite, which itself will look forward to the banquet of the kingdom" (Bovon, 3:143-44).

At the Last Supper (Luke 22:15-20), Jesus defined in advance the meaning of his imminent death and resurrection—by the words of institution over the broken bread ("This is my body, which is given for you") and the wine ("This cup that is poured out for you is the new covenant in my blood"). The "for you" pointed to the group sharing the meal with Jesus as the immediate beneficiaries of his death and new covenant. But, since Jesus called for the future repetition of the ritual ("do this in remembrance of me"), he wanted to confer on an indefinite number of others the saving benefits of his life, death, and resurrection. He desired to establish also with them his continuing place and presence in the meal fellowship he had instituted with a small, core group of disciples.[20]

The Last Supper came at the end of a life that began in Bethlehem with a birth outside the shelter of a public *kataluma*, moved through a ministry that included the parable of the Good Samaritan, assisted by the good innkeeper, and ended with a final celebration in a Jerusalem *kataluma*. The command "do this in remembrance of me" (Luke 22:19) extended beyond the ritual established on the eve of Jesus's death to concern his whole story, and hence the three inns that punctuated it. Thus "doing this in remembrance of me" can *also* be understood as an invitation to show the hospitality that failed at the birth of Jesus, but was inculcated by the parable of the Good Samaritan and supremely exemplified by Jesus the Good Innkeeper in an upper room of Jerusalem.

Ignatius proposed for retreatants a contemplation of the nativity that included overtones of the cross and resurrection. Attention to the three inns of Luke's Gospel fills out further possibilities for that contemplation. Like Mary at the end of the visit of the shepherds, we can "treasure all these words/events [*rēmata*] and ponder them in our hearts" (Luke 2:19 adapted).

9

PETER AS NEGLECTED WITNESS TO EASTER

(Luke 24:34; 1 Cor 15:5)

Four years after it appeared in German, Martin Hengel's *Saint Peter: An Underestimated Apostle* was published in English in 2010.[1] This learned book is a significant contribution on Peter and his role in the emergence of Christianity. It belongs not only with such earlier, landmark works as Oscar Cullmann's *Peter: Disciple, Apostle, Martyr* and the ecumenical study *Peter in the New Testament*,[2] but also with recent studies by authors like Christian Grappe and Rudolf Pesch.[3]

Hengel argues that "the historical and theological importance of the fisherman from Bethsaida has been generally underestimated within both evangelical [= Protestant] and Catholic exegetical circles." He applies his wide learning to establish Peter's "overarching importance" for all four Gospels and, more generally, for Jewish *and* Gentile Christianity.[4] Peter proved "the apostolic foundational figure" in the emerging church. The key texts for Hengel's argument are Jesus's promise to Peter in Matthew 16:17–19 and, to a lesser extent, the promise in Luke 22:31–32, along with the commission in John 21:15–17.[5] Yet Hengel, like so many earlier and later writers, has little to say about the resurrection of Jesus and Peter's decisive function as Easter witness. In Hengel's study (and elsewhere), it is that witness that continues to be "generally underestimated."

In this chapter I will first discuss the work of Hengel, Pesch, and Grappe, and then illustrate a pervasive inattention to the role of Peter as resurrection witness. That will prepare the ground for exploring, exegetically, historically, and theologically, the importance of the Easter function of "the fisherman from Bethsaida."[6]

Three Views of Peter

Martin Hengel

Hengel spends over one hundred pages arguing for the fullness of Peter's power that was exercised in proclamation and leadership for the emerging church. Apropos of Matthew 16:17–19, he elucidates the nickname that functioned as an honorific name, *Kēphā* as "Rock,"[7] insists that, as the one who alone has "the power of the keys," the Matthean Peter was not simply the "typical disciple,"[8] and argues that long before Matthew wrote his Gospel, Peter was already the foundational apostolic figure in the church.[9] In particular, he was *the* great witness to the teaching and activity of the earthly Jesus; shortly after the martyrdom of Peter, his disciple Mark wrote a Gospel that transmitted the witness of Peter.[10] Luke and, even more, Matthew were to draw on Mark, and maintained "the overarching importance of Peter," an importance reflected not only in John but also in Acts and in such Pauline letters as Galatians and 1 Corinthians.[11]

When reaching these and further conclusions about Peter, Hengel invokes many ancient and modern authors and generally establishes his case convincingly. He did not persuade me over a few items, like his late dating of Matthew's Gospel (around AD 95). But these are minor issues, with my questioning centering on what was said (or rather not said) about the resurrection of the crucified Jesus. Hengel names Peter as "the decisive apostolic witness,"[12] but—normally—without stating that the heart of this witness concerned the unique divine action in raising Jesus from the dead, which made the Lord's glorious existence the beginning of (a) the end for all history and of (b) a new life for a transformed world.

Hengel refers to the appearances of the resurrected one and what he did for the disciples (in the plural) by giving them "the experience of the forgiveness of their guilt."[13] Then he mentions Peter "as the first to see the Resurrected One," a vision that meant "both forgiveness and a new acceptance."[14] I had expected Hengel to say much more than that, by elucidating the appearance of the risen Jesus to Peter, who was named in the ancient "summary of the Gospel" in 1 Corinthians 15:5 not by his personal name "Simon" but as "Cephas." This marked the beginning of Peter's role as "the Man of Rock," who witnessed to the heart of the Christian gospel, the utterly startling resurrection of Jesus from the dead.[15]

When characterizing Peter as "the recipient of the first appearance (protophany) of the Resurrected One,"[16] Hengel nowhere cited or even referred to Matthew 28:9-10 (where Mary Magdalene and "the other Mary" are the first to encounter the risen Jesus) or to John 20:11-18 (where Mary Magdalene alone is the recipient of the first appearance). May anyone, without further discussion, simply assume that Peter was the first to see the risen Lord? For Hengel this question proved even more pertinent since he spent pages arguing persuasively for the centrality of Peter in Matthew's Gospel. If Matthew made Peter as foundational, apostolic witness even more central than Mark had done, why did the former evangelist introduce Mary Magdalene and her companion as the first persons to whom the risen Jesus appeared? The "rival" claims of Peter and Mary Magdalene to be recipients of the protophany need to be explored.[17] I cannot avoid the suspicion that, when the resurrection of Jesus is quietly taken for granted and its dramatic importance is not (fully) appreciated, the question of who received the protophany can also become quite secondary.

Glibly assigning Hengel's silence to male chauvinism would find no support from the way in which, when treating later in his book the family of Peter and other apostolic families, he happily drew on Richard Bauckham's *Gospel Women*, a work that champions the female disciples of Jesus.[18] It was rather a certain reluctance to recognize the full importance of Christ's resurrection and its first dramatic disclosure that seems to have affected Hengel. Rightly making much of Peter's new name, he took "Rock" to describe "the entire thirty-five years" of the apostle's activity, from "his call to his martyrdom in Rome."[19] But receiving a foundational appearance of the risen Christ stood out among the many items that made up the whole story—from call to martyrdom.

Some lecturing in Rome (at the Pontifical Biblical Institute) helped prompt Hengel's study of Peter. Hence it is no surprise to find him singling out Matthew 16:18-19; Luke 22:31-32; and John 21:15-18 as texts that impress "anyone who visits St. Peter's Basilica in Rome," and point "back to the reality of the special, unique 'apostolic service' that the Man of Rock performed for the growing church."[20] Hengel is not alone in privileging the three texts from Matthew, Luke, and John. Rudolf Pesch names them as the three "classical texts" establishing Peter's primacy.[21] But what of three other texts that, as we shall see, connect even more clearly the service of the Man of Rock with the resurrection of Christ: Mark 16:7; Luke 24:34; and 1 Corinthians 15:5?

Rudolf Pesch

As Hengel would do five years later, Pesch dedicates pages to the origin, age, and meaning of Matthew 16:16–19, but includes further scholars (such as Jürgen Roloff) in the discussion. Did these verses derive from the earthly Jesus himself (a few scholars), from Peter's Easter encounter with Jesus (Pierre Grelot), from an early Christian tradition, or from the evangelist himself (the majority of commentators)?[22] Like Hengel and other recent scholars,[23] Pesch associates the Gospel of Mark with Peter. This allows him to call Peter *the* "eyewitness and servant of the word" (Luke 1:2).[24] This authoritative eyewitness could hand on and guarantee the tradition about the earthly Jesus's teaching and activity. The authority of Peter stood, above all, behind the passion story in Mark's Gospel.[25]

As Hengel would do, Pesch simply states, without pausing to examine the case of Mary Magdalene, that Peter was the first to see the risen Jesus.[26] Likewise, Pesch does not clearly recognize the full import of Peter's seeing the risen Lord. A chapter on the authoritative roles of Peter lists six areas: authority for the mission, for exorcising and healing, for teaching, for discipline, for reconciliation (the "binding and loosing"), and for leadership.[27] In the section on teaching, Pesch spends less than one page on Peter as "the one who received the first Easter appearance" and "formulated Easter faith."[28] Something similar happens when Pesch sketches Peter's connection with various steps in the process of the church's emergence: "Israel's rejection of Jesus; the Last Supper; the condemnation of Jesus; the renewal of fellowship with the Risen One; the restoration of the 'figure of the Twelve'; Pentecost; the opening and ratification of the Gentile mission."[29] The unique divine act that was Jesus's resurrection from the dead towers over the other events; we will also see how Peter's authoritative role as witness to the risen Christ towers over his other roles.

Pesch does his exegetical work on Peter carefully and is frequently persuasive. But he fails to acknowledge the huge significance of the resurrection as the beginning of the new creation, a significance that shapes Peter's primacy as Easter witness. One finds a similar gap in the longer book by Christian Grappe, a professor of New Testament on the Protestant Faculty of Theology at Strasbourg.

Christian Grappe

In *Images de Pierre aux deux premiers siècles*, Christian Grappe explores nine images of Peter: as disciple, martyr, repentant sinner, pastor, writer, the receiver of revelations who guaranteed the tradition, the confessor of faith who became the destroyer of heresy, the foundation (the Rock) who founded communities, and the first disciple who became the necessary point of reference.[30] The classic ecumenical study *Peter in the New Testament* listed seven images: missionary fisherman, pastoral shepherd, martyr, recipient of special revelation, confessor of the true faith, magisterial protector, and repentant sinner.[31] That study noted the extensive presence of Peter in the Christian apocrypha, Gnostic works, and other postbiblical sources,[32] but did not draw on this material for its study of Peter. The scope of Grappe's work, however, involves him in examining the Apocrypha, the Gnostic writers (who claimed to receive further revelations), and such mainline second-century writers as Ignatius, Justin, Irenaeus, and Clement of Alexandria.

Grappe recognizes the significance of the witness to Christ's resurrection coming from Peter as being the first recipient of an Easter appearance. Unlike Hengel and Pesch, he recalls the "rival" cases of Mary Magdalene and James, and spends pages on what both the New Testament and second-century sources say about Mary's encounter with the risen Jesus.[33] Yet it was Peter's role as the first, official witness to the resurrection, expressed in the early confession of faith (1 Cor 15:5), that underpinned the apostle's central significance.[34] Like Pesch, Grappe understands Mark 16:7 to refer to the primary appearance to Peter.[35] Hence three texts testify to the protophany to Peter (Mark 16:7; Luke 24:34; 1 Cor 15:5), unlike the three "classical texts" (Matt 16:18-19; Luke 22:31-32; John 21:15-17) that do not invoke the resurrection and the risen Lord's appearance to Peter, or at least do not emphasize that primary appearance as such.

Yet Grappe, like Hengel and Pesch, does not seem to appreciate the enormous impact and significance of Christ's resurrection from the dead. He "downsizes" the resurrection and so downsizes the significance of Peter precisely as Easter witness (see his nine images above). This is to underplay the utterly amazing act of God, the resurrection of Christ, that inaugurated the transformation of the universe and the final kingdom of God. From this resurrection flows the power that will resurrect and transform human beings and their world (1 Cor 15:20–28). This makes the resurrection of the crucified Jesus the focal point of the gospel, which established the identity of Peter as *the* Easter witness. Proclaiming the resurrection of Jesus, Peter at the head of other Easter witnesses could guarantee its trustworthiness and bring into being the fellowship of Christians.

Lack of Attention to Peter as Easter Witness

Traditionally both those who champion the Petrine ministry and those who reduce or even denigrate it have generally shared the same conviction about the central texts to be studied in the New Testament. On October 17, 1978, Pope John Paul II expressed this wide consensus when, in the address that opened his pontificate, he cited Matthew 16:18–19; Luke 22:31–32; and John 21:15–17 and stated, "We are completely convinced that all modern inquiry into the Petrine ministry must be based on these three hinges of the gospel."[36] Two of these three texts are situated in the pre-Easter situation: the first text promises Peter "the keys of the kingdom of heaven" and the power to "bind" and "loose"; in the context of Jesus's imminent death, the second text promises that the faith of Peter will not fail and that he will "lend strength" to the other disciples. On the far side of the resurrection, the third text establishes Peter as the pastor who must shepherd Christ's "lambs" and "sheep." These three classic texts have featured persistently in the defense of the Petrine/Papal primacy (as well as in debates about and opposition to that primacy). They point to the function(s) of Peter instituted, or at least promised, by the pre-Easter Jesus.

These three texts about Peter have been repeatedly cited when examining or legitimating the pastoral ministry of Peter (and his successors) for the universal church. Let me cite several examples. The first (Matt 16:18–19) and the third (John 21:15–17) of the "big three" texts feature prominently in the First Vatican Council's teaching on the Petrine primacy,[37] while the second (Luke 22:31–32) of these three texts turns up in the Council's statement on the pope's infallible magisterium.[38] More than a century later, in its first report on "Authority in the Church" (Venice, 1976) the Anglican-Roman Catholic International Commission (ARCIC) mentioned only three biblical texts when it came to discuss "conciliar and primatial authority" with their attendant "problems and prospects": Matthew 16:18–19; Luke 22:31–32; John 21:15–17 (no. 24).[39] In its second statement on "Authority in the Church" (Windsor, 1981), ARCIC listed a range of Petrine texts from the New Testament (nos. 2–9), paying particular attention to the "big three" texts, each of which it mentioned twice.[40] The same three texts received the primary emphasis when Pope John Paul II presented the Bishop of Rome's "ministry of unity" in his encyclical of May 25, 1995, *Ut Unum Sint*, even if he added at once, "It is also significant that, according to the First Letter of Paul to the Corinthians, the Risen Christ appears to Cephas and then to the Twelve" (no. 91).[41] The Windsor statement from ARCIC had likewise remarked in passing on this "special appearance" of the risen Jesus to Peter, noting that it is also attested by Luke 24:34 (no. 3).[42] But both the Windsor statement of 1981 and John Paul's encyclical of 1995 privilege the "big three" texts when they reflect on the ministry of Peter (and his successors).

To conclude this picture of these three texts persistently taking attention away, or at least implicitly away, from Peter's role as Easter witness, let me mention two further authors: Jean-Marie-Roger Tillard and John Michael Miller. While being a valuable ecumenical work on Peter and the papacy, Tillard's *The Bishop of Rome* refers on only two pages to Peter as Easter witness.[43] Miller[44] identifies the scriptural foundation for the Petrine ministry, notes in that section the apostle's role as witness to the risen Lord, but makes very little of it. The twenty-one theses on the Petrine ministry of the pope with which he concludes his study refer to Christ's incarnation and divine sonship but include nothing about Christ's resurrection and the ministry of proclaiming it.[45]

In theology and in official teaching, but not in the New Testament, Peter as Easter witness has been left almost completely off the table. What if we take up a possibility offered by Paul, Mark, and Luke for interpreting the Petrine ministry: an interpretation based on understanding Peter's primary (but not exclusive) role in the emerging church to be that of spreading and gathering the community through the power of his Easter message?[46]

The Testimony of Paul, Mark, and Luke

The Testimony of Paul

In 1 Corinthians 15:3–5, we have a formula of Christian proclamation that Paul may have received as early as his stay in Damascus, after the meeting with the risen Lord that radically changed his life and gave him his apostolic vocation.[47] The three verses run as follows:

> I handed on to you as of first importance what I in turn had received: *that* Christ died for our sins in accordance with the scriptures, and *that* he was buried, and *that* he was raised on the third day in accordance with the scriptures, and *that* he appeared to Cephas, then to the twelve.

The fourfold repetition of "that" (*hoti* in Greek) emphasizes "each element in turn."[48] The two key affirmations are "that he died" and "that he was raised"; in both cases, a further affirmation "confirms" what the formula proclaims. We know that "he died," because "he was buried." We know that "he was raised," because "he appeared to Cephas, then to the twelve." Burial underlines the reality of the death. The resurrection reverses the burial and so indicates an empty tomb.[49]

The protophany to Peter is not the only appearance of the risen Christ to be reported. Paul adds at once an appearance "to the twelve," which presumably involved a second appearance to Peter, and also adds appearances to "more than five hundred" followers of Jesus, to James (presumably the brother of the Lord, who had not "believed" in him [John 7:5]), "to all the apostles" (with the "apostles" constituting a wider group than "the twelve"), and lastly to Paul himself (1 Cor 15:5–8). So the whole passage testifies to appearances to three individuals (Cephas, James, and Paul) and to three groups ("the twelve," the "more than five hundred" followers, and "all the apostles"). It is not totally clear where the pre-Pauline formula ends. A few scholars hold that the formula ends with "he appeared," while many maintain that the formula includes the name of "Cephas" and perhaps also "the twelve." The formula would be left hanging if it stopped at "he appeared," and with the inevitable question unanswered: "to whom did he appear?" Whatever one's view about this, Paul clearly depends on previous tradition(s) for his information about the names of those to whom the risen Jesus had appeared. It is also clear that, in writing to the Corinthians, to whom Cephas had most probably also preached (see 1 Cor 1:12; 3:22; 9:5),[50] Paul wants to affirm harmony in the apostolic proclamation of the resurrection and in the faith it had evoked: "Whether then it was I or they, so we proclaim [Easter kerygma] and so you have come to believe [confession of faith]" (1 Cor 15:11).

According to the kerygmatic (and creedal) formula cited by Paul (1 Cor 15:3-5), Cephas was the first disciple (or at least the first male disciple) to whom the risen Lord appeared. We will see below how a similar formula in Luke 24:34 upholds the protophany to Simon Peter. The testimony offered by Paul in 1 Corinthians 15 allows us to draw this conclusion: by witnessing to his foundational Easter experience, Peter as Cephas offered firm and rocklike witness to the very center of Christian faith, the resurrection from the dead of the crucified Jesus.

The Testimony of Mark

When transmitting the witness of Peter, Mark makes him serve as an "inclusion" that frames the whole Gospel. At the start Jesus calls Simon (Mark 1:16-18), to whom he soon gives the name of "Peter" (3:16). Then at the end of the Gospel, in an open and empty tomb, an interpreting angel says to Mary Magdalene and her two companions, "Go, tell his disciples and Peter that he [Jesus] is going ahead of you to Galilee; there you will see him" (16:7).

Joel Marcus agrees with many scholars in holding that "and to Peter" echoes the tradition that Jesus appeared first to Peter.[51] At the same time, he suggests a double entendre on the part of the evangelist. "On the one hand, the women are to announce the news *especially* to Peter, the first disciple to be called," "the first to recognize Jesus' messiahship," and the one who would soon "be granted the first resurrection appearance." On the other hand, the women were "to proclaim the message *even* to Peter," whose opposition to Jesus's coming fate "earned him the epithet 'Satan'" (Mark 8:33) and who three times denied knowing Jesus (Mark 14:66-72).[52]

THE GOSPELS

While acknowledging that 1 Corinthians 15:5 reports the protophany to Peter, Frederick Lapham claims that "nowhere in the Gospel record is there any hint that Peter was the *first* witness of the Resurrection."[53] To be sure, Mark's Gospel presents three women as those who discovered the empty tomb and heard from an angel the astonishing news of the resurrection. But they did not see the risen Jesus himself. Yet Marcus and other scholars, pace Lapham, find Mark hinting that it is Peter who will soon be granted the first appearance of the risen Lord. Moreover, and quite clearly, Luke adds his witness that, at some moment after visiting the empty tomb (24:12),[54] a visit that led Peter to "wonder" but not yet to believe in the risen Christ, the protophany was granted to Simon Peter (24:34).

The Testimony of Luke

At the end of the Emmaus story, Luke quotes a traditional formula: "The Lord was really raised, and he appeared [*ōphthē*] to Simon" (24:34 au. trans.), a formula that converges with what we have seen in 1 Corinthians 15:4–5 (Christ "has been raised" and "appeared [*ōphthē*] to Cephas").[55] Seemingly Luke introduces the early formulation about the appearance to Simon Peter to head off any impression that the Emmaus appearance is the primary one. The evangelist defers to the tradition of a first appearance to Peter. Even before Cleopas and his companion return, Peter's testimony to his meeting with the risen Lord has brought to Easter faith "the eleven" and "those who were with them" (Luke 24:33 au. trans.). Simon's encounter with the living Jesus has shifted the community in Jerusalem from their incredulity and persuaded them that the message that the women brought from the angels about the resurrection (24:9–11) is "really" true. The report from Emmaus and the subsequent appearance of the Lord reinforce and clarify this Easter faith, but do not create it for the first time.

Luke has prepared his readers for this role of Peter as agent of faith in the resurrection of Jesus. This is the thrust of what Jesus promises at the Last Supper, even while foretelling Peter's denial: "I have prayed for you that your own faith may not fail; and you, when once you have turned back, strengthen your brothers" (22:32).[56] The primary appearance of the risen Lord to Simon Peter enables the apostle to play just that role. He "turns back" and "strengthens" his fellow disciples by the power of his Easter faith. The connection between 24:34 and 22:32, as

Robert Tannehill points out, "is reinforced by the fact that they are the only places in Luke where Peter is called Simon after the formal indication in 6:14 that Jesus gave Simon a new name." Tannehill adds, "Simon is warned and charged with responsibility in 22:31–32, and he begins to fulfill that responsibility by bearing witness to the risen Jesus before Jesus' other followers."[57]

Testimony from Paul, Mark, and Luke converges to support a primary appearance to Peter. Yet, at first glance, they and other New Testament authors do not seem to contain any story of this protophany of the risen Christ. Do we then look in vain for a vivid narrative of an appearance to Peter that could be like that of Jesus appearing to Mary Magdalene (John 20:11–18)?

The Story of an Appearance to Peter

Like others, Andrew Lincoln is open to the idea that Luke knew of a postresurrection miracle involving Peter and a great haul of fish in Galilee but, given the evangelist's "exclusively Jerusalem-oriented ending," inserted the story earlier—in the context of the call of Peter and other first disciples (5:1–11). Peter's words ("Go away from me, Lord, for I am a sinful man") make good sense if they originally came after his denials during the passion and on the occasion of his meeting the risen Lord.[58] In modern times it has been Raymond Brown who, appealing to this Lukan passage and other passages, has stood out for arguing that a primary appearance to Peter at the Sea of Tiberias in Galilee lies behind the catch of fish in John 21:1–14 and the rehabilitation of Peter in John 21:15–17.[59] Where Luke 5 links the haul of fish to the calling of Peter, John 21 links it to his installation as leader.

Brown recognizes, of course, the prima facie difficulty that Peter has six companions in John 21, whereas Luke 24:34 ("the Lord appeared to Simon") and 1 Corinthians 15:5 ("he appeared to Cephas") seem to suggest an appearance to Peter alone. Yet the presence of "silent" companions in the appearance to Peter cannot be simply excluded. After all, Paul speaks of an appearance to himself (1 Cor 15:8), and Luke three times indicates that others were present when the apostle met the risen Jesus on the road to Damascus (Acts 9:7; 22:9; 26:13). Like Paul's companions on the road to Damascus, Peter's fishing companions, apart from the Beloved Disciple, whom the evangelist may well have added

THE GOSPELS

to the narrative, do not play an important part in the story of the risen Jesus appearing on the shore and then disappear entirely when we come to the dialogue that rehabilitates Peter. As Lincoln was to suggest (see above), Brown observes that the rehabilitation scene, "made to correspond to Peter's denials, is more intelligible in the context of Jesus' first appearance to Peter."[60]

Brown also proposes that elements from the story of the appearance to Peter "have been preserved in fragments from the Synoptic description of Jesus' ministry."[61] He cites three possible places for finding such postresurrection material: Peter's walking on the water (Matt 14:28–33), Peter as the foundation rock of the church (Matt 16:16b–19), and the call of Peter and miraculous catch of fish (Luke 5:1–11). An Easter location for some of the themes in these three passages is possible. As regards the third, it is more than possible and even quite probable that some of its elements originally belonged to a story of the risen Christ appearing to Peter when the latter was fishing.[62]

Having reached some exegetical conclusions (about Peter being a primary Easter witness) and a plausible view of where the appearance of the risen Lord to Peter took place (at the Sea of Tiberias), we need to face a central question already mentioned above: Was Mary Magdalene chronologically the first to see Christ risen from the dead?

Mary Magdalene as Easter Witness

All four Easter narratives found in the Gospels feature Mary Magdalene at the discovery of the empty tomb and always name her in first place, whether she has two other women as companions (Mark 16:1–8), only one woman companion (Matt 28:1–10), or more than two other women companions (Luke 24:1–11), or seemingly goes alone and returns alone to the tomb (John 20:1–2, 11–18). According to Matthew (28:9–10), along with her solitary woman companion ("the other Mary") Mary Magdalene encounters the risen Jesus and, after having been commissioned by an "angel of the Lord" to tell the "disciples" to keep the rendezvous in Galilee (28:7), is now commissioned a second time and by the risen Jesus himself to tell "my brothers" to keep the rendezvous. John 20:11–18 pictures her alone when the risen Lord appears to her and instructs her to tell "my brothers" that he is "ascending" to the Father.[63] According to the (second-century) appendix to Mark's Gospel, the risen Jesus "appeared first" to Mary Magdalene; she then "told those who had been with him" that Jesus "was alive," but they would not believe her (16:9-11). In all the Easter texts this is the only place that formally states that the resurrected Christ *first* appeared to anyone.[64]

The Gospels converge in presenting Mary Magdalene as *the* primary and preeminent witness to the discovery of the empty tomb. What of her being the recipient of the first appearance of the risen Christ (Matt 28:9-10; John 20:11-18)—something explicitly asserted by Mark 16:9, apparently in dependence on John 20:11-18?[65]

Any answer here must reckon with the fact that neither Mary Magdalene nor any other women are mentioned by Paul in the list of three individuals to whom the risen Jesus appeared (1 Cor 15:5-8): Cephas, James, and Paul himself. Paul also lists three groups: "the twelve," more than five hundred "brothers," and "all the apostles." While women did not belong to the first group, they were presumably represented in the crowd of over five hundred "brothers and sisters" or "fellow Christians," and could well have numbered among "all the apostles." At the end of Romans, Paul names his collaborators Andronicus and Junia (a married couple?) as "distinguished among the apostles" (16:7).[66] Understanding "apostles" to extend beyond "the twelve," Paul makes room for women among the apostles for two reasons: they could be witnesses to the risen Christ (for this qualification of apostleship see, e.g., 1 Cor 9:1) and sent on mission for Christ, like Epaphroditus (Phil 2:25; 4:18).[67] The concluding chapter of Romans opens by praising Phoebe and Prisca, includes further positive remarks about other women, and shows how comfortable Paul is with the prestige and leadership roles of women (16:1-16).

Did Paul know the tradition of an appearance to Mary Magdalene? It could be that he was aware of appearances in Galilee but not of appearances in Jerusalem, where Mary Magdalene met the risen Lord. If Paul knew about that meeting, why then did he not name Mary Magdalene in 1 Corinthians 15:5-7? He might have suppressed her name as an Easter witness, since he was sensitive to the fact that the testimony of women was, more or less, not accepted in Judaism and the community in Corinth included Jewish as well as Gentile Christians. However we construe the "silence" of Paul in 1 Corinthians 15, we cannot allege that the early church as a whole placed little or no value on women's testimony. Otherwise, we cannot convincingly account for the preeminence of Mary Magdalene and other (named) women both as witnesses to the empty tomb (all four Gospels) and as those who brought to the other disciples the angelic message about Jesus's resurrection (the Synoptic Gospels).

Two of the Gospels, Matthew and, at greater length, John, testify to a protophany to Mary Magdalene. For at least one good reason we can hold that this tradition is early and historically reliable. It runs counter to the trend to assign the first appearances to Peter and other male disciples.[68] With her "I have seen the Lord" (John 20:18), Mary emerged as equal to Peter and other male disciples in her witness to the resurrection. Did the appearance of the risen Jesus to her precede chronologically that to Peter? Matthew and John (pace Paul, Luke, and perhaps Mark) would encourage this conclusion, which has been long favored by the liturgical language used for her feast on July 22.

Some have pointed to conflicts between Mary Magdalene and Peter,[69] which are found in Gnostic and other apocryphal works of the second and third century and speak of the risen Christ appearing to her, communicating new revelations, and giving her an authoritative role that male leaders in the church then suppressed.[70] This material, even though it seems a later, odd spin-off from, rather than a reliable guide to, what was happening in mainstream Christianity, has been used to argue for serious divisions in the early church over apostolic authority. Here one should recall that, from the late first century to the end of the second century, such writers as Clement of Rome, Ignatius of Antioch, Justin Martyr, and Irenaeus have various things to say about issues and problems in the early church but nothing at all to say about any debates over women legitimately transmitting apostolic revelation and tradition and, in particular, nothing to say about any conflict between Mary Magdalene and Peter. Clement goes out of his way to praise women like Esther and Judith for what they had done for their people (1 Clement, 55), while Irenaeus places Jesus's mother as the New Eve alongside her son as the New Adam. The appendix to Mark (16:9–20), which many scholars date to the first half of the second century, has nothing to report about any debates over the testimony and authority of women. Rather it highlights the role of Mary Magdalene as primary Easter witness and the male disciples' failure to accept her testimony. If serious divisions existed in mainstream Christianity over the separate authority of Mary Magdalene and of male disciples headed by Peter, why does none of this conflict show up in the work of writers from Clement to Irenaeus? The case for such gender conflict during the early years of Christianity is, as Philip Jenkins shows, quite weak.[71]

Peter as Neglected Witness to Easter

Apropos of Mary Magdalene in her role as Easter witness, many cite Hippolytus of Rome referring in the third century to the women at the tomb of Jesus as "apostles," which developed into Mary Magdalene often being called *apostola apostolorum* (the apostle of the apostles). Soon after the Council of Chalcedon in 451, Pope Leo the Great named her a figure of the church (*personam Ecclesiae gerens*). In the following century Pope Gregory the Great referred to her as "another" Eve, since she announced to the other disciples life and not death.[72] But in emerging Christianity, it was Peter who had taken the primary role as official proclaimer of the Lord's resurrection.

Peter as Easter Witness

Peter functions as bridge figure for Luke, being the last disciple to be named in the Gospel (Luke 24:34) and the first to be named in the Acts of the Apostles (Acts 1:13). In Luke's second work Peter has significant things to do: for instance, taking the initiative to find a substitute member for the Twelve after the defection of Judas (Acts 1:15–26); conferring, along with John, the gift of the Holy Spirit (8:14–17); performing miracles by healing the sick and even raising the dead (3:1–10; 5:15–16; 9:32–42); and playing a key role in admitting Gentiles into the Christian community without imposing on them the observance of the Torah (10:1—11:18; 15:1–29).

But the major function of Peter is that of being, right from the day of Pentecost and along "with the eleven" (Acts 2:14) and "all" the other disciples (2:32), the leading, public witness to the resurrection of Jesus from the dead.[73] Just as Peter's "turning back" and witnessing to the resurrection had "strengthened" his "brothers" (Luke 22:32), so his witness to the risen Jesus now reaches out to those who have come to Jerusalem from the wider world. He speaks with and for a college or official group of Easter witnesses in announcing the good news: "This [crucified] Jesus God raised up, and of that all of us are witnesses" (Acts 2:32). Peter stands "with the eleven" (2:14) and proclaims a resurrection of which "*we* are witnesses" (3:15). For Luke, Peter leads the others in being the example par excellence of an authoritative eyewitness (to the risen Lord) and minister of the (Easter) word (Luke 1:2). The first half of Acts presents various dimensions of the leadership role that Peter exercised in the life of the early church. But the heart of the matter was his preeminence among the official witnesses to the resurrection of Jesus (e.g., Acts 3:13–15; 4:10; 5:30–32).

Neither Luke nor any other New Testament author allows us (1) to separate Peter from Mary Magdalene, the Twelve, Paul, and other Easter witnesses. Nor do they encourage us to (2) reduce the Petrine function simply to that of being a witness to the resurrection. Nor do they permit us (3) to isolate Peter's experience of the post-Easter Jesus from all that has gone before. The watershed of Easter does not invalidate or cancel what has happened to Peter through his closeness to Jesus and leadership of the Twelve. If Peter holds a special leadership role in the early church, this is associated not only with his function as *the* Easter witness but also with a position he has already enjoyed during Jesus's ministry. Nevertheless, it is Easter that brings Peter the new, worldwide function of being the leading Easter witness as missionary, shepherd, and rock—an activity that eventually leads to his final "witness" as martyr.

Understanding and interpreting this Petrine function primarily (but not exclusively) in the light of the Easter appearance to him looks attractive from the point of view of the liturgy and of God's self-revelation. First, this interpretation links Peter expressly with the center of the church's life of worship, the resurrection of the crucified Jesus. Not only baptism and the Eucharist but also all the sacraments focus on and draw their power from the paschal mystery. Second, this vision of his function expresses Peter's relationship with the climax of divine self-revelation: the resurrection of the crucified one, through which Jesus was revealed as the effective Messiah, Lord, and Son of God. Highlighting what the New Testament reports about Peter's role as Easter witness moves us to the center of our christological confession. The events of the first Good Friday and Easter Sunday form the highpoint of the saving self-communication of the tripersonal God, which was proclaimed by Peter and eventually enshrined in the Creed of the church.

Prioritizing Peter's role as Easter proclaimer has a further theological advantage. Those who follow Vatican II in setting the (prophetic) service of the word ahead of the (priestly) sacramental ministry and the (kingly) shepherding and leading of the Christ's flock should be attracted to my account of the Petrine function.[74] This account attends primarily (but not exclusively) to the prophetic service of the word in witnessing to the resurrection (on the basis of Peter's meeting with the risen Jesus).

When prioritizing Peter's Easter witness, we need to recall that the New Testament does not offer a single, monolithic tradition about him.

He can be depicted as fisherman or missionary (e.g., Mark 1:16–18; Luke 5:10), shepherd (e.g., John 21:15–17), rock (e.g., Matt 16:18), repentant sinner (e.g., Mark 14:72), and martyr (John 21:18–19; see 13:36). We can relate these different images to that of Easter witness. In the opening chapters of Acts, Peter's missionary "fishing" takes the form of proclaiming the resurrection. The shepherding vocation comes to him from the risen Christ. Peter's role as "rock" receives its legitimacy from the crucified and risen Jesus, who is "the living stone," "the cornerstone," and "the stone of scandal" (1 Pet 2:4–8 au. trans.). Peter's repentance has its context in the passion, death, and resurrection of Jesus (Luke 22:61–62; 23:49; John 21:15–17); he will suffer martyrdom in the service of the risen Lord (John 21:18–19). In short, the different images of Peter and traditions about him converge on his function as Easter witness. In the words of Raymond Brown and his colleagues, "The important tradition about Peter having been the first of the major companions of Jesus' ministry to have seen the Lord after the resurrection" provided "very likely" the "original context for much of the New Testament material about Peter."[75]

Peter and the Pope

As regards the way Peter's leadership should be or was in fact handed on, the New Testament contains no explicit directions. The Acts of the Apostles contains nothing about Peter's later life. It describes Paul's coming to Rome (28:11–31) but not his martyrdom there. John's Gospel points to Peter's martyrdom (21:18–19) but does not specify how[76] or where it took place. Nevertheless, Rome was the city where Peter and Paul suffered death for their Master.[77] The Church of Rome came to be recognized as exercising a unique responsibility for all the communities of Christians. As successor of Peter, the Bishop of Rome was acknowledged to be called in a special way to do two things. He was *both* to proclaim the saving truth revealed by Christ *and* to keep all Christians united in their faith.[78]

Here "called in a special way" does *not* mean "called as the only one" or "called exclusively." Peter's role of leadership did not isolate him from the other apostles. Paul and the other apostolic missionaries also witnessed authoritatively to the good news, centered on the resurrection of the crucified Jesus, and set themselves to maintain unity among the

THE GOSPELS

churches. Likewise, the special responsibility of the Bishop of Rome to uphold the truth about Christ and preserve Christian unity is a function also exercised with other bishops (and, indeed, all Christians).

What light could my presentation of Peter's primary role throw on the nature of the papacy? From his primary role as Easter witness let me briefly draw five conclusions for the ministry of the Bishop of Rome.

1. The church was founded on *all the apostles* (Eph 2:20), the official witnesses to Jesus Christ. They proclaimed the resurrection of the crucified Savior, admitted all nations into the new community, and authoritatively guided the emerging church. In this college of witnesses Simon Peter stood out as *the* foundational witness to Jesus's resurrection. His new name, "Cephas," suggested his special function. To him alone was addressed the promise: "On this rock I will build my church."

2. The mission given to Peter and the other apostles was partly but not totally handed on to their successors, the Bishop of Rome and the other bishops. I say "not totally" because certain functions died with the apostles. Under the risen Christ and through the power of the Holy Spirit they were called to preach the resurrection of the crucified one and so bring the church into existence. Once achieved, this founding of the church could never be repeated. Pope, bishops, and other believers bear—in different ways—the common responsibility of nourishing Christian life and mission and so keeping the church in a flourishing existence. They are all called to maintain the good state of the community, but not to found (or refound) the church.

   Hence the words "on this rock I will build my church" do not apply to the Bishop of Rome in precisely the way they apply to Peter. In the case of the pope the meaning would rather be "on this rock I will preserve my church in existence."

3. Nevertheless, the mission given to Peter and the other apostles was partly handed on to their successors. Let me sketch some details of this succession.

   The Bishop of Rome has a relationship to his fellow bishops that is *like* that of Peter to the other apostles.

Together they share the major responsibility for spreading the good news of the risen Christ, leading the church with authority, and maintaining the sacramental life of the community. In the life of the church, the bishops with the pope are the primary preachers, pastors, and celebrants of the liturgy.

Among all the bishops, the Bishop of Rome, like Peter, has a special role of leadership to serve the whole church with love (John 21:15-17) and through suffering (John 21:18-19). His special service aims at maintaining the true faith and unity of all Christians.

4. Grappe, Brown, and his colleagues, in listing "repentant sinner" among the major images of Peter (see above), drew attention to the shadow side in the chief apostle's exercise of his ministry. Rather than being surprised at human weaknesses and limitations in the ministry of Peter's successors, we should expect them. Even after the resurrection and the coming of the Holy Spirit, Peter could at least on one serious occasion appear to limit true Christian freedom (Gal 2:11-21).[79] Among all the disciples only Peter is reported to have confessed his sinfulness so strikingly: "Simon Peter…fell down at Jesus' knees, saying, 'Go away from me, Lord, for I am a sinful man'" (Luke 5:8).

The conclusion from this seems clear. The shadow side of the papacy, far from ruling out the Petrine succession, belongs to it. We should not be surprised if, like Peter, the Bishop of Rome at times fails in the way he exercises his special function of leadership for the whole church.

5. In this article I have shown how Peter fulfilled his ministry, primarily but not exclusively, through being *the* official witness to Christ's resurrection from the dead. This suggests that among the various titles exercised by the Bishop of Rome, the primary one could be recognized as being *the* proclaimer of the Lord's victory over death. I need to work this out in a little detail.

The pastoral jurisdiction and teaching function of the pope, defined by the First Vatican Council (1869-70), can be contextualized by recalling the Petrine ministry of being the primary witness to the risen Christ. Vatican I described the papal office as a "perpetual principle and visible foundation of the *unity*" that belongs to the bishops and the whole church (DzH 3051; ND 818; my italics). It is above all through being the primary, official proclaimer of the central truth, "Jesus is risen," that the pope expresses and supports this unity. Vatican I went on to describe the goal of papal primacy: "by preserving unity, both in communion and the profession of the same faith, the Church of Christ may be one flock under one supreme shepherd" (DzH 3060; ND 826). Now the church as a community of believers brings together those who confess Jesus as risen Lord and, through sharing this faith, are bound in love to each other. Their faith and communion are served by the pope (as primary teacher and pastor) proclaiming through word and deed *the event* that more than anything else founded the community of believers: the resurrection of the crucified Christ (along with the outpouring of the Holy Spirit).

The Second Vatican Council's Dogmatic Constitution on the Church (*Lumen Gentium*) put "preaching the Gospel" ahead of pastoral and liturgical roles as the most important duty of bishops (no. 25). No less than the other bishops, the Bishop of Rome must fulfill this duty, which in a 1975 apostolic exhortation Pope Paul VI called "the pre-eminent ministry of teaching the revealed truth" (*Evangelii Nuntiandi* 67). One might reasonably comment that "the Gospel" to be preached and "the revealed truth" to be taught primarily concern and essentially derive from the resurrection of the crucified Jesus.

In recent decades contacts between Catholics and other Christians have highlighted more and more the need to find real *unity* in confessing the *truth* of faith. How best can we describe that unity and truth? The central truth of Christian faith can be formulated by saying, "The crucified Son of God is risen from the dead to give us the Holy Spirit." The Easter mystery says it all. It is the basic truth to be maintained and passed on by Christians. They are baptized into Christ's death and resurrection (Rom 6:3–11) to live together as God's new Easter people.

Peter as Neglected Witness to Easter

What more could we expect from the Bishop of Rome than that like Peter he strengthen the whole church's faith in Christ's resurrection? How could he better serve the unity of an Easter people than by proclaiming insistently the event that brought the church into existence: the resurrection of the crucified Jesus followed by the coming of the Holy Spirit? To be sure, the pope must also lead the church with loving authority and celebrate the sacraments. But his great task for all the world is to announce through word and deed the news that lies at the heart of Christianity: Jesus is risen.

A Lutheran-Catholic report on which I have drawn observes that "no matter what one may think about the justification offered by the New Testament for the emergence of the papacy, this papacy in its developed form cannot be read back into the New Testament."[80] In general, one can only agree with this statement. Nevertheless, there is one yearly ceremony in which, by proclaiming the resurrection, the pope strikingly symbolizes and even parallels Peter's central function as Easter witness. Each year millions of people see on television or follow by radio the pope's Easter broadcast. In many languages he announces to the city of Rome and the world the glorious news that gave rise to Christianity: "Christ is risen. Alleluia!"

Of course, we should respect the great differences between our cultural and historical setting in the twenty-first century and that in which nearly two thousand years ago Peter carried out his ministry. Nevertheless, one need not strain to find some parallel between what the pope does at Easter and what Luke pictured happening at Pentecost. In Jerusalem Peter stood up to announce Jesus's resurrection to "Parthians, Medes, Elamites, and residents of Mesopotamia, Judea and Cappadocia, Pontus and Asia, Phrygia and Pamphylia, Egypt and the parts of Libya belonging to Cyrene, and visitors from Rome, both Jews and proselytes, Cretans and Arabs" (Acts 2:8–11). Today the television cameras catch the faces of those who have come to Rome from all over the world, so that they can stand in St. Peter's Square on Easter Sunday and hear from Peter's successor the great news that has forever changed human history: "This Jesus God raised up, and of that all of us are witnesses" (Acts 2:32). Peter's witness to the resurrection lives on strikingly in the pope's Easter proclamation. In that special way the Bishop of Rome visibly serves and strengthens the church's faith by reenacting before all the world the primary role of Peter as fundamental witness to Jesus risen from the dead.[81]

10

DID JESUS EAT THE FISH?

(Luke 24:42-43)

The highpoint of Luke's realistic presentation of the Easter appearances comes when the risen Jesus asked his disciples for something to eat. "They gave him a piece of broiled fish, and he took it and ate it in their presence" (24:42–43).

The passage is echoed twice in the Acts of the Apostles. While "eating with" the apostles (1:4),[1] the risen Jesus commands them to wait in Jerusalem for the coming of the Holy Spirit. During a meeting in Caesarea with Cornelius, Peter testifies to Jesus's resurrection in these terms: "God raised him on the third day and allowed him to appear, not to all the people but to us who were chosen by God as witnesses, and who ate and drank with him after he rose from the dead" (10:40–41). In Luke 24:43 only Jesus eats but he does not drink.[2] In Acts the disciples also eat with him (1:4), and they drink as well (10:41).

When the risen Jesus appeared to the disciples in Jerusalem, did he eat and drink (stage one of the tradition)? What place could such a motif of postresurrection eating with the disciples have enjoyed in the life of the early church (stage two)? Where do we see the intentions of Luke at work in this detail about eating (and drinking) in the postresurrection situation (stage three)?

In attempting to answer these questions and interpret Luke 24:43, we can also observe and report how various exegetes introduce a similar Easter tradition from another Gospel (John 21:9–14), corrective material from Paul (canonical criticism), theological/anthropological questions about Jesus's new state (e.g., can a risen body digest food and grow?), and reflections that go beyond the evangelist Luke's intentions to what the episode might mean today (actualizing hermeneutics).

Stage One of the Tradition

In his commentary on Luke, Joseph A. Fitzmyer judges Jesus's request for food and eating the fish in front of the disciples to be "Lukan embellishments" that belong only to stage three of the tradition.[3] Along with Luke, several other New Testament authors attest reliably stage one of the tradition: the risen Jesus appeared to groups of disciples when they were gathered together (1 Cor 15:5-7; Luke 24:36-49; Matt 28:16-20; John 20:19-29; 21:1-23). But when Luke represents Jesus as eating fish, he is "indulging a sort of realism" that sets him apart from the other evangelists.[4] In reaching this conclusion, Fitzmyer does not, however, appeal to Paul's reflections on the risen body (above all, 1 Cor 6:12-13; 15:35-54), which create problems for Luke's realistic presentation of the postresurrection Jesus.

Some modern exegetes maintain that the risen Jesus's eating with his disciples goes back to stage one of the tradition, the post-Easter events themselves. Thus I. Howard Marshall in *The Gospel of Luke* argues that in 24:43 Luke follows a historically reliable, "well-attested tradition." In support of his position, Marshall points to John 21:13; Acts 1:4; and Acts 10:41.[5] This, of course, is to slip over the fact that in Acts 1:4 and 10:41 it is the same author referring back to what he has already written in his first work. As we shall see, in the two subsequent passages he is qualifying or correcting what he has written in Luke 24:43. In John 21:13, it is by no means clear that Jesus himself eats: "Jesus came and took the bread and gave it to them, and did the same with the fish." Christopher Evans excludes the Johannine scene as a parallel witness to Christ's eating: "the Lord provides food but does not eat."[6]

Marshall faces two difficulties, one historical and the other anthropological/theological. He refers to "indisputable" evidence that "fish was readily available in Jerusalem" and so could have been eaten there by the disciples and the risen Jesus.[7] More importantly, Marshall recognizes that Luke's emphasis on "the physical reality" of Jesus's resurrection body leads to an apparent contradiction with Paul's dictum that "flesh and blood shall not inherit the kingdom of God" and the apostle's insistence on the spiritual nature of the resurrection body. But, Marshall argues, the conflict is apparent rather than real. Paul is concerned with the nature of the body in the new life after the resurrection of the dead, while Luke is concerned with the appropriate form of the manifestation of the risen Jesus in earthly conditions. Luke's narrative makes it plain that, although Jesus has flesh and bones, he is able to appear and vanish in a way that is not possible for ordinary human beings. Both Luke and Paul agree that resurrection is concerned with the body and not with the continuing existence of a bodiless soul or spirit.[8]

All the same, difficulties remain. Did "the appropriate form of manifestation of the risen Jesus in earthly conditions" include *really* eating (and digesting) food? If so, can this be reconciled with Paul's teaching that in the risen life eating and digestion will be set aside (1 Cor 6:13)? Or did the risen Jesus merely pretend to eat?

From an earlier generation, Plummer, who like Marshall understands Luke to report a historically reliable tradition in 24:42–43, shows himself aware of the objection of playacting:

> The objection, that if Jesus took food in order to convince them [the disciples] that he was no mere spirit, when the food was not necessary for the resurrection-body, he was acting deceitfully, does not hold. The alternative "either a ghost, or an ordinary body needing food," is false. There is a third possibility: a glorified body, capable of receiving food. Is there any deceit in taking food, which one does not want, in order to place others who are needing it, at their ease.[9]

Even if Paul is not explicitly mentioned here, one senses the pressure of the apostle's reflections on the risen state. Not everyone will be content with Plummer's version of a glorified body, which neither needs nor wants food but yet is "capable of receiving" (and digesting?) it. Eating something to put others "at their ease" seems an act of ordinary human courtesy. To attribute such motivation to the risen Jesus, however, risks banalizing the whole scene and picturing him as a kind of "resurrected gentleman." Yet something a little similar about such good manners turns up in a contemporary commentary by François Bovon: "Jesus asks for something to eat—politely, he does not say 'give me,' he says, 'do you have?'"[10]

At this point one could list exegetes who defend the historicity of the fish episode in Luke 24:42–43. Leon Morris is perfectly clear about what happened: "Jesus dispelled their disbelief by calling for some food which he proceeded to eat."[11] F. F. Bruce takes *sunalizomenos* in Acts 1:4 to mean "eating with," notes the reference to Luke 24:42–43 and Acts 10:41, and states,

> Plainly the resurrection body had no need of material food and drink for its sustenance. But Luke may imply that he took food in the company of his disciples, not for any personal need of his own, but in order to convince them that He was really present with them and they were seeing no phantom.[12]

Plummer, Morris, and Bruce, no less than Marshall, must face these questions: What happened to the food eaten by the risen Jesus? Can a risen body digest food and discharge waste—not to mention, increase in size?[13]

Alongside these four scholars, one can also line up Catholic exegetes who took the fish-eating episode *au pied de la lettre*. Josef Schmid commented that, while not needing any food, the risen Jesus dispelled the disciples' "unbelief" by truly eating the fish. "How he could take in this nourishment," Schmid admitted, "remains for us a mystery."[14] Pierre Benoit agreed that Jesus ate the fish—not because his glorified body needed to eat, but because with pedagogical condescension he gave "his disciples a proof that he can eat and therefore is not a mere phantom."[15]

This sampling of views about stage one of the tradition can suggest that the end (stage three) is where we more appropriately start. We should investigate what we actually have, the text of the evangelist, reflect on Luke's intentions and his literary product, and move back from there to stages two and one.

Stage Three of the Tradition

The fish episode comes within a single literary unit (Luke 24:36–53), a section that recounts "but one appearance of the risen Christ." Within this larger literary unit, verses 36–43 serve as a prologue to what is to come in verses 44–53. Although Luke does not begin this section of his narrative by explicitly portraying the disciples at table in a meal setting, the reader is meant to suppose that.[16] Fitzmyer may be pressing Luke's narrative intention too far when he takes Jesus's question, "Have you anything here to eat?," to mean "Do you still have anything here to eat, anything left over from your evening meal?"[17] It is one thing to recognize a meal setting for Luke's story. It is quite another to claim that the evangelist wants his readers to imagine that Jesus appears after the meal has ended. Nevertheless, Edwards seems to agree with Fitzmyer by proposing tentatively the translation, "Do you have any leftovers?"[18]

At all events Luke's "apologetic motif" is clear. By asking for something to eat and consuming it in their sight, the risen Jesus establishes his "physical reality."[19] Walter Grundmann also notes Luke's "apologetical" purpose: "the bodiliness of the resurrection in the sense of the resurrection of the flesh must be secured." Eating the fish establishes bodily resurrection in a way that "brushes aside every doubt." The "apologetical meaning of the fish" is clear: "the bodily resurrection is so real that the Risen One can eat."[20] It is in similar terms that Josef Ernst identifies Luke's primary concern: "someone who takes nourishment cannot be a ghost"; "any doubt about the bodily resurrection is excluded" when Jesus takes and eats food before the eyes of his disciples.[21]

One should add, however, that in the Jewish tradition, eating would not necessarily establish human bodiliness, whether risen or otherwise (see, e.g., the eating on the part of three divine visitors in Gen 18:8, two angels in Gen 19:3, and Raphael in Tob 3:16—12:22). In the Book of Tobit, the angel explains that he has not really been eating: "all these days I merely appeared to you and did not eat or drink, but you were seeing a vision" (Tob 12:19 RSV). Nevertheless, Luke's Gentile readers would presumably hold that angels and spirits do not eat and hence be satisfied that eating the fish establishes the risen Jesus's genuine bodiliness.

Behind the apologetic motif one can reasonably suppose two movements that the evangelist wishes to combat when writing his Gospel in the seventies or eighties. On the one hand, Luke could be answering those within the Christian community who overspiritualize the resurrection or even deny it while maintaining the continuing, personal presence of Jesus's spirit. On the other hand, the evangelist may be responding to outside critics who reject *tout court* that Jesus appeared as bodily risen from the dead and allege that the disciples experienced some ghostly phantom or even a mere figment of their imagination.

In this connection some exegetes (e.g., Ernst and Grundmann) have spoken of an "anti-docetic" concern Luke shares in common with John.[22] Marshall rightly points out that "the narrative is not concerned to refute Docetism in the proper sense of that term, since it is concerned with the nature of the risen Jesus and not with the [human] nature of the earthly Jesus."[23] Strictly speaking, Docetism was a tendency that considered the humanity, sufferings, and death of the earthly Jesus to be apparent rather than real. One might defend Ernst, Grundmann, and others by allowing them to use the terms *docetic* and *anti-docetic* in a broader sense that would *also* apply in controversies about the state of the risen Jesus.

Even if they did not share that strongly realistic version of stage one in the tradition that Marshall, Plummer, and others defended, Ernst and Grundmann felt the need to deal with the tension between Luke's realistic presentation of the risen Jesus and Paul's reflections on the spiritual body in 1 Corinthians 15:35–53. Grundmann attributes the difference to basically different interests. Paul's statements are "Christologically determined," while Luke follows an "anti-docetic intention,"[24] a distinction that does not throw much light on the question. If understood in the broader sense, an anti-docetic intention takes up christological issues that concern the risen Jesus. Grundmann's distinction does not reach the heart of the difficulty: can we reconcile Luke's very realistic portrayal of the risen Jesus with Paul's version of the spiritual body? Or should we go so far as to argue that Jesus's risen existence differs significantly from our (future) risen existence, so that, whereas he did on one occasion eat (Luke), this will not be true of us (Paul)?

Ernst does better in explaining why such "strongly materialistic elements" in Luke's account of Jesus's invitation to touch him (24:39) and his eating the fish (24:43) do not contradict Paul's statements on risen life and glorified bodiliness. Luke is not offering a "realistic description" but rather "helps to interpretation."[25] Yet Ernst does not enlarge on what such "helps to interpretation" might be. Let me return to these shortly.

The Making of Luke 24:42–43

What lay behind the intimate and vivid scene of Luke 24:42–43? Can we detect elements from stage one and two of the tradition that are particularly relevant for grasping the evangelist's intentions?

I suggest that five items converged in the making of Luke's narrative: (a) the feeding of five thousand with loaves *and fishes* (Luke 9:10–17 parr.); (b) the Last Supper (Luke 22:14–23 parr.); (c) an appearance of the risen Christ to the disciples when they were gathered together (1 Cor 15:5–7; Mark 16:7 parr.) in table fellowship (Mark 16:14) that involved a meal of bread and fish (John 21:13); (d) a memory of initial doubts on the occasion of that appearance (Matt 28:17; John 20:24–25); and (e) the celebration of the Eucharist in the early community (e.g., 1 Cor 11:23–26). Together with these five elements, which will feature below when we discuss Luke's message, we need to consider two features of Luke's style: (i) a use at times of imaginative, elaborated narratives, and (ii) a corrective self-commentary. Let us look at these two features in turn.

> (i) Unlike the simpler statements from John 20:22–23 and Romans 5:5 about the gift of the Holy Spirit, Luke introduces an elaborate scenario for the day of Pentecost (Acts 2:1–4). We find another example of (i) by setting Matthew's brief assertion about Mary being "found to be with child from the Holy Spirit" (Matt 1:18) alongside Luke's annunciation story (Luke 1:26–38). Both Matthew and Luke use a pregospel "annunciation of birth" tradition involving virginal conception through the Holy Spirit, but then Luke's story is more elaborated.[26]
>
> In general, a certain freedom to adapt and embellish shows up more strongly in the first two chapters and last chapter of Luke's Gospel (e.g., in the Emmaus story)—a freedom compatible with his promise to provide authentic information about the story of Jesus (Luke 1:1–4) and the origins of the church (Acts 1:1–2). Luke does not misleadingly create important episodes *ex nihilo*. But on occasions he takes a historically reliable tradition (e.g., the memory of an appearance to Cleopas and his companion) and writes it up in an elaborate way.[27] Gerhard Lohfink finds the initial key to this descriptive art of Luke in the remark that at the baptism the Holy Spirit descended on Jesus "in bodily form" (Luke 3:22). Luke likes to present matters in a visible and tangible way.[28]
>
> (ii) At times Luke deals more than once with the same material, qualifying and correcting an excessive realism that one passage alone could suggest. Thus, the simpler account of Jesus's parting from his disciples at the end of

the Gospel (24:50–51) offsets the vivid narrative of Acts 1:6–11. The promise of the Holy Spirit (Luke 24:49; Acts 1:4–5, 8) puts matters in a less spectacular way than the embellished version of the day of Pentecost (Acts 2). In these cases, the simpler versions forewarn readers not to interpret in a wooden, literalistic fashion the stories of the ascension and the coming of the Spirit that will be provided by Acts. Luke's corrective self-commentary may also run in the opposite direction. Later material can qualify and correct what readers have been given earlier. Acts 1:4 and, especially, Acts 10:41 work like that, qualifying and correcting the excessive realism of Luke 24:43.[29] In Acts 1:4, the apostles eat with or simply stay with the risen Jesus. Acts 10:41 does not speak of Jesus eating but of the apostles eating and drinking in his company after the resurrection.

Luke's Pluriform Message

It seems that Luke has three or, possibly, five things to say through the fish-eating motif taken within its immediate literary context (24:36–43). *First*, this motif obviously aims *apologetically* at establishing—through what Bovon calls "the physical demonstration of the resurrection"[30]—the bodily reality of the risen Lord, now alive and present to his disciples (so Bovon, Ernst, Fitzmyer, Grundmann, Marshall, and so on). Luke knows of those who, both inside and outside the Christian community, doubt or deny the bodily resurrection of Jesus. These doubters and deniers were represented by the disciples in Jerusalem. They "disbelieved" their senses and wrongly "supposed that they saw a spirit" when the risen Jesus stood among them. He finally removed their doubts, and they recognized his bodily presence among them (Luke 24:36–43). The bodily reality of the risen Jesus is stressed. At the same time the corrective self-commentary provided by Luke himself speaks against taking the fish-eating motif literalistically.

The Emmaus story (Luke 24:13–35) should prepare readers to be cautious about taking the fish-eating motif *au pied de la lettre*. The risen Jesus does not operate under the normal bodily conditions of this-worldly human beings: he appears and disappears at will; friends recognize him only when "their eyes are opened" (Luke 24:15–16, 31).

Here Marshall argues that Luke realizes that the Emmaus story could lead readers astray and hence introduces items like the eating of fish to stress the "physical" side of the resurrection: "if the previous story [Luke 24:13–35] has given the impression that the spiritual presence of Jesus is what ultimately matters, Luke redresses the balance in this narrative [Luke 24:36–43] in which the physical reality of the risen Jesus is heavily emphasized."[31] But does Luke want to reduce the now glorious (Luke 24:26), transformed bodiliness of Jesus to the state of a resuscitated corpse that eats and digests food?

An old tradition of Christ appearing on the occasion of a meal, at least as reflected in Acts 1:4, can hardly support such a "physical" apologetic. It expresses here "la familiarité ou la communauté de vie entre le Ressuscité et les disciples."[32] Acts 10:41, which obviously wants to recall the "meal" at Emmaus and the "eating of the fish" in Jerusalem in the Gospel's final chapter, serves not as an apologetic for the bodily resurrection but to underline the qualifications of the apostles as valid witnesses to the risen Christ.

Second, the fish-eating motif in Luke 24 also plays its part in establishing the credentials of the apostolic community as reliable witnesses to the resurrection. Cleopas and his companion receive an interpretation of the Scriptures before recognizing the risen Lord (Luke 24:31, 35). It is the opposite sequence for the eleven apostles and others in the Jerusalem community. They see the risen Jesus (Luke 24:36–43), and then have their minds opened to understand the Scriptures fulfilled in his resurrection from the dead (Luke 24:44–47). The evidence of the senses and a new insight into the Scriptures, along with the gift of the Holy Spirit, will qualify them to be foundational, universal witnesses (Luke 24:47–49). They can begin their mission to the world because they have been with him during his ministry (Acts 1:21), have seen him "in their presence" (Luke 24:43),[33] and now understand the deep meaning of the Scripture.

Third, the fish eating has a further, eucharistic level of meaning. It fits into a broad pattern of meals in Luke's Gospel: meals with Pharisees (7:36–50; 14:1–2); meals with sinners (19:1–10); the eschatological meal (12:37; 13:29); and so forth. In particular, some literary correspondences link 24:42–43 ("fish" and "he took and ate") with the Passover meal in 22:19 ("he took bread") and the supper at Emmaus in 24:30

("he took the bread"). As Guillaume states, the mention of fish in 24:42 "peut server de renvoi aux poisons (9:16) de la multiplication des pains," and so refer (at least indirectly) to the Eucharist.[34] Bovon comments, "By eating fish, as the multitudes did with the multiplication of loaves," Christ "eats the same food as his disciples. Luke suggests here the commensality, the fellowship, and even the eucharistic liturgy."[35]

To be sure, Luke's eucharistic vocabulary and reference come through more clearly in "the breaking of the bread" at Emmaus (24:30, 35). But they are also present, albeit more discreetly, in what one might call "the breaking of the fish" in Jerusalem. Ernst argues that the nature of the food in 24:42–43 (fish) is insignificant. But this is to miss the reference to the multiplication of loaves *and fish* in 9:10–17—an episode with strong eucharistic overtones.

One difficulty with recognizing a sacramental meaning in 24:42–43 comes from the fact that it is Jesus who eats, and he eats alone. But the literary correspondences between these verses and the earlier passages in the Gospel that unmistakably express eucharistic meaning encourage me to recognize also here a sacramental reference. Add too the eucharistic reference that also seems to be present when Luke takes up again the theme of table fellowship with the risen Lord in Acts 1:4 and 10:41. In particular, Acts 10:41 recalls Luke 22:30 ("you may eat and drink at my table in my kingdom"), language that suggests not only the joy of eternal life with God but also the banquet of the Eucharist.

Bovon comments on a widespread textual variant that adds honeycomb to the portion of fish offered to Jesus in Luke 24:42: "We know that in antiquity fish and honey often appeared on the communion tables along with bread and wine." The textual variant, while it does not belong to the original text, "demonstrates that there were many persons during the first centuries of the Christian era who gave this episode a eucharistic dimension."[36]

In the *fourth* place, Luke's fish-eating motif could signify that the risen Jesus offers *pardon* to his followers who have abandoned and (in the case of Peter) denied him. In this Gospel eating together with Jesus expresses forgiveness of sins and reconciliation with God (e.g., 19:1–10). The problem about reading 24:42–43 this way is twofold. Only Jesus himself is represented as eating; in the strict sense of the word there is no table fellowship. More importantly, Luke has played down the disciples' need for repentance and a postresurrection reconciliation. When Jesus is arrested, Luke does not add that the disciples "all fled" (Mark 14:50;

Matt 26:56). After Peter's third denial, it is only in Luke's account that "the Lord turned and looked at Peter" (22:61)—a look that expresses reproach and even more compassionate hope that Peter will fulfill his appointed role (22:31–32). According to Luke, not only some female followers of Jesus but also "all his acquaintances" witnessed the crucifixion (23:49). Finally, Luke reports an appearance to Peter alone (24:34), which took place before the risen Jesus's encounter with the group. Thus, Luke has reduced the need for post-Easter forgiveness to be expressed through renewed table fellowship with Peter and the others. Possibly the fish-eating motif also symbolizes such reconciliation, but this meaning does not seem prominent in Luke's text and intentions.

Fifth and finally, Eugene LaVerdière understands Luke 24:42 as an invitation to "the disciples and Luke's readers" "to extend nourishment to those in whom Jesus is really present." The passage "requires a commitment to the earthly lives of people"—in the spirit of giving food to visiting strangers because the risen Lord identifies himself with them.[37]

Perhaps this reflection works at the level of actualizing hermeneutics. But there is no evidence that by the fish-eating motif Luke himself had such a message in mind. It is through material drawn from the ministry of Jesus (e.g., Luke 16:19–31) or from that of his apostolic witnesses (e.g., Acts 4:32–35) that Luke delivers the call to meet various needs in "the earthly lives of people."

In part, LaVerdière's interpretation echoes the view of Richard Dillon that in Luke 24:36–43 Jesus represents the missionary to whom Christians should show hospitality: "The risen Christ seems to re-enact precisely the procedure he had prescribed for his itinerant representatives." Dillon refers to the mission scheme of Luke 10:2–12 and finds a "remarkable analogy" between that missionary instruction and the appearance story.[38] Luke 10:2–12 and 24:36–43 have some common features, above all the greeting of peace and the reference to eating. But, unlike the missionaries of Luke 10:7, 9, the risen Christ does not come to stay; he does not drink nor does he heal the sick. These and further differences cast doubt on Dillon's claim that the "risen Christ appears in the role of missionary to the chosen household."[39]

Conclusion

With other New Testament passages Luke 24:42–43 recalls a postresurrection appearance to the apostolic group on the occasion of their being together for a meal. But it does not follow that the risen Jesus quite literally ate (and drank) with his disciples (stage one of the tradition). In the life of the early church (stage two of the tradition) a eucharistic setting may have preserved the memory of the risen Lord's encounter with the disciples gathered for table fellowship. Since it is an item shared by Luke 24:42–43 and John 21:1–14, fish may have figured in stage two of the tradition.

Luke himself (stage three of the tradition) uses the fish-eating motif as one of his means for expressing at least three things: (a) the bodily reality of the risen Lord; (b) the qualifications of the apostles as witnesses; and (c) the ongoing eucharistic presence of the Lord. The main thrusts of the motif are apologetic (concerning the living Jesus himself), apostolic (concerning the foundational witnesses to the resurrection), and sacramental (concerning the eucharistic life of the community). But Luke does not want his readers to imagine that the risen Jesus quite literally consumed (and digested) some fish before the astonished eyes of his disciples. The Christ who had entered into his glory (Luke 24:26) was beyond all that.

11

MARY MAGDALENE AS MAJOR WITNESS TO JESUS'S RESURRECTION

(John 20:11-18)

The title of this chapter demands a definition of terms. Although most or even all readers will recognize Mary Magdalene as a historical person, some may still (wrongly) identify her with "the woman…who was a sinner" (Luke 7:37),[1] and the term *major witness* can be misunderstood in diverse ways. In first-century Judaism, women, like slaves, were not qualified to testify in trials as witnesses. Flavius Josephus wrote, "From women let no evidence be accepted, because of the levity and temerity of their sex; neither let slaves bear witness."[2] Thus, if "witness" had been applied to Mary Magdalene in the legal context of those times, this chapter's title would have involved an oxymoron.

The fact that some women, and specifically Mary Magdalene, were cited by the Gospels as witnesses for the resurrection of Jesus evoked scorn from those opposed to early Christianity. Origen needed to refute the charge that belief in the risen Jesus was based on the testimony of a "hysterical female" and "perhaps someone else" (Peter?).[3] This prejudice against accepting women in general and Mary Magdalene in particular as Easter witnesses continued through the centuries. Ernest Renan, for instance, constructed Mary Magdalene as *the* (hallucinated) witness, whose "strong imagination" made her imagine that Jesus was personally risen from the dead and whose testimony convinced the other disciples: "Divine power of love! Sacred moments in which the passion of one possessed gave to the world a resuscitated God!"[4] In the twentieth century even such a staunchly orthodox writer as Giuseppe Ricciotti downplayed her significance.[5] Some years later, Francesco Spadafora argued that the appearance to Mary Magdalene was not as important as those to the male disciples—the Jerusalem appearances were less significant than those in Galilee—since those in Galilee were connected with the foundation of the church.[6]

In the post-Pentecost situation, the early witnesses of the risen Jesus set Christianity going and growing. We know much about some and almost nothing about others. We have enough data to write books about Peter and Paul, but we enjoy scarce information about Mary Magdalene. These limits do not diminish her importance but demand that we rightly interpret the data. She was great enough for Pope Leo I, soon after the Council of Chalcedon (AD 451), to call her a "figure of the Church [*personam Ecclesiae gerens*]"[7] and, some years later, for Pope Gregory the Great to refer to her as another Eve who "announces" not death but "life to the men."[8] Ulrich Luz cites Jerome, Hilary of Poitiers, John Chrysostom, and Cyril of Alexandria who treated typologically the appearance to Mary Magdalene and "the other Mary" in Matthew 28:9–10: "Jesus removed the curse that had been put on women because of Eve."[9] Much earlier, in the third century, Hippolytus of Rome referred to the women at the tomb of Jesus as being "apostles,"[10] which developed into Mary Magdalene often being called the *apostola apostolorum* (the apostle of the apostles).

For the purposes of this chapter, we will define *witness* as someone who has firsthand knowledge of some fact or events.[11] A major witness is one whose testimony is of greatest importance or is the most complete. To analyze Mary Magdalene's role as major witness to Jesus's resurrection, we begin with the Gospels.

New Testament Data

Joseph Fitzmyer names six resurrection narratives found in the Gospels.[12] First, Mark 16:1–8 describes how three women (Mary Magdalene, Mary the mother of James, and Salome) discover the tomb of

Jesus to be open and empty. An angel charges them to go and tell the disciples and Peter that Jesus goes before them into Galilee, where they will see him. The women "flee and say nothing to anyone, for they were afraid." There are no appearances of the risen Christ.[13]

In Matthew 28:1–20, two women (Mary Magdalene and another Mary) find the tomb open and empty. An angel of the Lord and then Jesus himself appear to them; both the angel and Jesus tell the women to break the news of the resurrection to the others. Subsequently the risen Christ appears to "the eleven" on a mountain in Galilee, and commissions them to teach all nations and baptize them "in the name of the Father and of the Son and of the Holy Spirit."[14]

A third Easter chapter, Luke 23:56b—24:53, consists of six episodes: (a) the finding of the empty tomb by women (Mary Magdalene, Mary the mother of James, Joanna, and others). They are told by two angels in gleaming robes to recall the words Jesus had addressed to them while he was still in Galilee. The women leave the grave and report it all to the eleven, who regard the story as so much nonsense. (b) Peter alone goes off to see the tomb for himself (and the risen Christ appears to him). (c) Jesus appears to two disciples on the road to Emmaus. (d) He then appears to the eleven and their companions in Jerusalem. (e) He commissions them to be "witnesses" and to preach in his name; and (f) he leads them out to Bethany, where he parts from them and is carried off to heaven.[15]

Rudolf Schnackenburg considers it significant that Luke, who "does assign a certain role to the women," "does not know of an appearance by Jesus to them." This silence "carries weight," evidently weight against the historical and, as we shall see, theological significance of a Christophany to Mary Magdalene.[16] François Bovon, however, comments that "Luke ignores or chooses to ignore the personal appearance she was granted (Matt 28:9–10; John 20:11–18). If he maintains the presence of this one to whom he refuses greater honor, it is because the memory of the women followers of Jesus was inseparable from Easter morning."[17]

Others have different explanations. Zane C. Hodges writes, "For Luke, the extended manifestation to two male witnesses at once is the heart of his resurrection narrative and its effect is not to be diminished by even an allusion [to an appearance] to prior female witnesses."[18] Playing off "two male witnesses" in the Emmaus story against "prior female witnesses" runs up against the objection that the sex of Cleopas's companion is not disclosed; the person might, for example, have been his wife. In any case nothing is made of that person's gender. His or her authority as Easter witness can hardly have been reckoned notable, since this anonymous person's only place in Luke's two-volume work occurs in the story of Emmaus.

Luke does not mention an appearance to Mary Magdalene, either alone (John) or with a female companion (Matthew), but he recalls how she and the other women reported their experience at the open and empty tomb of Jesus to "the eleven and to all the rest" (24:9). He then repeats this news by saying that they reported "these things" to "the apostles," now specifying by name that this Easter message came from "Mary Magdalene, Joanna, and Mary the mother of James" (24:10). This way of twice presenting matters underlines the importance of the women witnesses and draws close to calling Mary Magdalene and her two companions "apostles to the apostles."

According to a fourth resurrection narrative (John 20:1–29),[19] Mary Magdalene, on discovering Jesus's tomb to be open and empty, informs Simon Peter and "the beloved disciple." This is followed by his appearing at the tomb to Mary Magdalene alone, an appearance to the disciples in Jerusalem on Easter Sunday evening, with Thomas absent, and his appearance a week later, with Thomas present. An epilogue (John 21:1–25) tells of an appearance to seven disciples on the shore of Lake Tiberias.

Fifth, in the second-century Markan appendix (Mark 16:9–20),[20] an appearance to Mary Magdalene precedes an appearance to two disciples who are walking "into the country." Then Jesus appears to the eleven, whom he upbraids for their disbelief and commissions to preach the gospel to all nations. He is taken up into heaven, and the disciples go forth to preach.

It should strike those who read this summary that Mary Magdalene is mentioned in all five Gospel narratives and, when mentioned, is always the first person named. Is this merely accidental or were the evangelists recognizing her importance? Apropos of the appearance to Mary Magdalene in Matthew 28:9–10, Luz remarks, "It seems to me that the appearance to a woman contradicts the dominant trend in the institution of the church to give the honor of the first appearance to Peter and the apostles, and for that reason it probably goes back to an early tradition."[21] As regards Luke's placing Mary Magdalene in first place among the women who visit the tomb of Jesus on Easter Sunday morning (24:10), Bovon observes that Luke "ignores or chooses to ignore the personal appearance she was granted," but adds, "If he maintains the presence of this one to whom he refuses greater honor, it is because the memory of the women followers of Jesus was inseparable from Easter morning."[22] Commenting on John 20:10, Raymond Brown says, "The real purpose of this verse is to get the disciples off the scene and give the stage to Mary Magdalene," to whom the risen Jesus then appears.[23]

Interpretation by Bultmann, Hoskyns, Dodd, and Barrett

In a classic commentary, Rudolf Bultmann compares the account of the Easter appearances in John 20 with those found in the Synoptic Gospels. He notes that in John's narrative Mary Magdalene recognizes the risen Christ when he calls her by name. Bultmann points to the meaning this detail undoubtedly has: "The shepherd knows his sheep and 'calls them by name' (John 10:3) and when they hear his voice, they recognize him. Perhaps we may also add: the naming of a name tells a man [sic!] what he is; and to be known in such a way leads a man to the encounter with the Revealer."[24]

Bultmann qualifies this by saying that Mary Magdalene cannot enter into fellowship with Christ until she has recognized him as the Lord who is with the Father.[25] Her message to the disciples is the core of Easter faith: understanding the offense of the cross. In contrast with Luke's account (Luke 24:11), nothing is said about how the disciples reacted to her message, either positively or negatively.

Edwin Hoskyns also writes of the shepherd-sheep image.[26] He states that the message Mary Magdalene had to deliver to the disciples was "that the new order, the order of the powerful action of the Spirit of God, the New Covenant, was now imminent." Hoskyns points out that while, in all three Synoptic Gospels, Mary Magdalene is first woman named in the Easter texts, in the Fourth Gospel "the emphasis rests entirely upon the appearance of the Lord to Mary and upon the words which he addressed to her."[27]

In *The Interpretation of the Fourth Gospel*, C. H. Dodd compares and evaluates the postresurrection scenes in the Gospels. He sums up Matthew 28 as meaning that Christ comes in glory to reign over all.[28] He insists on the evidential value that the appearances have for the apostles; they know that the Lord is alive (Luke 24:23) and will come again.[29] John's Gospel, however, presents the appearances as the renewal of Jesus's personal relations with the apostles.[30] Thus Dodd largely edits out the significance of Mary Magdalene.

C. K. Barrett takes John 20 to depend on the Easter tradition of 1 Corinthians 15:5-8 and Mark 16:1-8. In that earlier tradition nothing is said about an appearance to Mary Magdalene. Barrett believes that John 20 intends to give the central place to the Beloved Disciple.[31] This position seriously reduces the significance of Mary Magdalene.

Schnackenburg and Bovon

When Rudolf Schnackenburg comments on John 20, he notes that the events of Easter Sunday morning are held together by Mary Magdalene.[32] He argues that, even if concentration on her corresponds to the fourth evangelist's tendency to bring individual persons to the fore, her choice is not the creation of the evangelist but taken over from a source.[33] Mary's encounter with the risen Christ "represents for the evangelist the climax which, according to his Christological thought, he emphasizes strongly."[34]

Schnackenburg knows that, in the oldest list of postresurrection appearances (1 Cor 15:5-8), "a Christophany to Mary Magdalene is lacking." But he does not consider this a "serious counter-argument, because the primitive Church obviously did not place any value on the testimony of women."[35] Nevertheless, he ends by subordinating Mary's testimony to that of the male disciples: "For John, the value of the story [of the appearance to Mary Magdalene] is not on a historical but a theological level. In Mary's encounter with Jesus the meaning of Jesus's resurrection for the fellowship of the disciples may 'find expression.'" Yet "it forms a [mere?] prelude to Jesus's appearance before the disciples to whom the risen Lord gives the Spirit and grants authority."[36]

In an important article, Bovon recalls that some exegetes had considered the appearance to Mary Magdalene among "later and legendary" additions to the text.[37] He believes, however, that it is important to examine possible reasons for the Easter appearances being included in the Gospels and epistles. Since Peter was the first leader of the church, he was obviously mentioned in 1 Corinthians 15:5, as were James and other apostles in 15:7. The fact that Mary was mentioned at all shows that the early church considered her important and wanted to include her as an authentic Easter witness.[38]

Yet how do we explain that Mary Magdalene is missing from the names provided by 1 Corinthians 15:5-8? Bovon believes that the list provided by Paul represents a compromise between the Judeo-Christianity of Jerusalem (represented by Peter and James) and Hellenistic Christianity (represented by Paul himself). This compromise was made at the expense of other such groups as the Johannine church. To include Mary Magdalene in a kerygmatic list would have alienated some groups for several reasons: (1) those from a Jewish background would not accept a woman's testimony; (2) the church was concentrating on setting up a male ministry opposed to prophetic witness; (3) and a woman would detract from Peter and Paul, whom the early church was emphasizing.[39]

Elisabeth Schüssler Fiorenza

A scholar who from a feminist viewpoint has analyzed the role of women (and especially Mary Magdalene) as witnesses to the resurrection is Elisabeth Schüssler Fiorenza. She points out the continuity of fidelity on the part of female disciples, who had stood with Jesus in suffering, sought to honor him in death, and then became proclaimers of his resurrection.[40] She relies on the work done by Raymond Brown[41] to assert that the discipleship and leadership of the Johannine community included both women and men. The "Johannine Christians, represented by the Beloved Disciple, clearly [regarded] themselves as closer to Jesus and more perceptive than the churches who [claimed] Peter and the twelve as their apostolic authority."[42]

Schüssler Fiorenza recognizes two traditions that coexist in the accounts of the postresurrection appearances—the tradition of Mary Magdalene being the primary apostolic witness to the resurrection (Matthew, John, and the Markan appendix) and the tradition of the Petrine primacy (Paul and Luke). She finds it remarkable that these two independent streams of the gospel tradition have survived.[43] She points out that the role of women in the church has always been controversial. Patristic Christianity downplayed the significance of women, especially Mary Magdalene, as primary witnesses to the resurrection and highlighted male figures like Peter, Paul, and the Twelve. Noncanonical gospels, however, claimed women disciples as apostolic authorities for the reception of revelation and secret teaching.[44] Apocryphal writings of the second and third centuries that spoke of a competition between Peter and Mary Magdalene reflected the tension that existed about the

Mary Magdalene as Major Witness to Jesus's Resurrection

primacy of apostolic authority. In fact, the "argument between Peter and Mary Magdalene clearly reflects the debate in the early church on whether women are the legitimate transmitters of apostolic revelation and tradition."[45]

Before moving on, let us introduce three observations about Schüssler Fiorenza's position. First, while she recognizes different appearance traditions that coexist in the New Testament, she does not distinguish between them in the usual way: the appearances that took place in Galilee (to Peter, the Twelve, and the "more than five hundred"), those that took place in and around Jerusalem (to Mary Magdalene, James [and others], and Cleopas and his anonymous companion), and the appearance to Paul outside Damascus. These individuals and groups were distinguished by their geographical location rather than by their female or male identity.[46]

Second, early church writers (e.g., Clement of Rome, Ignatius of Antioch, Justin Martyr, and Irenaeus) remain quite silent about any controversy over women legitimately transmitting apostolic revelation and tradition. Clement goes out of his way to praise women like Esther and Judith for what they had done for their people (1 Clement, 55). Schüssler Fiorenza admits that it is (only later) Gnostic and other apocryphal writings that "claim women disciples as [separate?] apostolic authorities for the reception of revelation and secret teachings."[47] These writings belong to the second and third centuries. She does not appreciate the importance of Mark 16:9–11, according to which Jesus appeared *first* to Mary Magdalene. Yet in what follows (16:12–20) there is no suggestion of any conflict between Mary Magdalene and Peter as apostolic authorities. This important, second-century addition to Mark's Gospel (16:9–20) acknowledges Mary Magdalene's significance but fails to vindicate Schüssler Fiorenza's thesis.[48] We must ask ourselves whether the Gnostics have accurately preserved something that was present at the beginning. Are they reliable guides or simply a decadent spinoff? Bovon believes that the extra- and postbiblical traditions about Mary Magdalene were filled in and distorted, not by members of the universal church but by such marginal movements as Gnosticism and Encratism.[49]

Third, patristic Christianity at times played down the role of women. Yet, as we saw, Hippolytus of Rome, Leo the Great, Gregory the Great, and others could pay remarkable tribute to the person of Mary Magdalene.

THE GOSPELS

Pheme Perkins

Schüssler Fiorenza does not refer to an earlier work, Pheme Perkins's *The Gnostic Dialogue*,[50] that challenged the reliability of the Gnostic writings as guides to the origin and development of Christianity. Perkins wrote at a time when Elaine Pagels had popularized a theory of Gnostic/orthodox conflict.[51] She argued that Pagels was mistaken in portraying the Gnostics as "champions of individual creativity against an increasingly repressive and unimaginative orthodoxy."[52] Perkins summed up her case:

> She claims that gnosis represents the form in which Christian symbols continue to inspire great creative artists, otherwise alienated by a rigid orthodox Christianity. Gnostics insist on the right of the autonomous, creative human self. The preceding section [of my book] has already taken issue with the historical inaccuracies in such presentations of the Gnostic/orthodox relationship. We have seen that Gnostics did not have the picture of the autonomous, differentiated, creative self, presupposed in this argument. Such a view of the self is largely the product of modern thought and presupposes a consciousness of self and world radically different from that of second- and third-century people.[53]

In a later work Perkins refers favorably to Schüssler Fiorenza's view that women belonged to the larger group of witnesses (from which a successor to Judas was chosen) and were commissioned as missionaries.[54] Perkins approached her research, however, more from an exegetical point of view rather than from any attempt to recruit the early Christian story for a feminist theological reconstruction.[55]

When Perkins compares Matthew's Easter story with that of Mark, she notes how the former clarifies ambiguities found in the Markan account. Specifically, just as "Matthew makes the figure at the tomb unmistakably an angel, so he attributes to the angel [more emphatically] knowledge of the women's errand ['*I know* that you are seeking Jesus who has been crucified'] (Matt 28:5) rather than 'you are seeking Jesus who has been crucified' [Mark 16:6]." The women "are to go quickly and announce that Jesus has risen. Thus, they are messengers of the resurrection."[56] Matthew has replaced Mark 16:7 ("Go, tell his disciples and

Mary Magdalene as Major Witness to Jesus's Resurrection

Peter that he is going ahead of you to Galilee; there you will see him, just as he told you") with "Go *quickly*, tell his disciples that *he has been raised from the dead*, and behold he is going before you into Galilee; there you will see him. *Behold, I have told you*" (Matt 28:7 au. trans.). Perkins interprets Jesus's subsequent words to the women (Matt 28:10) as a further command to the women that they should carry out the commission to be messengers of the resurrection that they had already received from an angel of the Lord.

Perkins observes that, whereas the angel's commission in Mark 16:7 contains "and Peter," the words are missing in Matthew 28:7. She comments,

> Matthew gives Peter primacy in the gospel as spokesperson for the disciples, as guardian of Jesus' interpretation of the Law, and as representative of the typical disciple, but he does not place Peter above the others. He is firmly anchored within the circle of disciples to whom the ministry of the post-Easter church is entrusted. One might even wonder if some scholars have gone too far in pushing 1 Cor 15:5 to imply that the primacy that Peter enjoyed among the disciples was based on his rallying the others after his vision of the risen Lord.[57]

Perkins concludes her analysis of the resurrection accounts in Mark and Matthew by arguing that there are three traditions behind the Gospel narratives. They are (1) the kerygmatic tradition reflected in 1 Corinthians 15:3–5, (2) that of the empty tomb found by the female disciples, and (3) that of the Christian prophets who speak in the name of the Lord, proclaiming his messianic exaltation.[58]

In her comments on Luke 24:36–49, Perkins says that Jesus's commission to witness is intended for the entire group of those who have followed him from Galilee. This group explicitly includes a number of women disciples, and so this commissioning is also meant for them.[59] Perkins notes how "the eleven and those with them" say of Peter, "The Lord has risen indeed, and he has appeared to Simon" (Luke 24:34), whereas in John 20:18, Mary Magdalene says of herself, "I have seen the Lord." The language of John acknowledges Mary Magdalene's equality with other disciples as a witness to the resurrection.[60] Her words in

115

THE GOSPELS

John's Gospel recalls Paul's questions: "Am I not an apostle? Have I not seen Jesus our Lord?" (1 Cor 9:1).

Summary

Before we draw conclusions, we should summarize the data we have presented. To examine Mary Magdalene's role as witness to Jesus's resurrection, we began by defining terms. Whereas a witness is someone who has firsthand knowledge of something, a major witness is one whose testimony is of greater significance and more complete. The evidence to which the Easter witnesses testified concerned Jesus's postresurrection appearances to them and the discovery of the empty tomb.

We examined five resurrection narratives in the Gospels. Mary Magdalene is mentioned in all five, and, when mentioned, always in the first place. In 1 Corinthians 15:3–8, an earlier source, however, even if the presence of women is implied in verse 6 (the appearance to more than five hundred disciples), no mention is made of Mary Magdalene or any other female witnesses to the resurrection. The importance of Cephas (Peter) is stressed as the first recipient of a postresurrection appearance of Jesus. Some commentators react by subordinating the Gospels to Paul; others simply accept the coexistence of two different traditions.

To complicate the problem, we know that there was an ancient prejudice against admitting women as witnesses. In modern times some commentators have tended to stress that faith in Jesus's resurrection is based on the testimony of male rather than female disciples. Where his appearances were admitted as evidence of the resurrection, only those to Peter, Paul, and other male disciples were considered normative.

An examination of some of the classical commentators on John's Gospel—Bultmann, Hoskyns, Dodd, Barrett, and Schnackenburg—showed diverse opinions about the meaning and significance of the postresurrection appearances. Bultmann considered Mary Magdalene to bear the core of Easter faith, and Hoskyns portrayed her as delivering the message that the order of the new covenant was now imminent. Dodd, however, was interested in the appearances but not in a woman witness as such, while Barrett believed that only the Beloved Disciple was important in John 20, the gospel chapter that most fully describes

Mary Magdalene. Schnackenburg did better, but at the end he too subordinated her testimony to that of the male disciples.

Prejudice against women has been rightly challenged in recent decades, above all by feminist writers. A rethinking of traditional positions encourages us to recognize and value Mary Magdalene as a major witness to Jesus's resurrection.

Conclusions

While the postresurrection appearances are not as such the *object* of Christian faith (and hence never entered the major creeds of the church), they were the historical *catalyst* of that faith and enjoy primary significance in the birth of Christianity. In the Easter tradition of Christian origins, women and especially Mary Magdalene played a lead role. In John 20, she is the human figure who holds the events together.

Was the appearance tradition that highlighted the women witnesses (the Gospels) as important as that which depended on the tradition involving male leaders (1 Corinthians)? To the extent that we admit any evidence from the Gnostic and other apocryphal writings of the second and third centuries, we can recognize that even by then this question had not been universally resolved. There was still a debate in some (marginal) quarters as to whether women could be legitimate transmitters of revelation. By the sixth century, however, we find Pope Gregory the Great speaking of Mary Magdalene as being a new Eve who revealed true life to the male disciples.

Rather than arguing for a priority of importance, let alone contradiction, between the two traditions, Perkins assesses their differences. She concludes that Peter is (1) the spokesperson for the disciples, (2) guardian of Jesus's interpretation of the law, (3) representative of the typical disciple, and (4) part of the group in charge of the post-Easter ministry of the church. Some women (1) were the primary messengers commanded to announce first the resurrection, and (2) belonged to those commissioned to witness. In addition, Mary Magdalene was considered equal to male disciples as a witness to Jesus's resurrection.

This synthesis does not deny authority to Peter, the recipient of a special postresurrection appearance. It does, however, point up the converging roles of women, Peter, and other disciples as witnesses to the risen Christ. Among the female recipients of Easter appearances, Mary

Magdalene has the primary role. In the words of Andrew Lincoln, she "receives the first resurrection appearance, and, as part of this, is given the commission to make the key announcement to the disciples. It is not surprising that she has been called 'the apostle to the apostles.' If an apostle is one who has received a resurrection appearance and a commission, then Mary's testimony deserves to be called apostolic."[61] We should join Ann Graham Brock in desiring "a greater appreciation for her role as the first apostle."[62]

12

"HIS LIFE ROSE WITH HIM"

John 21 and the Resurrection of Jesus

Apropos of the resurrection of Jesus, I have treasured the words of an Anglican scholar and preacher, Henry Scott Holland (1847–1918): "When he [Jesus] rose, his life rose with him."[1] The new, risen state of Jesus embodies his human life and history that ended with the crucifixion and burial. The resurrection has made his history irrevocably and gloriously present. Does the New Testament and, specifically, John 21 support Holland's cryptic claim? Can we understand this final chapter of John to suggest that the history of Jesus, as portrayed in the Fourth Gospel, rose with him?

In exploring this vision of Jesus's resurrection, I follow Alan Culpepper[2] and others in understanding John 1—21 to be a literary unity.[3] Maurizio Marcheselli and other recent writers persuasively interpret John 21 as rereading John 1—20. It is by reference to the previous text (John 1—20) that the final text (John 21) acquires its significance and importance. Marcheselli writes of this *relecture* as "involving a certain number of main themes that have appeared in John 1–20" or a "re-reading" of "some of the great themes of Johannine theology."[4] This rereading retrieves details that present what Jesus said, did, and suffered during his human life. Through deft echoes and allusions, the story of Jesus rises with him in John 21. Marcheselli himself understands the rereading displayed by John 21 as primarily (but not exclusively) ecclesiological.[5] I think a good case can *also* be made for a christological rereading that would underpin Holland's vision of Jesus's life and history rising with him.

Craig Keener speaks of John 21 providing "a model for the disciples' continuing experience of Jesus beyond the resurrection."[6] To do that, the chapter yields a model of Jesus's own history rising with him. This risen existence makes the disciples' ongoing experience of him possible.

Word, Light, and Life

The Gospel of John opens by proclaiming, "In the beginning was the Word [*Logos*] and the Word was with God, and the Word was God" (John 1:1).[7] After stating that "the Word became flesh and lived among us" (1:14), the Gospel no longer uses the title *Logos*, but speaks of "the word [*logos*]" of Jesus. The royal official whose little son was seriously ill "believed the word that Jesus spoke to him" (4:50). Jesus called on Jews who believed in him: "If you continue in my word, you are truly my disciples" (8:31). He encouraged people to "keep" his word (8:51; 14:24). The Fourth Gospel frequently attributes to Jesus the related verb *legein*, right from his very first utterance (John 1:38). At times we find Jesus expressing himself with striking emphasis: "Amen, amen, I say [*legō*] to you" (e.g., 3:3, 5, 11; 5:19, 24, 25).

John 21 ten times talks of the risen Jesus's speaking: *legei* in the third person (21:5, 10, 12, 15[2x], 16, 17, 18, 19, 22), and once in the first person, *legō* (21:18). In that chapter he is credited with saying 101 words. After Peter's threefold protestation of love, Jesus warns him that he will be violently put to death, evidently by crucifixion (21:18–19),[8] and introduces this warning in the solemn way that, from 1:51, he used twenty-four times during his public life: "Amen, amen, I say unto you" (21:18 au. trans.).[9] The Word who spoke his words with truth and authority during his human life speaks words in his risen existence. The *Logos* continues to express himself by speaking (*legein*).

After identifying Jesus Christ as the Word of God, the Prologue of the Fourth Gospel insists on his being "the light [*phōs*] of all people":

> The *light* shines in the darkness [*scotia*], and the darkness did not overcome it. There was a man sent by God, whose

"His Life Rose with Him"

name was John. He came as a witness to testify to the *light*, so that all might believe through him. He himself was not the *light*, but he came to testify to the *light*. The true *light*, which *enlightens* everyone, was coming into the world[10] (John 1:4–9).

The Fourth Gospel will use "light [*phōs*]" twenty-two times and sometimes in counterpoint with "darkness." In the course of bringing sight to a man who had been born blind and lived in physical darkness (9:1–39), Jesus calls himself "the light of the world" (9:5).

As light, Jesus is self-revealing. Returning from the dead, Jesus reveals himself at the end of John's story; he manifests himself "just after daybreak" (John 21:4). He is there on the beach as dawn comes and darkness slips away. The scene takes the reader back through the cure of the blind man and the claim to be the light of the world to the Gospel's Prologue, which has pictured Christ as "the true light, which enlightens everyone." During his human history he has shown himself to be light for others; now resurrected from the dead, he comes to drive away darkness and share his light.

Right at the start, John's Gospel has identified the creative Word as being not only light giving but also life giving: "What has come into being in him was *life*, and the *life* was the light of all people" (1:3–4). The Fourth Gospel uses "life [*zōē*]" thirty-seven times. After multiplying five barley loaves and two fishes to feed five thousand hungry people, with the fragments of the loaves filling twelve baskets (6:13), Jesus presents himself as the very *bread of life* (6:22–61).[11]

"Life" figures in a promise Jesus made for the sheep of his flock: "I came that *they may have life, and have it abundantly*" (10:10). As the good shepherd, he will "lay down [his] life for the sheep." But he lays it down "in order to take it up again" in his resurrection from the dead (10:11–18). Before raising Lazarus from the dead, he reveals himself as "the resurrection and *the* life" (11:25). On the eve of his crucifixion, he calls himself "the way, the truth, *and the life*" (14:6). He is life itself and will continue to dispense life, even more richly, in his resurrection from the dead.

In the closing chapter of John, Peter and six other disciples have fished all night and caught nothing. Now Jesus, a mysterious figure on the lakeside, tells them to cast their net on the right side of their boat. They do so and make an enormous catch of 153 large fish (21:6, 8, 11)—a symbol of extravagant fullness[12] and of *life in abundance* (10:10).

This abundant supply of fish matches the earlier excess of bread and the generous quantity of wine made available at the marriage feast of Cana.

Mission of Disciples Led by Peter

After John 20, the situation we meet in 21:1–3 is astonishing. Summoned by Mary Magdalene's unexpected discovery of the open and empty tomb, Peter has visited the tomb of Jesus (20:3–10). On Easter Sunday evening, along with the other "disciples" (20:19), he rejoices to see the risen Lord, receives the Holy Spirit, and is sent on mission (20:21–22). Thomas, who was absent on Easter Sunday evening and expresses his crass doubts about the resurrection, a week later sees the risen Lord and blurts out his confession, "My Lord and my God" (20:24–29). Then we suddenly find Peter, Thomas, Nathanael,[13] "the sons of Zebedee," and two other "disciples" (one must be the Beloved Disciple and the other perhaps Andrew, Peter's brother)[14] out fishing, almost as if Jesus had never turned their lives around by his ministry, death, resurrection, and gift of the Spirit. Peter's announcement, "I am going fishing" (21:3), seems to ignore the association with Jesus that has shaped his recent past. It even suggests an uncertainty about the way Peter and his fellow disciples should begin their ministry to the world.

The text assumes what we already know, not explicitly from John but from the Synoptic Gospels: Peter and the sons of Zebedee were fishermen when Jesus first called them from their boats and nets on a new mission to fish for human beings (Mark 1:16–20 parr.).[15] That Peter, Andrew, James, and John had been fishermen must have been widely known among early Christians. Peter, who has been called and renamed by Jesus very early in John's story, albeit only after the calling of Andrew and his anonymous companion (the Beloved Disciple?) (John 1:35–42),[16] acts as spokesman for the Twelve in professing faith in Jesus (6:66–71). At the Last Supper, Peter plays a notable role: for instance, by enlisting the help of the Beloved Disciple in unmasking the identity of the traitor (13:21–30) and by rejecting what Jesus foretells about Peter's triple denial (13:36–38), which then takes place later in the evening (18:15–18, 25–27).

At the Last Supper, John's Gospel has repeatedly pointed to the coming *mission* to be exercised by the *disciples* of Jesus (14:12; 16:2–3; 17:18–23). Jesus speaks of "the enduring fruit" that his disciples' mission will bring (15:16). Earlier, Jesus has presented the image of himself as the "true vine" and warned of the fruitless results that come from remaining apart from him (15:4–5). The fishing exhibition of the seven disciples led by Peter evokes the sense of the disciples lacking resources if they remain on their own (21:5). Their precrucifixion relationship with Jesus will now be transformed by the risen Lord. The history of Jesus—specifically, in his association with Peter and the other six men—rises from the dead.[17] This transformed association will affect both Jesus and their *discipleship* of *mission*, imaged as a fruitful fishing and shepherding led by Peter, rehabilitated as chief fisherman and now appointed as shepherd of the Lord's flock. As the story evolves in John 21, there emerges a wonderful, unconscious irony in Peter's words to the other disciples: "I am going fishing" (21:3). He will be commissioned for the Lord's mission, symbolized as "catching fish" (see n. 15).

The Self-Manifestation of the Risen Jesus

Right from its Prologue (John 1:1–18), the Fourth Gospel introduces language for the *divine self-revelation that elicits human faith*: "word," "light," "witness," "glory," "truth," and "make known." Fairly soon other significant terms for revelation turn up: for instance, "sign" and "manifest" (*phaneroō*). John begins his ministry of "witness" (1:19) in order that Jesus might be "manifested" to Israel (1:31). Through the "sign" of water changed into wine, Jesus "manifested" his "glory" at Cana (2:11). The "brothers" of Jesus exhort him to "manifest himself publicly" (7:4). In his closing prayer at the Last Supper Jesus says that he has "manifested" God's name (17:6).

In its final chapter, the Fourth Gospel twice states that the risen Jesus "manifested [*ephanerōsen*] himself to the disciples by the Sea of Tiberias" (John 21:1 au. trans.).[18] It does that by subsequently calling this Easter appearance the "third" manifestation to the "disciples" of Jesus raised from the dead (21:14)—more precisely his third to a group of disciples, as he has also appeared to Mary Magdalene alone (20:11–18).[19] Three times in John 21 we find the verb *manifest*, the same word that closes the story of Jesus miraculously remedying a lack of wine by changing water into wine: "Jesus did this, the first of his signs, in Cana of Galilee, and *manifested his glory*; and his disciples believed in him" (John 2:11 au. trans.).[20]

The choice of the verb *manifest* and the naming of "Nathanael of Cana in Galilee" as one of the six other "disciples" with Peter (21:2) should prod readers into remembering how it is in Galilee (1:43) that Jesus meets Nathanael and calls him to be his disciple. Before encountering Jesus "from Nazareth," Nathanael famously expresses his low expectations: "Can anything good come out of Nazareth?" (1:45–46). Then Nathanael's confession of Jesus in 1:49 ("Rabbi, you are the Son of God! You are the King of Israel") forms "the climax of the responses of the first disciples to Jesus."[21] It prompts Jesus into promising Nathanael that he will "see greater things" (1:45–51). Nathanael and the disciples he represents see this promise being fulfilled in the first sign Jesus performs.[22] At "a wedding in Cana of Galilee" they witness his "glory manifested," when Jesus changes around 150 gallons of water into wine, indeed the "best" wine (2:1–11). Nathanael and a further six disciples *will also see something "greater"* when, according to John 21, they meet Jesus gloriously risen from the dead and witness the sign of the extraordinary catch of fish.[23] The lavish number of fish parallels the amount of excellent wine that Jesus, the heavenly bridegroom (3:29), provides.[24] Here we should recall how "glory" (*doxa*) signals the presence of God (e.g., Exod 24:16–17; Lev 9:23; Num 16:19; 1 Kgs 8:11). In John 21 Nathanael and the other disciples, especially Peter and the Beloved Disciple, enjoy a touchingly intimate, face-to-face encounter with the "glory," or the presence, of the risen Lord. What manifests Jesus's glory during his human history at Cana in Galilee now recurs with fresh intensity when he appears in resurrected life on the shores of Lake Tiberias.

Thus, the Nathanael connection deftly implies what has happened to Jesus's initial relationship with the first disciples. The history of that relationship rises with Jesus, in a gloriously enhanced form, through his resurrection from the dead.

Questions, Irony, and Love

Three characteristics of Jesus's story told in John 1—20 are resurrected to new life in the Easter narrative of John 21: questioning, irony, and love.

Right from the start of John's Gospel, Jesus shows himself a *questioner*. His very first words take the form of a question to Andrew and his anonymous companion (presumably the Beloved Disciple): "What are you looking for?" (1:38). Many striking questions turn up as the story unfolds, such as Jesus's question to the Twelve ("Do you also wish to go away?" [6:67]) and his questions at the Last Supper (e.g., "Do you know what I have done to you?" [13:12]). To be sure, the other Gospels contain questions asked by Jesus, but they are a special feature of the Fourth Gospel. Throughout, the questions bring out many central themes that the evangelist wishes to convey.

When rising to new life, Jesus is reinstated as the divine questioner. At the outset, he asks a question: "Children, you have no fish, have you?" (21:5). Then, famously, the chapter features the only question Jesus ever repeats, and he puts it three times to Peter: "Do you love me?" (21:15–17). After the resurrection, an old habit is restored and intensified. Peter faces Jesus the questioner, from whom he receives forgiveness and a lasting commission.

Irony has also characterized the story of Jesus as told by the Fourth Gospel.[25] The meaning of what people say and do can go beyond what they intend and even be at odds with what they intend. Thus, the high priest Caiaphas gives his advice to the council: "It is better for you to have one man die for the people than to have the whole nation destroyed" (11:50). The evangelist at once draws attention to the truth about the redemption of all people that has been unconsciously expressed (11:51). Sometimes irony emerges in the words of Jesus himself; he knows the true import of what he says or asks, but the persons he addresses do not yet grasp the truth. This is the case when he puts the question, "Children, you have no fish, have you?" (21:5).

The risen Jesus knows that the disciples have failed to catch any fish and that he himself will supply them with a huge quantity of fish. "Ironically," Brendan Byrne comments, "he gives the impression of being disappointed at their inability to provide him with anything to eat, while all along knowing that it is he who will provide them with food in abundance."[26] A characteristic that pervades the Fourth Gospel's account of the human history of Jesus, irony, does not disappear at the crucifixion but is reinstated with the resurrection.

The Fourth Gospel, as it draws to its highpoint, emphasizes the *love* Jesus shows to others: "Jesus loved Martha and her sister [Mary] and [their brother] Lazarus" (11:5). The anonymous Beloved Disciple reclines next to Jesus at the Last Supper (13:23),[27] and Jesus names as "friends" all the disciples present and urges them to "love one another" (15:12–17). Fulfilling his commands (14:15) means loving one another as Jesus has loved them (13:34). In presenting the life and mission of Jesus, the author of the Fourth Gospel focuses on love "as the sole fruit and requirement for life within the community."[28] Love pervades the last discourse of Jesus (13—17): the verb *agapaō* is used twenty-one times, the noun *agapē* six times, the verb *phileō* three times, and the noun *philia* three times.[29] It should be noted that the two verbs, *agapaō* and *phileō*, are used interchangeably throughout the Fourth Gospel.[30]

The bond of love rises with Jesus's victory over death. His first word to the seven disciples, "boys/children [*paidia*]" (21:5), recalls his address at the Last Supper, "little children [*teknia*]" (13:33) and the role of the "*paidarion*" (boy) at the multiplication of the loaves and fishes (6:9),[31] and breathes forth tender affection, familial intimacy, and a sense of "continued dependence" on him.[32] On his side, the Beloved Disciple's eyes of love allow him to see "in the abundant catch of fish a sign" that the stranger "who has hailed them from the lakeshore" is indeed the risen Lord (21:7), just as love has enabled the Beloved Disciple's leap to Easter faith "through discerning the significance of the folded and separately placed face-cloth" (20:6-8).[33] In both cases it is love that enables the disciple to read signs of the resurrection.

Language for the love that bonds Jesus and his disciples is resurrected: in the final Easter chapter *agapaō* appears four times (21:7, 15, 16, 20) and *phileō* five times (21:15, 16, 17). Above all, in the sections dedicated to Peter and Jesus (21:15-19) and the Beloved Disciple and Jesus (21:20-25), a verbal language of love pervades the narrative.

Early in the Fourth Gospel a majestic statement has announced that the human history of Jesus is a story of love: "God so loved the world that he gave his only Son" (3:16). Chapter 21 takes the theme further in the key of resurrected love.

Miraculous Catch, Hauling One Net/One Sheepfold, a Discourse Following a Sign

The extraordinary catch of fish, the only such miraculous event in the Easter stories of the four Gospels, recalls the miracle of the loaves *and fishes* (John 6:1-15). Jesus, when he multiplied fish and loaves to feed the hungry, enlisted Andrew the brother of Simon Peter and other disciples to take care of the distribution (6:8) and the collection of the fragments left over (6:12–13). In the postresurrection situation, Jesus now directs seven of his disciples to catch fish in abundance. He uses some of those fish to supplement the breakfast of *"fish and bread"* (21:9) that he has already prepared.

A warm humanity shines through what Jesus does in directing the disciples to throw out their net on the right side of the boat and catch a remarkable number of fish (21:6). During his earthly ministry, the miracles involve and reveal his humanity rather than compromising it. On the occasion of his most striking miraculous sign, bringing Lazarus back from the dead, Jesus is remembered as weeping (11:35).[34] The human style of Jesus's miracles rises with him in John 21. But here the "raising" of what has happened in the ministry of Jesus goes beyond that style.

The discourse that followed the sign of the loaves and fishes throws up a term to be resurrected in John 21. In that discourse, Jesus speaks symbolically of people being *"hauled* [*helkuō*]*"* to him by the Father (6:44). The verb recurs in a promise associated with the future exaltation of Jesus: "And I, when I am lifted up from the earth, will haul all people to myself" (12:32 au. trans.). During the earthly ministry, the Father is named as the One who "hauls" people to Jesus, or Jesus himself is named as the agent who will do the hauling.

Now John 21 resurrects this "hauling," when it is Peter, not independently but following a command from Jesus, who "hauls" ashore an unbroken net containing 153 large fish and brings some of them to the risen Jesus (21:10–11). Adding some fish to those Jesus has already prepared for breakfast symbolizes the unified, fruitful mission that the risen Lord is launching.[35] Initially the whole group of the disciples in the boat cannot "haul" aboard the great catch; all they could do was "drag" the net toward the shore (21:6, 8). It takes Peter to bring the catch to shore—an action that can suggest Peter's role in "hauling" people to the risen Lord. At the arrest of Jesus, Peter had "hauled out" his sword, struck Malchus, a slave of the high priest, and cut off his right ear (18:10). By translating the verb as "drew," the NRSV respects the English idiom of "drawing one's sword" but hides a subtle link to a very different act that Peter will perform for Jesus in the postresurrection situation. Symbolically, Peter the fisherman is now engaged, not in hauling out his sword and engaging in an armed scuffle, but in personally hauling others to Jesus and, in the service of the risen Lord, gathering "the dispersed children of God" (11:52).[36]

The remarkable way in which the net remains unbroken, despite its enclosing so many large fish, brings to mind the unity of believers that the earthly Jesus promised through the image of uniting all in "one flock" (10:16) and prayed for at the Last Supper (14:12; 15:5; 17:18). The death of the "one shepherd" (10:16–17) brings salvation for all humanity (3:16–17), now gathered under this "one shepherd." The images of fish and sheep differ. At the time of Jesus few people bred fish in artificially constructed ponds, and hardly anyone, either then or later, cared for shoals of fish in the way that human beings may care personally for flocks of lambs and sheep. But the images of the unbroken net and the one flock converge in symbolizing the prayer that "rises with" Jesus: "that they may be one" (17:18) and that his church might hold all together in unity.

In the Fourth Gospel, explanatory discourses follow some *signs*. Such a discourse (5:19–47) comes after the healing at a pool in Jerusalem (5:6–9); the discourse on the bread of life (6:22–59) follows the feeding of the five thousand (6:1–15); another discourse (9:39—10:18) comes after the healing of a man born blind (9:6–7). The risen Jesus resurrects the sequence of a sign explained by a discourse, with the discourse becoming a dialogue with an individual (21:15–19) rather than a discourse to a large group of people (as in the three examples just given). After he "provides fish for his followers, he summons their leader [Peter] to continue to provide for his followers."[37]

The abundant catch of fish does not, however, function like the signs that occur during the life of Jesus. They worked to reveal his identity. His signs rise with him, but now introduce reasons for recognizing the identity of Peter (as agent of unity) and the Beloved Disciple (as trustworthy witness).[38]

A Meal

Early in John 21, the theme of food and eating surfaces when Jesus asks the seven disciples, "You have no fish [or: you have nothing to eat], have you?" (21:5). The question retrieves the story of Jesus's contact with the Samaritans (4:31–38) and, specifically, the moment when the disciples offer him something to eat, and he responds by

"His Life Rose with Him"

saying mysteriously, "I have food to eat that you do not know about." At once he explains, "My food is to do the will of him who sent me and to complete his work" (4:32, 34). His food is the fruit of missionary work, into which he will induct the disciples (4:38; 17:18; 20:21). In the Samaritan setting, the mission is pictured as harvesting grain, from which bread will be made (4:35–38). The image of food will be resurrected in John 21, which highlights the mission of the disciples—in particular, that of Peter and the Beloved Disciple (see below).[39]

In John 21, when the disciples reach land, they see that Jesus has already provided some fish and bread for them (21:9). By personally preparing a cooked meal (here of fish), the risen Jesus does something they have never seen him do during his earthly lifetime. But then with words and gestures he evokes what he has done when multiplying the loaves and fishes for the five thousand (6:8–11). Asking the disciples to bring some of the fish they have just caught and adding them to the fish he has already prepared (21:10), he "takes" and "gives" them bread and fish (21:13). We think of his "taking" and "giving" for a large crowd during his earthly history (6:13) and of his promise that those who come to him "will not hunger" (6:35). "The Son of Man will *give* you food that endures for eternal life" (6:27 au. trans.); he promises that "the bread that I will *give* for the life of the world is my flesh" (6:51).[40] As the host at breakfast, he resurrects what he has done as host during his lifetime and also done on the shores of the same Lake Tiberias (6:4–13).[41] It is only in the Fourth Gospel that this lake is called the Lake of Tiberias (6:1 and 21:1). The setting for John 21 recalls what happened in chapter 6, and also introduces something similar that is about to happen—not least a prominent role for Peter (6:66–71) who will be given a shepherding role (21:15–17).

The postresurrection breakfast signifies the risen "Jesus' *ongoing presence and provision* for his own. He is the life-giving Lord," who feeds the seven disciples and through them the entire church. This "life-giving and life-sustaining work continues" through Peter who "will serve as a shepherd" in tending the flock, and through the Beloved Disciple, who "will offer his distinctive witness, a testimony that underwrites the Gospel itself."[42]

The "charcoal fire" around which the disciples take their breakfast (21:9) retrieves a memory of the charcoal fire in the high priest's courtyard where Peter has dreadfully failed Jesus by denying that he even knows him (18:18, 25). Despite an explicit recall of the Last Supper that comes in John 21:20,[43] what may pass unnoticed is the way in which the lakeside breakfast resurrects the memory of earlier meals. Those earlier meals have proved occasions of deadly threats against Jesus (12:1–11), disputes about "wasting" precious nard to anoint the feet of Jesus (12:4–8), the betrayal of Jesus by one of his disciples (13:21–30), and a "misunderstanding" when the wine runs out at a marriage feast (2:3–4). The miraculous feeding of the five thousand is also significant here. It leads to a discourse on the bread of life, which ends with many disciples leaving Jesus and the first warning about Judas's treacherous betrayal (John 6:22–71). That meal throws up a double crisis.

In a loving, healing way, the Easter breakfast at dawn resurrects meals and associated crises that have shaped the history of Jesus. The breakfast of *bread* and fish promises the saving activity of the risen Jesus that will continue through eucharistic meals. From the second century, Christians will take up the image of *ichthus* (fish) as a title and image for Christ, with "Jesus Christ, Son of God, Savior" in Greek (*Iēsous Christos Theou Huios Sōtēr*) giving rise to the acrostic *Ichthus* symbolizing the presence of their glorious Lord. The fish symbolism represents Christ and the Eucharist.[44]

Peter and the Beloved Disciple

The last phase of Jesus's history links him with a special pair, Peter and the Beloved Disciple—at the Last Supper (13:21–30). Commentators identify the Beloved Disciple with "another disciple," who brings Peter into the courtyard of the high priest, where Peter miserably denies his relationship with Jesus (18:15–18, 25–27). Peter is absent at the crucifixion, whereas the Beloved Disciple is present and declared a son of Jesus's own mother (19:25–27). Peter and the Beloved Disciple are linked by a visit to the empty tomb, but Peter does not share the faith in Jesus's resurrection that the arrangement of the grave clothes brings to the Beloved Disciple (20:2–10). In John 21:7, the "privileged knowledge" of the Beloved Disciple, who identifies the stranger on the beach ("It is the Lord"), is passed on: "Peter is shown to be dependent on the insight and word of the Beloved Disciple for his recognition of the risen Jesus."[45] The Beloved Disciple outran Peter in the race to the empty tomb but allowed Peter to enter first into the empty tomb (20:4–6). As Lincoln observes, Peter is now "determined to be the first to get to shore" and so be the first to meet Jesus.[46] Risen from the dead, Jesus resurrects his relationships with both Peter and the Beloved Disciple. The earlier history of those key relationships rises with Jesus.

At their very first meeting, before changing his name to "Peter," Jesus has addressed him as "Simon son of John" (1:42).[47] He picks up and repeats three times the same address at their postresurrection encounter: "Simon son of John, do you love me?" (21:15–17). The risen Jesus brings back to new life his relationship with Peter. The recent terrible failure of Peter is wiped away through his threefold profession of love for Jesus. The risen Jesus now guides Peter to a self-knowledge and love that will allow him to live up to the name Jesus gave him at their first meeting (*Cēphas*) and truly prove a "rock."

In the imagery of the Good Shepherd and his sheep, the Good Shepherd calls his sheep by their names (10:1–8). Called by his original name, "Simon son of John" is now commissioned to feed the Lord's lambs and sheep.[48] It is not that Peter replaces "Jesus as Shepherd." Rather, "Jesus entrusts to him for safekeeping and nurturing the flock," which remains the flock of the Good Shepherd.[49]

The great catch of fish with which John 21 opens might have shaped the missionary charge as "cast my net, catch my fish." Yet in Johannine imagery it is not fishing but shepherding the flock that involves danger and even death (10:11–15, 17–18). Peter the fisherman becomes Peter the shepherd. His commission calls him to utter self-sacrifice in the service of the flock. No longer will it be a matter of his deciding whether or where to go or stay (6:67–68). He will be carried where he does not wish to go (21:18–19)—with Jesus making a fairly clear reference to the way Peter will share his Master's destiny by also being crucified.[50]

Like Philip at the beginning of the Fourth Gospel (1:43), Peter at the end hears from the risen Christ the simple but radical call to faithful discipleship: "follow me" (21:19, 22). Shortly before his passion and death, Jesus says, "Whoever serves me must follow me, and where I am, there will my servant be also" (12:26). At the Last Supper, Peter hears Jesus speaking of his impending death and telling Peter, "Where I am going, you cannot follow me now; but you will follow afterward" (13:36). Peter is now "bidden to do what previously had been impossible for him"—follow Jesus in a violent death.[51] The history of Jesus rises with him in the sense that he now definitively calls Peter to follow him and do so on the road to martyrdom.

The risen Jesus renews his relationship with Peter, reinstates him in his leadership role, and points to a future where he will heroically *glorify* God. The Fourth Gospel has associated the glorification of God with the coming death of Jesus (12:28; 13:31-32; 17:1, 5). As William Loader remarks when commenting on John 15:8, "To glorify God is also the task of the disciples as they fulfil the commission given them." He recalls John 17:19 and notes that "already during his earthly ministry Jesus was glorified by the disciples' response."[52] The risen Jesus resurrects this language by inviting Peter to glorify God through a martyr's death on a cross.

The closing chapter of John's Gospel ends by highlighting the distinctive relationship of *the Beloved Disciple* to Jesus (21:20-25). He witnesses the start of Jesus's ministry (1:35-40) and is close to Jesus at the Last Supper and the crucifixion (13:23; 19:25-27). He testifies to the piercing of Jesus's side on the cross (19:34-37).[53] Unlike Peter, he has never denied his Lord and needs no rehabilitation. After the resurrection he will continue, through the completed Fourth Gospel, his unique witness to the light and life communicated by the Son of God. The Gospel as a whole is attributed to the testimony of the Beloved Disciple, "the disciple who is witnessing to these things and has written them." The community of believers ("we know that his witness is true") confirms the truth of this ideal witness (21:24), just as the community confirms the truth of the incarnation at the start of the Fourth Gospel ("we have seen his [the Father's only Son's] glory" (1:14; see also the "we" of John 1:16).

The cryptic remark of Jesus about the Beloved Disciple "remaining until I come" (21:22-23) concerns the role the Beloved Disciple played. Some or many disciples have *misunderstood* the remark and supposed that the Beloved Disciple "would remain alive until Jesus's eschatological return."[54] John 21:23-25, by correcting this misunderstanding, resurrects something that happens throughout the Fourth Gospel's story of Jesus: individuals and groups of people misunderstand Jesus (e.g., 3:4; 6:60-65).

Like Peter, by the time the Fourth Gospel was finally composed, the Beloved Disciple has already died but not as a martyr. Yet the contribution of the Beloved Disciple as witness and disciple is "not diminished either by the fact or the manner of his death."[55] Despite his death, the Beloved Disciple does "remain" (21:24) and "makes an irreplaceable contribution to the entire believing community" through his witness to the saving events and "the written record of that testimony that he has 'authored' in the shape of the gospel." "Authored" does not mean that the Beloved Disciple "physically wrote all that is contained in the text." Rather "it means that he instigated its composition as a record of his unique witness to the life-giving revelation disclosed in Jesus."[56]

Here at the end the Fourth Gospel retrieves two themes with which it opened its account of the history of Jesus: *witness* (the verb *martureō* and the noun *marturia*) and *truth* (the noun *alētheia* and the adjective *alēthēs*). The witness of John the Baptist (1:7, 8, 15, 19–36) ushers in the story of Jesus's historical ministry. At the Last Supper, Jesus tells the disciples that they are qualified for the task of witnessing to him, since they have been with him from the beginning (15:27). The Gospel ends by resurrecting the theme of witnessing to Jesus and does so in his relationship with the ideal witness, the Beloved Disciple (21:20–24). Jesus is risen from the dead and so too has human witness to him.

The theme of *truth* (26 times) and *true* (12 times) pervades the Fourth Gospel. Identified as "full of grace and truth" (1:14), Jesus promises that "the truth will set you free" (8:32), calls himself "the truth" (14:6), and insists that "my witness is true" (8:14). The closing words of the Gospel qualify the witness of the Beloved Disciple as "true" (21:24). True witness, which has testified to the earthly Jesus, continues with his resurrection from the dead. Let us summarize the case for interpreting John 21 as the history of Jesus rising with him.

Word, Light, and Life

The attributes of word, light, and life, which permeate the Fourth Gospel's portrayal of the historical Jesus, are resurrected in the final, Easter chapter. The word (*logos*) rises again when the risen Jesus speaks (*legei*) and says just over one hundred words (*logoi*). He uses once (21:18) a solemn expression that has turned up twenty-four times in the Gospel's portrayal of the earthly Jesus: "Amen, amen, I say unto you." The Word has spoken with authority and truth during his human lifetime and does so once again when risen from the dead.

The key theme of "light (*phōs*)," found twenty-two times in the Fourth Gospel's account of Jesus's history, returns in the final chapter. The risen Jesus shows himself "just after daybreak" (21:4). Light is streaming into the sky when Jesus appears on the shore of the lake. Resurrected from the dead, he proves himself now and forever the light of the world. His history, which has been a history of light shining in the world, has risen with him.

So too has his *life*-giving attribute. At a wedding feast in Cana Jesus supplies a generous amount of wine for the marriage guests; later, near Lake Tiberias, he provides abundant life by feeding five thousand with five loaves and two fish. An enormous catch of fish, not to mention the preparations for breakfast (21:1–14), shows how the history of the One, who is "the bread of life" (6:22–59) and even "life" itself (14:6), is risen with him.

The Disciples, Their Mission, and Christ's Self-Manifestation

In their fruitless fishing exhibition, the seven disciples (symbolizing all Jesus's followers) exemplify the empty results of any mission apart from him (15:4–5). By "manifesting" himself, the risen Jesus now reveals the something "greater" that he has promised to Nathanael (1:50): the divine glory disclosed in the resurrection. The Nathanael connection recalls the history of Jesus's initial relationship with his disciples, which now returns in an enhanced form.

Questions, Irony, and Love

In John 21, the history of Jesus also rises through three characteristics that have shaped his earthly life: questions, irony, and, very strikingly, love. Rising to new life, Jesus is reinstated as the divine Questioner—above all, through the threefold question he puts to Peter. Irony has qualified the story of Jesus as told in the Fourth Gospel. Irony returns in the question he puts to the seven disciples: "Boys/children, you have no fish, have you?" (21:5). The love that has bonded the earthly Jesus with his disciples rises with renewed intensity in the Easter chapter. The language of love pervades the passages dedicated to the relationship between Jesus and two of his followers, Peter and the Beloved Disciple.

"His Life Rose with Him"

The Meal, Peter, and the Beloved Disciple

The story of Jesus's earthly existence is also evoked by further themes in John 21: the miraculous catch, the question about food (= 21:5 recalling 4:31–38), Peter's "hauling" ashore the unbroken net, Jesus's language about his sheepfold, and a discourse that follows a sign (the catch of fish). But we must also include *the meal* of fish and bread and what it recalls about the feeding of the five thousand, the promise of the Eucharist, and Peter's denial that has taken place at another "charcoal fire." The breakfast on the shore of Lake Tiberias also brings back various meals that have occasioned shadows and even crises in the story of Jesus's ministry.

We also saw how Jesus's relationship with *Peter* is resurrected and transformed in the Easter narrative of the Fourth Gospel. Here the violent death, which Jesus predicts for Peter, reminds us that Jesus's own history is made up not only of what he does and says but also of what he *suffers*. The suffering history of Jesus rises in the coming crucifixion of the apostle, who will also "glorify" God by his martyrdom.

As for *the Beloved Disciple*, the risen Jesus values him as the ideal witness, who through his Gospel continues his testimony to the revelation and salvation brought by the Son of God. A full account should also factor in the themes of misunderstanding and true witness, which characterize the Fourth Gospel's narrative of Jesus's earthly story.

Conclusion

Scott Holland's claim that "when Jesus rose, his life rose with him" finds ample warrant in the closing Easter chapter of John's Gospel. In *Studi sul vangelo di Giovanni*, Marcheselli stresses the ecclesial message of John 21.[57] But we can *also* (or even better) read that chapter christologically. The allusions, images, and terms with which John 21 persistently evokes and rereads earlier chapters allow us to say that the "life of Jesus rose with him."

II
ACTS OF THE APOSTLES

13

BURIED BY HIS ENEMIES?

(Acts 13:28-31)

According to the Acts of the Apostles, Paul made a major address in a synagogue in Pisidian Antioch (13:16b-41). He spoke of "the residents of Jerusalem and their leaders" failing to recognize Jesus and

> condemning him. Even though they found no cause for a sentence of death, they asked Pilate to have him killed. When they had carried out everything that was written about him, they took him down from the tree and laid him in a tomb. But God raised him from the dead, and for many days he appeared to those who came up with him from Galilee to Jerusalem, and they are now his witnesses to the people. (Acts 13:27-31)

When we compare this account with what Luke had already written at the end of his Gospel and at the start of Acts, it differs over the disposal of Jesus's body. According to Luke 23:50-56, Joseph of Arimathea asked Pilate for permission to take the dead Jesus down from the cross, before wrapping him in a shroud, and burying him in a new tomb in which no one had yet been buried. Mark 15:42-47 and Matthew 27:57-61 tell more or less the same story of Jesus's burial, while John adds that Joseph was, generously and courageously, helped by Nicodemus (19:38-42).

ACTS OF THE APOSTLES

Fitzmyer, Holladay, and Bock

In Acts 13, as we have just seen, "the residents of Jerusalem and their leaders" not only prevailed on Pilate to crucify Jesus but also were apparently those who took Jesus down from the cross and buried him in a tomb. Joseph Fitzmyer comments briefly that those in the Gospels "to whom the crucifixion [of Jesus] is ascribed are not the same as those who take him down from the cross [Joseph and Nicodemus]."[1] Fitzmyer notices, but does not attempt to resolve, the difference between two seemingly incompatible accounts of those who took Jesus down from the cross and buried him.

In a more recent commentary on Acts, Carl Holladay also notes the difference: the Jewish leaders are "credited with removing Jesus from the cross and burying him in a tomb." This is not, however, "as likely as the Gospel tradition that Jesus was buried by one of his followers."[2] However, Holladay does not explain why the gospel tradition is more "likely" nor how the difference might have arisen.

Darrell Bock appeals to something that occurs in New Testament Greek, as it does in modern English and other languages—what he calls "generic" usage. This describes the third-person plural implicit in the Greek original but not expressed, as it is by English, in "they found," "they asked," "they carried out," "they took down," and "they laid." Bock writes, "The reference to 'they' is generic, an allusion to Joseph of Arimathea and probably to Pilate's permission that allowed Jesus to be buried and the opposition that caused his death. This 'they,' then, includes those who rejected Jesus (Jewish leaders and Pilate) and those who respected Jesus (Joseph of Arimathea)."[3] Bock defuses in this plausible way a seeming contradiction between what Luke wrote in his Gospel and what he wrote in the Acts of the Apostles.

In Acts, Luke's plural, being a generalizing plural, focuses more on the actions rather than on clearly specifying the agents. As regards the actions, there is no difference between Luke's Gospel and Acts. In both cases, Jesus was taken down and buried in a tomb. But, besides explaining the "they," we need to attend also to the *literary* nature of the passage in which such a "generic" or generalizing usage of verbs occurs.

Buried by His Enemies?

Pervo, Keener, and Bovon

Richard Pervo calls Acts 13:27–31 a summary, that is not only "concise" but also "crabbed." In fact, "so short is this summary that a reader might conclude that Jesus was buried by his enemies!"[4] But it is not merely any "reader" but, as Craig Keener remarks, "some scholars" who can draw this wrong conclusion.[5]

Keener states, "Some scholars think that the text claims that Jesus's elite Jerusalemite accusers buried Jesus." He simply comments, "They probably read too much into a concise summary."[6] But he does not name any of these scholars nor explain why they could be reading too much into the passage.

One notable scholar, François Bovon, not only reached the conclusion rejected by Keener but also gave it a high degree of historical reliability: "Jews hostile to Jesus and not a friendly Joseph of Arimathea buried the crucified one. The tradition must be older and historically more reliable than the data of the Gospels."[7]

Bovon was aware that his firm judgment about "the tradition" in Acts involved holding that, for apologetic purposes, the first Christians had created the story of Joseph of Arimathea burying Jesus: "if the first Christians wanted to use the empty tomb as an argument, it obviously had to be able to be identified and located."[8] Presumably, if Jesus had been buried by his enemies and not by Joseph, with some or even many female disciples as witnesses to Joseph's intervention (e.g. Mark 15:47; Luke 23:55–56), it would have been difficult, if not impossible, for the followers of Jesus to identify and locate the tomb that briefly contained the corpse of Jesus. Hence, if they were going to appeal to an open and empty tomb as an argument for resurrection of Jesus, as, for instance, Matthew (28:1–15) and, seemingly, Luke (Acts 2:24–32) did,[9] they would have to create the story of a friendly Joseph of Arimathea burying the dead Jesus. Much then is at stake for those who interpret Acts 13:28–31.

Settling the literary nature of this passage in Acts is crucial. We need to decide between a Lukan "summary" (Pervo and Keener) and an inherited "tradition" (Bovon) used by Luke. Hans Conzelmann showed himself firmly on the side of a "summary." Rejecting "the assumption of a special tradition, according to which the Jews buried Jesus," he insisted that "the form here is kerygmatic, not narrative. This is simply a concise summary of the events."[10] Before exploring further the nature of such a summary, let us recall two classical solutions to the apparent conflict between what Luke wrote in his Gospel and in Acts.

Two Classical Solutions

(1) The apparent conflict between the burial of Jesus by Joseph of Arimathea (Luke's Gospel) and by enemies (Acts) long ago prompted a response from John Calvin. Combining the burial story with the setting of a guard (found only in Matt 27:62–66) and obviously accepting the historicity of both, Calvin wrote, "He [Jesus] was buried by Pilate's permission, but, on the other hand, guards were placed at the sepulcher by the decision of the priests. Therefore, even if Joseph and Nicodemus committed Christ to the sepulcher, it is [only] incorrect, but yet not absurd, to attribute that [the burial] to the Jews."[11] Calvin understood "the residents of Jerusalem and their leaders"—namely, "the chief priests" (to whom Matthew adds "the Pharisees," 27:62)—to be involved in the burial of Jesus inasmuch as they asked Pilate's permission to post a guard at the tomb.

To explain partly the "incorrect but not absurd" conflict between what Luke wrote in his Gospel and what he wrote in Acts, Calvin used a story from Matthew and threw in a detail found only in John (Nicodemus's role in the burial of Jesus). The precise issue, however, concerns what Luke himself wrote in different sections of his own "two-volume" account of Christian origins. Furthermore, whatever their judgment about the presence of Nicodemus at the burial, many scholars now doubt the historicity of the guard story, a key element in Calvin's solution.[12]

Calvin might have argued that Joseph of Arimathea, friendly and all as he showed himself to the cause of Jesus, was a member of the Sanhedrin and attested in all four Gospels as responsible for securing the burial of Jesus. In that sense one could attribute the burial "to the Jews."[13]

(2) It was in terms of identical authorship that Barrett confronted the difference between Luke 23:50–56 and Acts 13:28–31: "Luke himself knew that they were friendly hands that took down the body of Jesus

from the cross. It is difficult to believe that the man who wrote this in the gospel seriously wished to attribute to Paul the view that it was Jesus' Jewish opponents who buried him."[14] As far as I know, Barrett is the only commentator to make this point, which is surely a significant observation about the author of the Third Gospel and Acts. Far from being a careless compiler, Luke showed himself from the outset a careful and self-conscious writer (1:1–4), not someone likely to contradict himself about an event as significant as the burial of the crucified Jesus.

Barrett himself believed that Ernst Haenchen, when commenting on the passage in Acts, "says all that is necessary."[15] Haenchen wrote, "In reality Luke has only shortened the account as much as possible."[16] We saw above how Conzelmann also firmly endorsed the view that Acts 13:28–31 represents a concise summary.

Jacob Jervell

The comments of Jacob Jervell allow us to refine further the interpretation of Acts 13:28–31. Noting how ascribing the deposition from the cross and burial of Jesus to Jewish opponents does not agree with what Luke wrote in his Gospel, Jervell observes, "Wir haben hier aber eine verkürzte Berichterstattung. Die Beerdigung ist der Hintergrund, das Kontrastschema für die rettende Tat Gottes."[17]

This calls for expansion. We find a similar, if less elaborate, *Kontrastschema* in Peter's address on the day of Pentecost: "This man [Jesus of Nazareth], handed over to you according to the definite plan and foreknowledge of God, you crucified and killed by the hands of those outside the law. But God raised him up, having freed him from death" (Acts 2:23–24). The scheme is basically bipartite: an evil human action ("you crucified" Jesus), contrasted with a life-giving divine action and reversal ("God raised him up"). Jews (in particular, those "who live in Jerusalem," 2:14) and Gentiles ("those outside the law") committed the evil deed. Reference to the resurrection is not completed by introducing appearances of the risen Christ. Subsequently Peter speaks implicitly of the empty tomb of Jesus and explicitly of the whole apostolic group as witnesses to the resurrection (2:25–32).

The same bipartite scheme of God reversing a human sentence is repeated in a second sermon of Peter: "You handed over and rejected [Jesus] in the presence of Pilate, though he had decided to release him.

But you rejected the Holy and Righteous One and asked to have a murderer given to you, and you killed the Author of life, whom God raised from the dead. To this we are witnesses" (Acts 3:13-15). Once again, the killing of Jesus is followed and set over against God's raising him from the dead. The identity of "those outside the law" is now specified by mentioning Pilate. Here Peter adds at once, "to this we are witnesses."

In Acts 13, however, Luke offers his fullest version of the *Kontrastschema*: Jewish and Gentile responsibility for the sentence of death passed on Jesus; his crucifixion; his deposition from the cross and burial; the resurrection; the postresurrection appearances; and the apostolic witness to the resurrection of Jesus. The scheme now essentially includes four parts: (a) the death of Jesus, (b) the reality of which is emphasized through his burial in a tomb, (c) the resurrection, (d) revealed by the appearances (to be followed by the witness of apostolic proclamation). This fourfold scheme corresponds to the fourfold shape of the Pauline testimony in 1 Corinthians 15:3-5: Christ died (a death confirmed by burial), has been raised from the dead, with a resurrection confirmed by the Easter appearances (and followed by the witnesses proclaiming all this [1 Cor 15:11]).

Conclusions

In the interests of fashioning a tight, four-part scheme in Acts 13, Luke has allowed a certain ambiguity to creep in about the identity of "they," the agents responsible for the deposition of Jesus from the cross and his burial. Bock helpfully notes how a generalizing "they" functions. It focusses on the *activity*, the deposition from the cross and the burial, rather than on the identity of the *agents*. In any case, Calvin was right in remarking that what we read is Acts 13 is not totally false. After all, John's Gospel recalls that "the Jews" were concerned that the body of Jesus (and those crucified with him) should be taken down before sunset (19:31). In any case, it was two members of the Jewish Sanhedrin (Joseph of Arimathea and Nicodemus) who ensured that the body of Jesus was removed and buried.

When interpreting Acts 13:27-31, we are better advised to join Conzelmann, Haenchen, Jervell—not to mention Barrett, Keener, and Pervo—in recognizing here a Lukan *summary* rather than follow Bovon in detecting an old *tradition* (of Jesus's burial by enemies), which

Buried by His Enemies?

would tell against the historicity of what Luke's Gospel attests, a burial by the friendly Joseph of Arimathea. In particular, Jervell's notion of a summary that takes the form of a *Kontrastschema* can be convincingly filled out by recalling earlier, simpler versions of such a scheme already deployed in the Acts of the Apostles.

III
PAUL'S LETTERS

14

THE LANGUAGE OF RECONCILIATION

(Rom 5:8-11; 2 Cor 5:18-21)

The extraordinary use of ordinary words often characterizes religious discourse and writing—a situation that is clearly exhibited in the letters of St. Paul.[1] The apostle tries, sometimes subtly and sometimes with alarming casualness, to express the message of the gospel in language that, while adequate for ordinary human affairs, remains less than fully capable of handling the dealings of God with ordinary human beings. As a result, he can force expressions that have their grounding in the world of created realities to do substitute service for the unsayable. An inevitable consequence of this situation is that, if we wish to understand Paul rightly, we need to introduce important qualifications into the rules that govern the use of these expressions—to the point that we continually hang precariously on the edge of paradox, if not outright contradiction.

The concept of reconciliation (*katallagē*), with the verb "to reconcile" (*katallassō*), with God as the subject (something previously unattested), occurs in a prominent way in Romans 5:8–11 and 2 Corinthians 5:18–21. In using this language, Paul did not follow the Old Testament Scriptures, but drew on his Greco-Roman background and especially (but not exclusively) on military-diplomatic usage. There *reconciliation*, used in a social, secular sense, denoted a change from a state of alienation and hostility between individuals and groups to a relationship of peace and friendship.[2]

Before investigating how Paul employs the concept of reconciliation and the limitations imposed on our translating and adopting his language, however, we should first examine the use of the concept on the home ground of ordinary discourse. Only then will we able to see why the apostle might have thought the term an appropriate one for his purposes, and how far we can accept the consequences of his usage without landing ourselves in absurdities. If it is proper to urge theology (and biblical studies) to pay attention to the religious uses of language, then theology, no less than philosophy, is bound by Ludwig Wittgenstein's charge "to battle against the bewitchment of our intelligence by our language."[3]

There are three main uses of the words *reconcile* and *reconciliation* that could be relevant to our purposes here, and we shall examine each of them briefly. They have to do, respectively, with (1) the acceptance of situations or facts; (2) the removal of contradictions or incompatibilities; and (3) the removal of enmity or conflict.

Three Usages of *Reconcile*

1. An accident victim may become reconciled to the fact that he will never walk again, or a diabetic may become reconciled to the necessity of taking daily insulin injections. It must be noticed here that what is involved is not just the acceptance of situations, but of limitations. People do not become reconciled to winning a million dollars in the lottery. The element of struggle needs to be present. A medical student does not become reconciled to discontinuing her studies if she has not previously struggled against adverse circumstances and failed to overcome them. At the same time, there is also an irreducibly positive aura about the use of the term in these circumstances. Being reconciled to the facts is a very different thing from giving up.
2. It may be the task of an insurance investigator to reconcile the descriptions of an accident given by several witnesses. A doctor can be asked to reconcile his position on the dangers of cigarette smoking with his own heavy smoking.

The Language of Reconciliation

An accountant may reconcile the statement produced by a bank with the different figures shown in some company's books. In all these cases there is a perceived incompatibility that must be resolved, some kind of conflict that should be removed or at least dealt with, but *there need not be any personal conflict* in such situations. In fact, there can be amicable personal relationships even where differences exist that cannot be reconciled. Two politicians may be close personal friends, in spite of the fact that they hold irreconcilable positions on a number of issues.

3. A husband and wife can be reconciled after a separation that might have ended in divorce. This is St. Paul's secular sense of *katallassō* in 1 Corinthians: "let her [the wife]… be reconciled to her husband" (7:11). Here the verb in the passive form ("let her be reconciled [*katallagētō*]") is "most probably deponent and has an active (reflexive) meaning: 'let her reconcile herself to her husband.'"[4] Two families might be reconciled after many years of dispute and even enmity. A wayward or headstrong son can be reconciled with his father after a long period of mutual animosity and rejection. The differences that are reconciled here are often related to type two, except that there exists *personal* involvement on a deep level. Reconciliation in these cases can take place, if (a) one party in the dispute admits error and acknowledges the rightness of the other's position. A son may give up his dissolute lifestyle and admit that his father's disapproval was justified. As is the case between God and human beings, only one party in the unreconciled situation may be at fault (the son) and need to be reconciled. Reconciliation can also take place, however, provided (b) both parties compromise or at least come to recognize a transcendent value that can unite them, in spite of continuing to hold tenaciously to deeply felt incompatible positions. This occurs when the parties agree not to allow differences to continue to permeate and poison their whole relationship.

It is not possible to be reconciled in this third sense to a stranger, or to some person with whom I am related only superficially. A man is not reconciled with someone whom he has angered by colliding with him on a crowded sidewalk. Furthermore, it would be odd to talk of the reconciliation of corporations or states (although not of families), since the dimension of personal involvement is often lacking in such cases. It would be proper to speak of the reconciliation of the *positions* taken by two nations (for instance, at peace talks), but this is reconciliation in sense (2) above. In cases where such talk of reconciliation seems less odd, the nations in question tend to take on the aspects of families and become personified, as is sometimes the case in accounts of the Palestinian-Israeli conflict.

A clear *presupposition* behind this third sense of reconciliation is that there exists some sort of significant personal relationship between the parties involved, and that there be some kind of conflict or dissonance to be resolved. It is through this latter feature that sense (3) of reconciliation enjoys its similarities to the previous two senses. It is also *presupposed* that some sort of interaction take place between the agents involved; it is not possible that one party to the dispute remains simply passive. A one-sided argument, in which one of the parties refuses to engage the other and remains indifferent to him or her both in dispute and resolution, does not display an element of real conflict. Any resolution that is reached here, therefore, can be called reconciliation only in a Pickwickian sense.

What is *not presupposed* by this third sense of reconciliation is that the parties to be reconciled necessarily enjoyed a relationship of close friendship *prior* to their state of conflict, although this *may* be so. In the examples given above, the husband and wife were, presumably, joined in loving intimacy before their separation took place. The estranged families once stood on good terms with each other. The father and his wayward son loved one another prior to the onset of mutual rejection and animosity. What precedes the state of conflict, however, may be simply no personal relationship at all. Two officers who were previously unknown to each other could join the same army unit and take an instant dislike to one another. Their deep personal animosity might so disrupt the life of the unit that a superior officer could be forced to intervene in the hope of settling their differences and so reconciling these warring parties.

Reconciliation, then, need not always imply the following three stages: (i) the parties were previously on terms of intimacy and friendship; (ii) a serious breach led to their becoming more or less totally estranged; and (iii) the good relationship was restored by the resolution of the conflict. Even where stage (i) is absent, we can still speak of reconciliation taking place. Gordon Kaufman ignores this possibility when he simply assumes that these three stages are always involved: "Reconciliation is the bringing together of parties who had become alienated and reuniting them; relations which had become strained and distorted are brought back to harmony and peace and fulfilment of friendship and love."[5] One could multiply almost indefinitely examples of this unwarranted assumption on the part of theologians and scripture scholars.

Reconciliation in Romans and 2 Corinthians

Let us turn now to examine Paul's use of the language of reconciliation. In Romans 5:8–11 we read,

> God proves his love for us in what while we still were sinners Christ died for us. Much more surely then, now that we have been justified by his blood, will we be saved through him from the wrath of God. For if while we were enemies, we *were reconciled* to God through the death of his Son, much more surely, *having been reconciled*, will we be saved by his life. But more than that, we even boast in God through our Lord Jesus Christ, through whom we have now received *reconciliation*.

Later in Romans, in the context of a warning to Gentile Christians in Rome, Paul said, "If their [my own people's] rejection is *the reconciliation of the world*, what will their acceptance be but life from the dead!" (Rom 11:15).

Second Corinthians 5:18–21 runs as follows:

> All this is from God, who *reconciled* us to himself through Christ, and has given us the ministry of *reconciliation*; that is, in Christ God *was reconciling* the world to himself, not counting their trespasses against them and entrusting the message of *reconciliation* to us. So we are ambassadors for

Christ, since God is making his appeal through us; we entreat you on behalf of Christ, *be reconciled* to God. For our sake he made him to be sin who knew no sin, so that in him we might become the righteousness of God.

Both 2 Corinthians 5 and Romans 5 clearly presuppose an antecedently existing hostility between God and human beings, in which human beings are the enemy of God. Clearly, however, the relationship is not symmetrical. While Paul seems to conceive the situation as that of human beings seeing God as enemy, God does not see human beings in that way.[6] Otherwise, he would not have taken the initiative to remedy the relationship, despite being the offended party in the conflict. As James D. G. Dunn puts it, "The image is not of God as an angry opponent having to be cajoled or entreated, but of God, the injured partner, actively seeking reconciliation."[7] Margaret Thrall concurs: "The reconciliation rested wholly on the divine initiative."[8]

What these two passages do *not presuppose* is that human beings *fell* from a situation of friendship with God into one of conflict and enmity, as happens when the *BDAG* defined *katallagē* as reconciliation with God: "*re-establishment of an interrupted or broken relationship.*"[9] Joseph A. Fitzmyer likewise read this sense into Paul's words by speaking of "the *return* of man to God's favor and intimacy after a period of estrangement and rebellion through sin and transgression."[10] Thrall does the same: "The basic idea of reconciliation is the *restoration* of friendly relationships after a period of enmity or estrangement."[11] Two stages account for the apostle's language: (i) a situation of hostility, followed by (ii) a resolution of the conflict and a state of friendship. This reconciliation means bringing hostility to an end or uniting those who were formerly separated, but not necessarily causing to be friendly *again* or bringing *back* into harmony. In other words, this Pauline language does not necessarily suppose an *original* state of harmony that was ruptured and then restored.

We should not ignore some difficult or at least odd aspects in Paul's passage on reconciliation in Romans. First, he pictures our reconciliation with God (i) as having already been accomplished, and (ii) as effected by a "third party." However, if (i) our reconciliation with God has already been brought about by God alone, it might seem that we do not need to do anything. Further, (ii) one must ask how Christ has accomplished the reconciliation with God. One can readily understand how reconciliation between alienated persons can be brought about

The Language of Reconciliation

through the "good offices" of a third party, as in ancient secular examples of the reconciling function of judges and envoys.[12] But it seems clear that the status of this third party must be acknowledged by both sides. If, however, our reconciliation has already been effected, before we were able to acknowledge and accept the good offices of Christ, in what sense was he representing our interests in the matter? One might argue that since we are the guilty party in the conflict, we have no interests to represent. But even so, it would still seem necessary that we be in some way actively involved in the process of reconciliation. If we continue to be passive while our reconciliation with God is accomplished, indeed if we remain ignorant of the event until after Christ's intervention, then *reconciliation* is being used in a logically extended sense. Even if Christ enjoys an ontological status as "the universal human being" and does not need to be commissioned by humankind as its representative, it would still seem necessary that individual human beings acknowledge Christ's status if they are to be reconciled with God. The "reconciliation," spoken of here by Paul as having already been accomplished, is then reconciliation in potentiality only.

Some of these problems return and seem compounded in 2 Corinthians 5:18–21. Once again (i) reconciliation is presented as a fait accompli; it has happened before we knew or did anything about it. In Thrall's words, "it is an act of God accomplished whilst humanity was still hostile towards him."[13] The conflict has already been resolved even though we had no possibility of interacting. It is all very well for Jan Lambrecht to insist on "God's reconciliation of humankind to himself. In the New Testament humans do not reconcile God to themselves."[14] Nevertheless, there is a radical mutuality in the language of reconciliation (in both Greek and English) that needs to be respected. At least in sense (3), both sides need to be actively involved, albeit in different degrees and ways, for reconciliation to take place.

(ii) Even less than in the passage from Romans 5 (where Paul fills out the "through Christ" in terms of his death and life), in 2 Corinthians 5 the apostle does not present Christ as a distinct agent. It is God the Father who emerges as the sole active protagonist who (in and through Christ) has accomplished our reconciliation.[15] Not only are we human beings excluded from participation but even vicarious participation through Christ seems excluded. It is the Father, not Christ, who is active.

Add too (iii) the plea that Corinthian Christians "be reconciled with God." This seems incompatible with what has just been said about

God having already forgiven human sin and reconciled the world to himself. But perhaps Paul intends to say here that, since God has already forgiven and saved human beings, the Corinthians are being asked to be reconciled to this fact and to order their lives accordingly. At least partially, this seems like a case of (1) above: God has saved the Corinthians, and they are being asked to accept this situation and what it involves. If God's antecedent reconciling activity is to "come to full fruition," there needs to be a "positive human response."[16]

J. Paul Sampley recognizes the puzzle posed by Paul's command "be reconciled with God": "Uncharacteristically, 2 Corinthians 5:20 is the only place in the Pauline corpus where the reconciling is to be done by people. In the other instances, Paul either uses the passive, such as 'we were reconciled' (Rom 5:10), where God is understood actor, or directly states that God is the reconciling one (2 Cor 5:16)."[17] What Sampley does not clearly acknowledge is the problem created by regularly and one-sidedly limiting the activity of reconciliation to God or to God acting through Christ.[18]

By doing so, Paul leaves behind sense (3) above, the frequent Greek (and for that matter English) usage of the verb *reconcile*, which we see him using in the case of a husband and wife who were at odds with each other: "Let her...be reconciled to her husband" (1 Cor 7:11). In such a case, reconciliation takes place by both parties interacting at the same time with a view to the desired reconciliation. Both parties need to be consciously and willingly involved in the very process of restoring the relationship between them. This is not the case when the activity of reconciliation is attributed to God alone, as in 2 Corinthians 5:19. Thrall understates the problem: "God and man are not seen by Paul as equal partners in the process [of reconciliation]."[19] The apostle speaks of a unilateral action of God, and not merely of an event in which human beings were unequal partners.

The Reconciliation of the World

Paul's remarks about "the reconciliation of the world" (Rom 11:15; 2 Cor 5:19) also invite comment. He may think of the impact of the Christ event on the entire cosmos. Fitzmyer, for one, held that Romans 11:15 points not merely to human reconciliation with God but also to a "cosmic extension of that effect to the whole universe."[20] Yet in both passages, Paul might have in mind *kosmos* in the sense of the whole of humanity. Or he might intend humanity in its entirety in 2 Corinthians 5:19—"the human world," as Thrall puts it[21]—but intend only the Gentiles in Romans 11:15.[22] In neither case is it clear that reconciliation extends beyond humanity to the entire created world.

A letter that may not have been written directly by Paul is, however, clear about the cosmic dimension of reconciliation: "In him [Christ] all his fullness [the fullness of God?] was pleased to dwell, and through him to *reconcile* to himself all things, whether on earth or in the heavens, making peace by the blood of his cross" (Col 1:19–20 au. trans.).[23] Ernst Käsemann saw Christ's assumption of lordship over the world as resulting in a kind of cosmic peace or unity.[24] However we interpret "all the fullness," our question here concerns something else: only conscious and willing agents can, properly speaking, be at enmity and then reconciled with each other in a new, peaceful situation. Despite the language of Christ "making peace through the blood of his cross" (Col 1:20), it makes better sense to think of this "reconciliation" not as primarily establishing friendly relations between personal agents but as Christ making "all things" conform to the divine plan. This is not precisely an interpersonal conflict that needs to be resolved, but rather an incompatibility that needs to be dealt with and removed. Thus Christ, through his death and resurrection, has made "all things" peacefully conform, at least in principle, to the wise plan of God. It makes sense to assimilate this use of "reconcile" to meaning (2) above.

Andrew T. Lincoln talks of "enmity" that has "invaded the cosmos" through "the activity of hostile cosmic powers." While not previously mentioned, it is presupposed that "at some stage the cosmos with its original harmony, as God had created it in Christ, was put out of joint, so that it became in need of being restored to harmony through Christ."[25] The principalities needed to be stripped of their power if all things were to be reconciled to Christ. Without using my classifications, Lincoln invokes in fact meaning (2): a disharmony or incompatibility that should be dealt with. As Eduard Lohse puts it, "In order to restore the cosmic order, reconciliation became necessary and was accomplished by the Christ-event. Through Christ, God himself achieved this reconciliation….The peace which God has established through Christ binds the whole universe together again into unity."[26]

Conclusion

Many people feel instinctively drawn to the warm, relational language of reconciliation, as we find it in two major letters by Paul and in a wonderful hymn in Colossians (1:15–20). Obviously, it is a language that continues to communicate well. In all three passages we have examined, the NRSV, NJB, REB, and other modern version render *katallagē*, *katallassō*, and *apokatallassō* as "reconciliation" and "reconcile."

Yet, as we have just seen, we may need to remind ourselves that the New Testament employs such language in ways that go beyond its ordinary, secular meaning in the Greek of that time and in the English of today. Paul, who introduced the language of "reconciliation" into Christian discourse, used this language in a logically extended fashion. The challenges he faced were different from ours because his purpose was to communicate rather than to analyze. By realizing how the concepts may lead us astray, we can come to appreciate better Paul's purposes in using the expressions in question.

Any speech drawn from human states of affairs cannot be expected to apply *tout court* to God's redemptive work toward sinful men and women. In the New Testament, reconciliation does not point to God being changed or reconciled to human beings; rather it is God or God through Jesus Christ who effects reconciliation by changing us. This example says much about the "character" and purposes of our all-loving God (Rom 5:8).

15

LOVE AS A VERB

(1 Cor 13:4-8a)

First Corinthians 13:4–8a contains, Joseph A. Fitzmyer writes, "sixteen Greek verbs that express characteristics of love [*agapē*], seven positive and nine negative."[1] He expounds the meaning of each of these sixteen verbs in the course of his commentary on Paul's "rhetorical encomium of love" (1 Cor 13:1–13).[2] He explains that "Paul's discussion of love is meant to exhort Christians of Corinth to consider their behavior in light of it." By the time of the apostle, *agapē* had "acquired a more general, ethical connotation: a spontaneous inward affection of one person for another that manifests itself in an ongoing concern for the other and impels one to self-giving." In short, "love is not a mere feeling, but it evokes a mode of action."[3]

Why Sixteen Verbs?

Like other commentators, Fitzmyer asks whether chapter 13 as a whole should be described as a "hymn, ode, or psalm." It is, he concludes, "rather a descriptive, didactic and hortatory passage composed with no little rhetoric, and differs considerably from the style of the rest of the letter, as well as from other New Testament passages that are usually considered hymnic: Philippians 2:6–11; Colossians 1:15–20." Fitzmyer adds, "It has no liturgical traces, no parallelism, and contains no mention of Christ," and "even lacks all explicit reference to God." Nevertheless, he maintains the usual title, "hymn to love," even though he recognizes that the passage is "structured prose, scarcely poetical or lyrical."[4] Fitzmyer recalls parallels to the way love is treated in 1 Corinthians 13, argues that this passage forms a climax to Paul's teaching about spiritual endowments, expounds a division of the chapter into three sections, and carefully examines the meaning of *agapē*.[5]

Thus, Fitzmyer offers his answers to a number of questions. But he does not raise the question, Why does the apostle choose sixteen verbs to express sixteen "characteristics of love"? These are characteristics of "behavior" or "a mode of action." But why does Paul depict all these characteristics through verbs (active in meaning and in the present tense) and not through other such verbal forms as participles and imperatives or through other such parts of speech as adjectives or nouns?

Elsewhere the Pauline letters note various characteristics of love (*agapē*), but do not always use verbs when pointing to these characteristics. Galatians 5:6, to be sure, introduces a verb (specifically, a participle) when calling love the way in which Christian faith "works itself out." But Paul employs nouns when naming love as "the fruit of the Spirit" (Gal 5:22) and "the fulfillment of the law" (Rom 13:10). An adjective turns up when he describes love as "genuine" or "sincere" (Rom 12:9). This variety raises a question for 1 Corinthians 13:4–8a: Why does Paul use only verbs (active in meaning and in the present tense), and not a mixture of verbs, nouns, and adjectives, when presenting sixteen characteristics of love?

Fitzmyer's language about love as "a mode of action" hints at an answer. C. K. Barrett offers a similar hint. Commenting on this section of 1 Corinthians 13, he speaks of being "actuated by love" and Paul's answering the questions, "What does love do and what does it not do?"[6] Gordon Fee writes of love as characterizing "our existence" and, more specifically, names love as "behavior."[7] In a classical study of *agapē*, Ceslas Spicq noted Paul's use of verbs in 1 Corinthians 13:4–8a, and spoke of the "activity" of love: it "never ceases to act" and "is always at work."[8] Such talk of "activity" and being "always at work" calls for further explanation, as do the comments from Fitzmyer, Barrett, and Fee about "action," being "actuated," "doing" or "not doing," and "behavior."

Love as a Verb

Craig and Thiselton

Nearly seventy years ago, Clarence Tucker Craig commented that "the nature of love is expressed by Paul in a series of verbs, the active character of which may not be fully indicated by adjectives," even though many translations have adopted adjectives: for instance, "love is patient, love is kind."[9]

Years later Anthony C. Thiselton quoted Craig, spoke of "the nature and *action* of love" (my italics), and stated that "our translation strives to preserve the verbal structure of the Greek, as against the adjectival structure of many English versions." He observed that "static" adjectives "describe the nature of love timelessly," and so fail to indicate fully its "active character." Thus, he refused to render the first two verbs of 1 Corinthians 13:4 as "love is patient, love is kind." Thiselton understood Paul's "choice of the dynamic verbal form" over adjectives to be "deliberate" and aimed at playing "its part in a chain of active temporal processes." Hence, he translated the opening words of verse 4 as love "waits patiently" and love "shows kindness."[10] He pressed on to preserve "the verbal structure" of most of the other sixteen verbs used by Paul—right through to 13:8a, love "never falls apart."[11]

Unlike Thiselton, Fitzmyer showed no particular sensitivity to the choice of verbs over adjectives and translated verses 4–8a as

> [Love] is patient; love is kind. Love is not jealous; [love] does not brag; it is not arrogant. It is not rude; it does not seek its own interest; it does not become irritated; it does not reckon with wrongs. It does not delight in wrongdoing, but rejoices with the truth. It puts up with all things, believes all things, hopes for all things, endures all things. Love never fails.[12]

Here five of the apostle's sixteen verbs were rendered "is" followed by an adjective.

Set this translation over against Thiselton, with his concern to follow Paul's choice of dynamic, verbal forms:

> Love waits patiently; love shows kindness. Love does not burn with envy; does not brag—is not inflated with its own importance. It does not behave with ill-mannered impropriety; is not preoccupied with the interests of the self; does not

become exasperated into pique; does not keep a reckoning up of evil. Love does not take pleasure at wrongdoing, but joyfully celebrates truth. It never tires of support, never loses faith, never exhausts hope, never gives up. Love never falls apart.[13]

Twice Thiselton translates by using "is" followed by an adjectival participle ("inflated" and "preoccupied"). In the first case, he might have rendered *ou phusioutai* as "does not behave arrogantly." In the second, "is not preoccupied with the interests of the self [*ou zētei ta heautēs*']" could have been translated "does not seek its own interests [plural rather than Fitzmyer's singular, 'interest']."

Here and there Thiselton's version verges on a paraphrase, which may bring out what Paul means but does not quite match what the apostle more cryptically says: for instance, "is not inflated with its own importance" (as opposed to Fitzmyer's "is not arrogant"), "does not behave with ill-mannered impropriety" (as opposed to Fitzmyer's "is not rude"), and, even more questionable, "does not become exasperated into pique" (as opposed to Fitzmyer's "does not become irritated"). In the first two cases, Fitzmyer's "is not arrogant" might be happily changed to "does not behave arrogantly," and "is not rude" could be changed to "does not behave rudely."

Drawing on both translations[14] and aiming to honor throughout the verbal character of Paul's encomium to love, I suggest the following:

> Love waits patiently; love shows kindness. It does not burn with envy. It does not brag, does not become conceited or behave rudely. It does not seek its own interests, and does not become irritated. It does not keep a reckoning of wrongs. It does not delight in injustice, but rejoices together with the truth. It always gives support, always believes the best, always hopes for the best, always stands firm. Love never falls apart.

Wallace and the Meaning and Tense of the Verbs

More should be said about the sixteen verbs that Paul deploys. All of them occur with an active meaning and in the present tense, with three of them having middle and passive forms but active meanings (see n. 1).

Grammatically speaking, as Daniel Wallace explains, "in general it can be said that in the active voice the subject *performs, produces*, or *experiences the action* or *exists* in the *state* expressed by the verb" (his italics). He then distinguishes the "simple active" from other possible forms of the active. Wallace recognizes that such a simple active is "by far the most common" usage: whether the verb is transitive or intransitive, "the subject *performs* or *experiences* the action" (his italics).[15]

The *Oxford Dictionary of English* (3rd ed., 2010) defines *verb* as a "word used to describe an action, state, or occurrence." Like Wallace's account of the active voice of verbs in the New Testament ("the subject *performs, produces*, or *experiences the action* or exists in the *state* expressed by the verb"), the *Oxford Dictionary of English* definition highlights how verbs describe actions (physical, mental, or both) and occurrences, even more than states in which the subject exists.

All sixteen verbs in Paul are in the present tense, and so "represent an activity as in process" (or in progress).[16] Once again this description from Wallace converges somewhat with what the *Oxford Dictionary of English* says of the present tense in English as "expressing an action now going on or habitually performed, or a condition now existing."

This convergence (not identification) between the use of verbs with active meaning and in the present tense found in both New Testament Greek and contemporary English encourages us to try to follow suit when translating the sixteen verbs deployed in 1 Corinthians 13:4–8a. That is what I attempted in my translation.

Love as Verbal

We saw above that Fitzmyer, Craig, and Thiselton, when writing on 1 Corinthians 13:4–8a, note the presence of sixteen verbs that describe sixteen characteristics of love. But these commentators scarcely hint at possible reasons for Paul going out of his way to choose verbs (with active meaning and in the present tense). Other commentators do not even register the use of these sixteen verbs, let alone attempt to explain the apostle's usage.[17]

Elsewhere, notably in Romans 12:9–21, Paul identifies the behavior of love (and a good Christian life) in similar ways, uses various verbal forms (participles sixteen times, the imperative six times, and an infinitive twice), as well as an adjective four times.[18] But this passage from Romans 12 does not present that characteristic behavior by personifying love and sixteen times introducing a verb (with an active meaning and in the present tense). In 1 Corinthians 13:4–8a, the apostle's repeated choice and usage of verbs emphasize the activity of love. To echo Wallace and the *Oxford Dictionary of English*, the person characterized by love performs or produces love as an activity.

We might sum up what Paul's teaching implies by saying that love is not so much a permanent set of habitual characteristics. Rather love consists of actions that occur when love does certain things or actively refrains from doing other things. In short, love is verbal, a constant performance. We might even say that love exists in action or it does not exist at all.

16

THE APPEARANCES OF THE RISEN CHRIST

(1 Cor 15:5-8)

In an exchange of letters with an American scholar a few years ago, the question emerged about the preferable way to translate *ōphthē*, as it occurs four times in 1 Corinthians 15:5–8, as well as in Luke 24:34; Acts 13:31; and 1 Timothy 3:16. Contemporary translations into English (for instance, the NIV, NJB, NRSV, REB, and RSV) render this aorist passive indicative of *horaō* as "he appeared." My correspondent suggested an alternative, a divine passive: "Jesus was shown by God to Cephas" (1 Cor 15:5), and then to the others. He recalled not only that in the early Christian tradition God is the agent of the resurrection (e.g., 1 Thess 1:10; Rom 10:9), but also that Galatians 1:15–16 ("he revealed his Son to me" or "in me") presents God (and not Christ himself) as the agent of this revelation or appearance to Paul. He might have added that a divine passive occurs very close to the fourfold use of *ōphthē* under discussion: "he [Christ] was raised [*egēgertai*]" or, if you like, "was woken from sleep" (from the sleep of death; 1 Cor 15:4). In this verse a scholarly consensus recognizes a divine passive and understands this resurrection or waking from sleep to have been effected "by God." It might be argued that finding a divine passive in verse 4 could encourage us to detect such a divine passive also in verse 5 (*ōphthē*).

This correspondence prompted me into revisiting the question of translating *ōphthē*, as well as thinking further about the language used by the New Testament witnesses to report the Easter encounters. Are contemporary translations correct in translating "he appeared," or should we render the fourfold usage of *ōphthē* in these passages, "he was made manifest" or "he was shown" (and in both cases one is to understand "by God") or even as "he was seen by"? Let me first examine some wider data and possible translations.

Eliminating One Possibility

A few earlier translations, notably the Authorized Version (AV) or King James Version (KJV), the New Testament in Modern English by John Bertram Phillips (1958; rev. 1970),[1] and the first edition of the New American Bible (NAB, 1970, but not its revised version of 1986) rendered *ōphthē* followed by the dative (!) in 1 Corinthians 15:5-8 as "he was seen by." The AV translated the verb as "he was seen of." First Corinthians has earlier used the active (perfect) form of the same verb (*horaō*) when Paul asks, "Am I not an apostle? Have I not seen [*heōraka*] Jesus our Lord?" (1 Cor 9:1). If we have the active form in 1 Corinthians 9:1 ("I have seen Jesus"), does the passive form correspond in 1 Corinthians 15:5-8 (Christ was seen by Cephas, and others, including Paul)? The Revised New Jerusalem Bible (RNJB) of 2019, unlike its two predecessors (the JB of 1966 and the NJB of 1985), rendered *ōphthē* as "was seen" by—not only in the four occurrences in 1 Corinthians 15 but also in Acts 13:31 and 1 Timothy 3:16. However, for some reason, it maintained "appeared" to Simon Peter in Luke 24:34.

Nevertheless, if we think of accepting the translation "he was seen by," we should expect the verb to be followed by *hypo* and a noun or pronoun in the genitive. That is the case, albeit with the aorist passive indicative of another verb (*theaomai*), in Mark 16:11: "he was seen [*etheathē*]...by her [Mary Magdalene]." But instead of *hypo* and the genitive occurring in 1 Corinthians 15, we have *ōphthē* followed by the dative ("he appeared to Cephas" and so forth), just as we have in similar New Testament passages, universally it seems, translated today "appeared": for instance, "there appeared to him [Zechariah] an angel of the Lord" (Luke 1:11); "there appeared to them Elijah with Moses" (Mark 9:4 parr.); "there appeared to them divided tongues, as it were

166

The Appearances of the Risen Christ

of fire" (Acts 2:3).[2] In all three of these passages the RNJB translates "appeared," and not "was seen by."

For any translation of 1 Corinthians 15:5–8 and Luke 24:34, it is clearly relevant that there are numerous examples of a Hebraism preserved in the Septuagint, which, when (generally) translating the Hebrew *wayyērā* (niphal imperfect), uses *ōphthē*. Joseph Fitzmyer calls this a case of a "semitized Greek verb."[3] The first such occurrence in the LXX comes with a theophany found in Genesis 12:7: "The Lord appeared to Abraham and said...."[4] It was this usage of *ōphthē* for theophanies that was applied to the encounters with the risen Christ.[5] Here, as Fitzmyer explains, the aorist passive "took on an intransitive meaning, 'appeared.'"[6] In an earlier generation, Joachim Jeremias recognized this same usage as being originally Hebrew and Aramaic, and translated *ōphthē* in 1 Corinthians 15 as "Christ appeared."[7] Even earlier Joseph Thayer had proposed "showed himself" (or "appeared") as the appropriate rendering of the verb as used in 1 Corinthians 15.[8]

The origin of the kerygmatic fragment that Paul quotes in 1 Corinthians 15:3–5 might affect the translating of *ōphthē*. (a) Did the fragment render in Greek a Semitic original coming from an Aramaic-speaking community (perhaps Jerusalem)? (b) Or was it drawn from a Greek original, borrowed from a Jewish-Gentile, Greek-speaking church (perhaps Antioch)? Jeremias argues for (a), but Fitzmyer shows that the evidence is far from conclusive.[9]

However, the disagreement between Jeremias and Fitzmyer over the origin of the fragment does not seem to affect the translation: "he let himself be seen" or "he appeared." Neither of them proposes a divine passive: "he was shown" or "he was made manifest [by God]." Fitzmyer speaks of the passive taking on "an intransitive meaning." Raymond Collins renders *ōphthē* as "he appeared," translating it "in an intransitive sense."[10] Anthony Thiselton, who renders the verb as "he appeared" or "he became visible," points out that "he appeared" occurs with a dative ("to Cephas") and in a "reflexive sense."[11] Wolfgang Schrage, who also prefers to translate the verb as "he appeared" or "he let himself be seen," writes of a "deponent or middle form."[12] But the labels ("intransitive," "reflexive," "deponent," or "middle") seem a secondary matter. Collins, Fitzmyer, Jeremias, Schrage, and Thiselton all endorse the common translation: Christ "appeared," "became visible," or "let himself be seen." Like all current English translations, none of them propose "he was seen by." Despite its passive voice, *ōphthē* does not have for them a passive meaning.

We have cited current English translations of and commentaries on 1 Corinthians. What do the authors of New Testament grammars and dictionaries say? Daniel B. Wallace observes that when "*ōphthē* is used in the New Testament with a simple dative, the subject of the verb consciously *initiates* the visible manifestation. In no instance can it be said that the person(s) in the dative case initiate(s) the act. In other words, volition rests wholly with the subject, while the dative noun is merely recipient."[13] In other words, the verb, while passive in form, is intransitive in meaning: the subject "appeared to" whoever is mentioned in the dative. The older Blass-Debrunner *Grammar of the New Testament* also recognized what it called a "passive with intransitive meaning" in *ōphthē* as used in 1 Corinthians 15:5–8, specifying this further as an "intransitive-deponent meaning."[14]

Rather than speaking, like Wallace, of *ōphthē* in its four occurrences in 1 Corinthians 15 as being "intransitive" in meaning or, like Blass-Debrunner, of an "intransitive-deponent" meaning, the Bauer-Danker *Greek-English Lexicon of the New Testament* categorizes them as passive but in "the active sense: became visible, appear." It cites various examples not only of the risen Christ "appearing" (as in 1 Cor 15) but also of "appearances" of angels (e.g., Luke 1:11; 22:43) and of Moses and Elijah at the transfiguration (Mark 9:4).[15] Bauer-Danker has its own label ("the active sense") but it lines up with the commentaries and grammars we have examined by understanding *ōphthē* in 1 Corinthians 15 to mean "Christ appeared," "became visible," "showed himself," or "let himself be seen."

"He Was Made Manifest by God"

Unlike Collins, Fitzmyer, and Thiselton, in his commentary on 1 Corinthians Schrage examines some earlier suggestions coming from Karl Heinrich Rengstorf, Gerhard Friedrich, and Josef Pfammatter, and considers the possibility of a divine passive and hence of interpreting *ōphthē* as being a paraphrase (*Umschreibung*) for the divine action: "God has let Christ become visible (*Gott hat Christus sichtbar werden lassen*)." Schrage points to the parallel with a passive form in 1 Corinthians 15:4 that we recalled above (*egēgertai*). Since Christ has been raised or woken from the sleep of death by God, he has also been made visible or manifest by God. Second, Schrage thinks that one might also appeal to a parallel in Acts 10:40: "God raised him [Jesus] from the dead and allowed him to appear (*edōken auton emphanē genesthai*)."[16] Third, Schrage recalls that for Paul, as for the earliest Christians, God is the agent of the resurrection (e.g., Rom 10:9), and adds, "It goes without saying that, for Paul, ultimately it is God himself who brings about the appearance of Christ." Fourth, after stating that the gospel he preaches came "through a revelation of Jesus Christ" (Gal 1:12), Paul makes it clear that Christ is the object rather than the subject of this revelation by declaring, "God…was pleased to reveal his Son to [or in] me" (Gal 1:15-16). In the apostle's own comment on his Damascus road encounter, it is the initiative of God that is to the fore.[17]

Nevertheless, Schrage emphasizes that the subject of the formula, *ōphthē Kēpha* (1 Cor 15:5), a formula found also in 1 Corinthians 15:6, 7, and 8, is Christ, just as in the LXX God "is repeatedly named as the subject of a theophany signified with *ōphthē*."[18] In a footnote Schrage refers to Genesis 12:7 and four further examples of such theophanies reported in Genesis. Like Fitzmyer and others, Schrage finds the LXX background of theophanies decisive and translates the verb accordingly in 1 Corinthians 15: Christ "appeared" or "let himself be seen." He deals with the parallel to *egēgertai* (1 Cor 15:4) by detecting a chiasm between active and passive elements in the formula: "(a) he died; (b) he was buried; (b) he has been raised; and (a) he appeared." The chiastic structure holds the formula together, as well the central affirmations, "he died" and "he has been raised," being confirmed, respectively, by "he was buried" and "he appeared."

We should agree with Fitzmyer, Schrage, and the other scholars and translations mentioned above that in all four instances in 1 Corinthians 15:5-8 *ōphthē* is to be translated "he appeared."[19] This leaves it open, however, to consider "he was made manifest by God" as a legitimate (theological) paraphrase of or (theological) comment on what we can call "Christophanies," even if it is not a strict translation (from a philological point of view). The *theological* paraphrase draws support from the *grammatical* category of the divine passive (in particular, 1 Cor 15:4). Theology cannot be totally separated from (biblical) philology.

In the LXX *ōphthē* is used for what have been called "theophanies" (e.g., Gen 12:7; 17:1) and "angelophanies" (e.g., Exod 3:2; Judg 6:12). This has encouraged Fitzmyer, Schrage, and others to speak of Christophanies reported by 1 Corinthians 15:5–8 and similar passages in the New Testament (e.g. Luke 24:34).[20] Apropos of the Christophany to more than five hundred faithful (1 Cor 15:6), Fitzmyer remarks, "One has to rule out a purely internal experience of these recipients of the appearance."[21] If this Christophany may not be reduced to "a purely internal experience," what does the New Testament witness encourage us to say about it and similar episodes? Let us begin with Paul and then take the discussion further.

The Nature of the Christophanies

Among the various witnesses—some would say eyewitnesses[22]—to encounters with the risen Christ, Paul's is the only case where we can be confident of hearing that testimony directly from the person in question. He presents his encounter as closing a series of appearances: "last of all…he appeared also to me" (1 Cor 15:8). Earlier in the same letter Paul defends his apostolic authority through two questions: "Am I not an apostle? Have I not seen Jesus our Lord?" (1 Cor 9:1). Here the perfect indicative (*heōraka*) expresses "the present effect of Paul's earlier experience of encounter with the raised Christ at the moment of his missionary and apostolic commission on the way to Damascus."[23] As Collins puts it, "Paul's vision of the Lord…is the foundational warrant for his apostleship."[24] Apart from these two verses in 1 Corinthians, Paul *never again* speaks either of his having "seen" the Lord or of the Lord "appearing" to him.[25] While this encounter with the risen Jesus set Paul apart by conferring apostolic authority on him, it was never repeated; for the apostle, it was a once-and-for-all, foundational experience, which made him the last in the series of official witnesses to the resurrection (1 Cor 15:8).[26]

In another letter Paul interprets his Damascus road experience as revelatory: it was a "revelation [*apokalupsis*]" of Jesus Christ as God's Son risen from the dead, a (foundational) revelation that commissioned Paul as an apostle (Gal 1:12, 16). Paul also uses the language of revelation in other contexts: for instance, he speaks of going up to Jerusalem with Barnabas and Titus "in response to a revelation" (Gal 2:1–2). To counter the impact of false apostles, he reluctantly speaks of "visions [*optasias*] and revelations [*apokalupseis*]." Although he uses both nouns in the plural, he presses on to recall only one personal experience, that of being taken up "to the third heaven" fourteen years earlier (2 Cor 12:1-4). While a deeply significant "revelation" characterized the Damascus road encounter, other episodes in Paul's life could also be called "revelatory."[27]

In his letter to the Philippians, Paul describes the dramatic, personal change he experienced through encountering the risen Christ (Phil 3:2—4:1). But he speaks here not of "seeing" Christ but of "knowing" him (Phil 3:8, 10).

Elsewhere in the New Testament,[28] *ōphthē* is used in an ordinary way when Stephen recalls how Moses "appeared" or "came to" some of his fellow Israelites when they were quarreling (Acts 7:26). In the Book of Revelation, the use of this verb is anything but "ordinary." After the seventh trumpet sounded in heaven, God's temple was opened and the ark of the covenant "appeared" (perhaps better "was seen") within the temple (Rev 11:19). Then followed immediately the vision of the woman, the child, and the dragon: "A great portent appeared in heaven: a woman clothed with the sun....She was pregnant and was crying out in birth pangs....Then another portent appeared in heaven: a great red dragon, with seven heads" (Rev 12:1-3). All three "appearances" (the ark, the woman, and the dragon) happen "in heaven," even if the dragon is obviously an evil portent.

Then we should also recall the use in the New Testament of *ōphthē*, followed by the dative, to designate (a) appearances of angels (Luke 1:11; 22:43; Acts 7:30, with *opthentos* followed by the dative in 7:35, referring to an appearance of an angel in 7:30), and (b) the appearance "to them" (Peter, James, and John) of Elijah with Moses (Mark 9:4; Matt 17:3). Luke 9:31 uses the related participle (*opthentes*) to speak of Elijah and Moses "appearing in glory." In citing these passages about the "appearances" of (a) angels and (b) of Elijah and Moses, my intention is to clarify language rather than to argue for the historicity of these episodes and their details. Nor do I want to press any comparison between Paul's experience of the risen Lord and any experiences of Zechariah in the temple (Luke 1:11), Peter, James, and John on the mountain (Mark 9:4), and Jesus in Gethsemane (Luke 22:43). Distinctions between various kinds of appearances should be respected and explored. The appearance of the angel to Zechariah, for instance, could be examined in the light of angelophanies in Genesis, the prophetic literature, and other passages in Luke and Acts. But in recalling the angelophanies and further appearances,

I simply follow the example of Bauer-Danker, which cites these *ōphthē* events under the heading of "become visible, appear."[29]

Apart from one reference to an Old Testament theophany (Acts 7:2)[30] and the appearance of a Macedonian in a night vision to Paul (Acts 16:9), the central role of *ōphthē* in the New Testament concerns appearances of Christ in the aftermath of his resurrection (Luke 24:34; Acts 13:31; 1 Cor 15:5, 6, 7, 8). In short, *ōphthē* was "used to identify visionary experiences of the risen Christ."[31] Ananias uses the related participle *ophtheis* to speak of "Jesus, who appeared to you [Paul] on your way here" (Acts 9:17). The risen Jesus himself says to Paul, "I have appeared [*ōphthēn*] to you for this purpose, to appoint you to serve and testify to the things in which you have seen me and to those in which I will appear [*ophthēsomai*] to you" (Acts 26:16). Here and below, when dealing with the three accounts in Acts (in chs. 9, 22, and 26) of Paul's Damascus road experience, my interest is in exploring the language of "seeing" or "appearing" that Luke uses rather than in pressing claims about the historicity or otherwise of particular details.

Add here the use of *ōphthē* in a hymnic or, more likely a creedal, fragment in 1 Timothy: "he [Christ Jesus] appeared to messengers" (1 Tim 3:16 au. trans.).[32] Normally *aggelois* has been translated "to angels," creating a question: how would we envisage the risen Christ appearing to beings of the other world, angels? But in the New Testament, no less than in the LXX, *aggeloi* can also designate human messengers: for example, John the Baptist (Matt 11:10; Mark 1:2; Luke 7:27), messengers sent by John (Luke 7:24), and Paul himself (Gal 4:14). Hence some major commentaries translate the phrase from 1 Timothy as "he appeared to messengers," understanding these to be witnesses who went on to proclaim the resurrection. The phrase unifies the individuals and groups that Paul lists in 1 Corinthians 15:5–8 as those to whom the risen Christ appeared.[33]

Clearly linked with this Christophany language are the many references to "seeing" the risen Christ: for instance, "he [the risen Christ] is going before you into Galilee; there you will see [*opsesthe*] him" (Mark 16:7; see Matt 28:7, 10). "Seeing" him on the mountain, the eleven disciples adored him (Matt 28:17). Mary Magdalene joyfully announces, "I have seen [*heōraka*] the Lord" (John 20:18). Barnabas explains that Saul "saw [*eiden*] the Lord on the road" (Acts 9:27). Thomas comes to faith because he has "seen" the risen Christ; those are blessed who come to faith without having "seen" Christ, as the original witnesses did (John

20:29; see 1 Pet 1:8). Likewise, Paul (in 1 Cor 9:1) implies that the Corinthians have not experienced what he has experienced: his "seeing" (the risen Lord) should be distinguished from any other "coming to faith."[34] When the New Testament refers to some of the first disciples experiencing the risen Christ, the language of seeing predominates.[35] Their decisive experience of the risen Christ came through seeing him.

But was this (a) in some sense a seeing with their eyes when Christ became visible? Or was it (b) merely a seeing with their mind as Christ became interiorly visible in a divine self-manifestation? Kremer, while remarking that the power of God and the angels "to appear visibly is ascribed to the risen Christ," defends (a): we "ought not deny *ōphthē* any visual element, as though it were simply a formulaic term for revelation."[36] Collins endorses (b): "the traditional Jewish understanding of divine transcendence[37]...suggests that the use of this traditional language with regard to a manifestation of the divine did not imply physical sight."[38] For Collins, no less than for Kremer, it was Christ who at least immediately[39] made the appearances possible; he showed himself and "allowed himself to be recognized."[40]

In presenting his interpretation, Collins remarks that "in the biblical accounts of a manifestation of the divine, auditory [rather than visual] elements predominate."[41] But it is precisely because of this predominance of the auditory that those manifestations of God and angels in the LXX fail to prefigure precisely the *ōphthē* in Luke 24:34; Acts 13:31; and 1 Corinthians 15:5–8 (four times). When Gabriel "appeared" (*ōphthē*) to Zechariah, much is said on both sides (Luke 1:5–20). Likewise, at the transfiguration, when Elijah "appeared" with Moses, there were auditory elements in the sense that they "were talking with Jesus" (Mark 9:4). But the six references (just listed) to the appearances of the risen Christ—or seven if we include 1 Timothy 3:16—make no reference to anything that was said; the language is simply "visual" (he appeared or let himself be seen).

Besides these six (or seven) occurrences of *ōphthē*, we find *ophtheis* (Acts 9:17) and two other passive forms of *ōphthēnai* and the active *eides* ("you have seen me," Acts 26:16) used by Luke when reporting Paul's encounter with the risen Christ. In the context of the postresurrection appearances, further texts introduce the active voice of the same verb *horan* ("to see") (1 Cor 9:1; Mark 16:7; Matt 28:7, 10, 17; Luke 24:24, 39 [twice]; John 20:18, 20, 25 [twice], 27). Luke 24:37, 39 and John 20:12, 14 use, also in the active, another verb "to see" (*theōrein*), while John

21 uses the active voice of *phareroun* ("to show," 21:1 twice) and once the passive *ephanerōthē* (21:14). At the end of the story about the two disciples at Emmaus, "their eyes were opened, and they recognized him [the risen Christ]; and he vanished [*aphantos egeneto*] from their sight" (Luke 24:31). In reporting the appearances of the risen Jesus to Mary Magdalene, to two disciples, and to the eleven, the longer ending to Mark employs the passive voice of *theaomai* (Mark 16:11) and *phaneroō* (Mark 16:12, 14) and the middle voice of *phainomai* (Mark 16:9). Acts speaks of the risen Christ "presenting" (*parestēsen*) himself and "appearing" (*optanomenos*) (Acts 1:3) and being "allowed to appear" (*emphanē genesthai*) (Acts 10:40).

This last paragraph, far from pressing any claims about historical details in the appearance narratives of the Gospels and Acts, aimed simply at establishing how they converged with Paul. In their choice of verbs, they witnessed to the Easter encounters as somehow being ocular and visual. In some narratives (classically in the Emmaus story of Luke 24), the disciples fail to recognize immediately the risen Lord. But such delayed recognition does not take away from the ways in which the Gospels and Acts use the language of sight in their Easter narratives.

The Easter stories of the Gospels also employ verbs expressing movement that imply the risen Christ being seen. He "came to meet" two women (Matt 28:9); he "came near" two travelers and "walked" with them (Luke 24:15, 36). He "came" to the disciples (John 20:24, 26). The evangelists similarly introduce verbs of "presence": Jesus "stood among them" (Luke 24:36; John 20:19, 26), or he "stood on the shore" (John 21:4). Unquestionably, one can and should raise the question, What would it be like for someone gloriously risen from the dead to "come" to others, to "meet" them, to "walk" with them, or to "stand" there before them? Nevertheless, such verbs imply that Jesus was seen by his disciples. Once again, in recalling these and other details from the Easter narratives in the Gospels, I do not want to read particular details back into 1 Corinthians 9:1; 15:5–8 (let alone into Gal 1:12, 16). My primary aim is to recall and clarify the language the evangelists adopted and relate it to Paul. In 1 Corinthians (and Galatians) Paul was using common language. Some clarity about that language might help us to sort out its relationship to what Paul and other New Testament witnesses had experienced.

All in all, when witnessing to the encounters with the risen Christ, the New Testament so privileges the language of seeing that Kremer seems justified in allowing for some "visual element" (see above). Nevertheless, the appearances did not imply *merely* physical sight or a *purely* ordinary seeing of an external object. As Paul implies, the postresurrection appearances involved seeing a "spiritual" (*pneumatikon*) body and not some "physical" (*psuchikon*) body of this world (1 Cor 15:44).[42] It was a perception that led to recognizing someone who now enjoys an exalted, heavenly existence, "Christ Jesus my Lord" (Phil 3:8, 10, 20), whose body is now "glorious" (3:21) and who now incorporates (3:9) and will "transform" (3:21) others into his risen life (3:11). John implies that "seeing" the risen Lord (John 20:18) presupposes his call and self-disclosure (20:16), along with the freedom of the one addressed to enter into a relationship of faith with him (20:27). It brings the recipients to "know" him (21:12). John pictures this freedom of faith through Mary Magdalene needing to "turn around" once again (20:14, 16), this time spiritually and not merely physically, "before she can acknowledge the risen Lord."[43]

When we recall how Paul links "knowing" the risen Christ with the hope of sharing in his glorious resurrection, we can agree with Thiselton: "Christ's risen presence serves as God's eschatological self-manifestation."[44] This is not to follow Willi Marxsen and others who have identified the encounter promised in Mark 16:7 ("there you will see him") with the parousia.[45] In this and other references to the postresurrection appearances, there is not a hint of those apocalyptic images and signs (proposed in Mark 13:6–27 and elsewhere) that are to accompany the parousia. While anticipating and even inaugurating in advance the end, the Easter appearances with their "seeing" do not yet embody the final "seeing" of which Hebrews speaks: "Christ…will appear [*ophthēsetai*] a second time, not to deal with sin, but to save those who are eagerly waiting for him" (Heb 9:28; see Luke 17:22).

The language used by Paul, the Gospels, and further New Testament witnesses supports the following account of how they wanted to express their experiences: (a) the appearances depended on the initiative of the risen Jesus, (b) were events of revelation, (c) disclosed the eschatological and (d) christological significance of Jesus,[46] and (e) called the recipients to a special mission through (f) an experience that was unique[47] and (g) was not merely interior "seeing" but also involved some exterior, visual perception.

The last point invites further reflection. Seeing the risen Jesus called for a graced and enhanced powers of perception. As Origen put it, he "appeared after his resurrection not to all people but only to those whom he perceived to have obtained eyes which had the capacity to see the resurrection [= to see him in his risen state]."[48] Centuries later St. Thomas Aquinas stated that, on the one hand, "the apostles could offer eyewitness testimony to the resurrection of Christ." But, on the other hand, this was because "they saw Christ alive after his resurrection with faith that works through eyes [*oculata fide*]."[49]

Here we need to allow not only for a graced seeing on the part of the witnesses but also for the transformation in the One who is perceived. The resurrected Christ constitutes the beginning of the end of the world (1 Cor 15:20, 23), the realized presence of the new creation. Through his risen bodiliness, matter has been elevated to a final destiny that goes far beyond the bodiliness we experience in this world. "Exalted at the right hand of God" (Acts 2:33), Christ manifests himself as sharing in the divine mystery and is not to be manipulated, weighed, measured, or in other ways treated like an ordinary object that takes up space in this world. He appears where and to whom he wills, and disappears when he wills (e.g., Luke 24:31). He now enjoys a "spiritual body," which Paul struggles to express in 1 Corinthians 15:12–58.

Those who accept this new state of the risen Christ should find little difficulty in acknowledging what it entailed: graced powers of perception on the part of those who "saw" him. To see the risen Christ required a transforming grace for the recipients of that experience. To see him they needed to be made in some sense like him. In all cases and, strikingly, in the case of Paul (and also, presumably, in that of James "the brother of the Lord" (1 Cor 15:7), some healing grace was needed "before" (understood ontologically and not chronologically) they could see and believe in the crucified and risen Christ.

What I have just been arguing for does not purport to be merely exegetical comments on what Paul or any other New Testament author allegedly put in these terms. My argument exemplifies rather how pondering their witness leads us on to theological reflection and interpretation.

Dealing with Objections

The account just offered about the Christophanies, or appearances of the risen Christ, faces various objections. Let me take up three of

The Appearances of the Risen Christ

them: the purported "appearances" in 1 Corinthians 15:5-8 (and elsewhere) are simply formulas to legitimate the authority of the recipients; the "appearances" were merely ecstatic, unreliable experiences; the "appearances" pointed only to internal phenomena, revelations to the mind of Paul and others of Christ's reality and status.

(a) Those who have developed the thesis of "legitimation formulas" go far beyond what we have noted above: being a recipient of an appearance of the risen Christ conferred apostolic authority on Paul. Peter and other members of the "Twelve" had already been given some measure of authority by the earthly Jesus (Mark 3:13-19; 6:7-13; Luke 22:29-30). Now they were confirmed in those leadership roles by receiving one or more appearances of the risen Christ. Those who press the theory of "legitimation formulas" claim that the "appearances" were only a rhetorical device to confer authority on those competing for leadership in the emerging Church. In short, "appearances" were invented to underpin claims to authority.[50]

Schrage and others have drawn attention to fatal difficulties facing the "legitimation formula" theory. Paul lists among the Easter witnesses "more than five hundred" disciples. But there is not the slightest hint that this was a device to establish their *special* authority. The longest and, for many, the most beautiful account of a postresurrection appearance is the story of the risen Jesus joining Cleopas and his anonymous companion on the road to Emmaus (Luke 24:13-35). Yet there is no suggestion that Christ commissioned them to undertake some authoritative role. Finally, there is no reliable evidence that conflicts between leading early Christians such as Mary Magdalene, Peter, and Thomas triggered the invention (or at least the embellishment) of resurrection appearances.[51]

(b) Those who want to explain or rather explain away the Easter "appearances" as (unreliable and highly subjective) ecstatic experiences point to Paul's account of being taken up to "the third heaven" (2 Cor 12:1-4) and try to identify this with his postresurrection encounter with the risen Christ (1 Cor 9:1; 15:8). But Paul writes here of an episode that took place "fourteen years" earlier: that is to say, around AD 42 and so, years after his Damascus road encounter with Christ, which is dated at the latest to AD 38. Moreover, when "caught up into Paradise," Paul "heard" things that are "not to be told" and that "no mortal is permitted to repeat" (2 Cor 12:4).[52] In 1 Corinthians 9:1 and 15:8, he recalls "seeing" someone, and certainly feels free to witness to that experience.

There is a qualitative difference between the appearance that made him an apostle and these later experiences.

Some have proposed that the "appearances" were simply experiences of the Spirit and that, in particular, the "appearance" to the more than five hundred disciples (1 Cor 15:6) was simply a different tradition about the Holy Spirit descending on the 120 followers of Jesus at Pentecost (Acts 2:1–13). But the traditions are radically different: 1 Corinthians 15:6 witnesses to a Christophany (with no reference to the Holy Spirit), Acts 2 to the outpouring of the Holy Spirit (with no Christophany). In general, Paul writes about the experience of the indwelling Spirit (e.g., Gal 4:6) and various gifts of the Holy Spirit (e.g., 1 Cor 12:1–13; 14:1–40). But he never identifies that common experience of the Holy Spirit and the spiritual gifts as the once-and-for-all encounter with the risen Christ that gave him his own special mission (1 Cor 9:1; 15:8; Gal 1:12, 16).[53]

(c) A third and final issue centers on the meaning of *horaō*. As we saw above, this verb, which altogether occurs 449 times in the New Testament,[54] features centrally in the Easter witness. In their classical work James Hope Moulton and George Milligan proposed three categories for appreciating the meaning of the verb: (i) see literally or with one's eyes; (ii) experience; and (iii) see with the mind.[55] This scheme provides part of the structure for the entry on the transitive uses of *horaō* set out later in the Bauer-Danker lexicon: (i) "perceive by the eye," (ii) "experience," and (iii) "perceive mentally."[56]

(i) Under "perceive by the eye," Bauer-Danker lists passages about the Easter appearances that we have recalled above: for example, "there [in Galilee] you will see him" (Mark 16:7) and "I have seen the Lord" (John 20:18). In these and other similar cases of "seeing" and "appearing" (or "becoming visible" or "letting himself be seen"), personal nouns or pronouns are involved as subject and object (or indirect object) of the verb: thus "you" (Peter and the other disciples) will see Jesus in Galilee (Mark 16:7); Mary Magdalene has seen the Lord (John 20:18). This holds true of what we have recalled from 1 Corinthians 15: Christ appeared to Cephas and the others. To follow Bauer-Danker, in all such cases the risen and living Christ was, at least in some sense, "perceived by the eyes" of Mary Magdalene, Peter, and the further Easter witnesses. They perceived him, and not merely some truth about him.

(ii) Under "experience," Bauer-Danker cites Luke 3:6, a quotation from the LXX that illuminates the preaching of John the Baptist and the baptism of Christ: "all flesh shall see [*opsetai*] the salvation of God." The lexicon could also have cited the words of Simeon in Luke 2:30: "my eyes have seen [*eidon*] your salvation." "Experience" conveys something of the new situation that has arisen with the birth of Jesus and the ministry of John (which culminated in the baptism of Jesus). Both cases include a "sensory" dimension. Simeon saw the Christ child and took him in his arms; the general public ("all flesh") saw John engaged in his ministry and eventually baptizing Jesus himself. In these two cases, persons (Jesus and John) were there to be perceived by the eyes of other persons.

(iii) It is the meaning of the third category in Bauer-Danker, "perceive mentally," that may raise questions about the Easter appearances. First the lexicon examines several cases (Acts 8:23; Heb 2:8; and Jas 2:24) in which some "sensory aspect [is] felt." To such cases where *horaō* is used and some sensory aspect is felt, we can add Matthew 13:14–15 and Mark 4:12.

There remain, however, two cases in which Bauer-Danker recognizes that the "focus [is] on the cognitive aspect": Romans 15:21 (a quotation from the LXX of Isa 52:15, "those who have never been told of him shall see [*opsontai*], and those who have never heard of him shall understand"), and 3 John 11 ("whoever does evil has not seen [*heōraken*] God"). Bauer-Danker translates the first case, "they who have never been told (of Christ) shall look upon him." Here, however, I think the parallel between "shall see" and "shall understand" suggests not "looking upon him," but a less personal "complement." The context in Romans 15 implies "seeing" in the sense of understanding and accepting the truth of the gospel that Paul has been commissioned to preach.[57] It is not, as in the Easter appearances, a question of "seeing him." As regards 3 John 11, Bauer-Danker refers to 1 John 3:10 ("no one who sins has either seen [*heōraken*] him [the Son] or known him"). The lexicon proposes the translation, "No one who sins has become conscious of him and known him." Raymond Brown is a more helpful guide here. Instead of being concerned with literally perceiving with one's eyes God (3 John 11) or Christ (1 John 3:10), or not doing so, these matching passages are saying that those who commit sins are not Christians. The author of the two epistles phrases this in terms of never having seen Christ or never having seen God. Those who sin prefer darkness to light; they deny the truth and are alienated from God; they have no true Christian experience of God.[58]

To sum up this lexical examination. Apart from the two cases, Romans 15:21 and 3 John 11 (taken together with 1 John 3:10), which focus on the cognitive aspect, *horaō* regularly includes a sensory aspect: that is to say, some kind of perceiving by the eyes.[59]

Conclusion

That Jesus lives and *that* we can hope to live with him is more important than *how* we know this. But how we know this—which means knowing this in dependence on the first witnesses to the life, death, and resurrection of Jesus—is still vitally important. I am grateful to my correspondent for prompting me into examining once again the expressions of the first witnesses as to how they came to know that Jesus had been raised from the dead, or how it was "manifested" or "shown" to the first Christians that Jesus had been "woken from the sleep of death." Obviously, some accounts of *how* they came to know this will put into doubt *that* they did so and could then confidently witness that they had done so. This chapter has limited itself to clarifying how they expressed the major experience through which they came to know that Jesus had been "woken from the sleep of death": the appearances. The full story of how they came to know this would involve examining much more and, not least, further details of the appearance narratives, the discovery of the empty tomb, and the gift of the Holy Spirit.

Finally, this chapter has put the case for acknowledging that the postresurrection appearances of Jesus involving some kind of ocular, visual element. The language used by Paul and other New Testament witnesses seems to imply that. Nevertheless, one should never forget that the Apostles' Creed and the Nicene-Constantinopolitan Creed do not profess faith in any account of the Easter encounters. They confess Jesus's glorious resurrection from the dead, without including particular details either about the experiences of the apostolic witnesses or about the way(s) in which they expressed what they had experienced.

17
"POWER MADE PERFECT IN WEAKNESS"

(2 Cor 12:9-10)

In a form-critical and *religionsgeschichtlich* analysis of 2 Corinthians 12:7–10, Hans Dieter Betz shows how this passage can affect and even determine one's interpretation of the whole letter.[1] Within these four verses the apostle's references to "power" and "weakness," while obviously touching the substance of his meaning, may leave our exegetical heads spinning. Let us look first at the basic options open to exegetes in dealing with these notions.

I

What does Paul intend by the "power" that coincides with his "weakness" (v. 10), or—as he puts it a verse earlier—the "power" that "is made perfect" in "weakness"? Does he simply mean the situation of "weakness" brings some previously hidden power to his own notice and that of others? In other words, is he alerting us to the (personal and public) *revelatory function* of "weakness"? Or does Paul understand this "power" to increase or even first become available in the face of "weakness"? In that case the apostle would be affirming something about the order of *ontological reality*. In brief, is Paul speaking primarily about the order of knowledge (his own knowledge and that of others) or about the order of reality? A third possibility is that he thinks of both orders. Under circumstances of "weakness" something happens (power intervenes), and both Paul and others become aware of this new development.

Among exegetes, Alfred Plummer in the International Critical Commentary stands out by his insistence on the revelatory function of "weakness"—to the explicit exclusion of any "ontological" explanation. His explanation reflects a dialectic between hiddenness and revelation, between superficial appearances and what human beings must be "taught." He comments on verse 9 as follows: "where human strength abounds, the effects of divine power may be *overlooked*....Where it is *manifest* that man was powerless, God's power becomes, not *more real, but more evident*." His exegesis of verse 10 continues to expound this notion of Christ's power becoming "conspicuous" in weaknesses: "experience has *taught* him [Paul], and has *taught* those who have been witnesses of his work, how much he can accomplish when he is *apparently* disabled by his infirmities and afflictions."[2]

Rudolf Bultmann favors such a "revelatory" interpretation for 2 Corinthians 12:9. When discussing "the origins of righteousness," he invokes this verse and explains that God's grace does not come to man as "a prop for his failing strength, but as a decisive question: Will you surrender, utterly surrender, to God's dealing—will you know yourself to be a sinner before God?"[3] This searching question intervenes to make humanity aware of its real situation. Later Bultmann argues that "Paul's dictum 'for power comes in weakness to perfection' (2 Cor 12:9) is spoken as a basic principle and holds true for any 'weakness.'" Through "the understanding of suffering learned beneath the cross...the believer's sufferings have become transparent to him."[4] In the encounter with suffering the believer becomes "aware of his weakness and insignificance" and "learns" the truth of human reliance upon God.[5]

In opposition to such a revelatory explanation, other scholars adopt a more or less "ontological" view of 2 Corinthians 12:9–10. Thus, in his paper "God's Righteousness in Paul," Ernst Käsemann maintains, "According to 2 Corinthians 12:9 and 13:3–4, God's *power* operates at the same time as a gift within us."[6] We will return later to other aspects of Käsemann's exegesis. For the moment, I wish to draw attention only to the fact that its trend is heavily "ontological." In the ninth edition of the Meyer commentary on 2 Corinthians, Hans Windisch shows himself partial to a basically similar view. He comments on 12:9b: "At the cost of his own weakness Paul draws down upon himself Christ's power. The renunciation of his own worth, the humble and open confession of his own helpfulness, is thus the pre-condition for the entrance of this heavenly reality into him."[7] Windisch's interpretation carries him beyond Käsemann: the humble admission of weakness constitutes both a moral duty and a precondition for the communication of divine power. We will come back to this point. It is enough here to note that for Windisch the "power" that comes to fulfillment in "weakness" forms an actual force communicated in different degrees. In his *Paulus und Christus* he draws the conclusion that the "power" increases proportionate to the suffering (*je mehr Leiden, desto mehr Kraft*).[8] A further comment on 2 Corinthians 12:9 makes this "physical" interpretation of the apostle's words startlingly clear. For Paul, "the situation and circumstances of weakness are especially the occasions in which he feels the divine power of Christ streaming into himself and incarnating itself in his own person."[9]

Robert Strachan accepts much the same explanation in the *Moffat New Testament Commentary*, albeit Pelagian implications surface in his remarks. Heavenly help provides an alternative source for the apostle's energy when his own strength fails. "Grace," Strachan writes, "indicates not only 'favor' but power, exerting its fullest power when human incapacity is at its meanest and weakest. The source of Paul's heroic energy and missionary fervor is found in the 'grace of God,' which is heavenly strength bestowed on men [!] at those moments when they need it most, and can contribute none of their own."[10]

This quick glance at some past interpretations leaves us with three important issues. Should we accept the view of Bultmann and others that Paul wishes to formulate a general principle that remains valid for any "weakness"? Second, what logic controls the connection between "weakness" and "power"? Is "weakness" a cause or precondition of "power"? Third, do Paul's statements about "power" and "weakness" concern primarily the order of knowledge or the order of reality? Are they "epistemological" or "ontological"? With these questions in mind let us turn to the exegetical details of our passage.

II

Paul refers in 2 Corinthians 12:7b to his plight ("a thorn…in the flesh" given to keep him "from being too elated…considering the exceptional character of the revelations"), states how he prayed for deliverance from the affliction (v. 8), and, without explaining how this disclosure took place, records an answer that came from the Lord (v. 9a). The reply (the only words of the risen Lord found in Paul's letters) may include only "my grace is sufficient for you." The following words ("for power is made perfect in weakness") would then form a comment added by Paul himself to provide a theological justification for the Lord's response. However, it seems more plausible to take verse 9a as a single logion with two parts.[11]

We can conveniently begin with the second half of the logion and the verb *teleitai* ("it is brought to fulfillment," "it is made perfect"). In 1 Corinthians 15:43 (*spereitai en astheneia, egeiretai en dunamei*), Paul supposes a two-stage process in which "power" succeeds "weakness." Here, however, the two notions are made simultaneous: "power" is brought to fulfillment in "weakness." He then reformulates the word of the Lord and sharpens the paradox: "whenever I am weak, then I am strong" (2 Cor 12:10b).

Some scholars explain Paul's choice of *teleitai* as deliberate, anti-Gnostic polemic. Thus, Erhardt Güttgemanns writes,

> The concept of *teleiōsis* plays a great role in Gnosis. There *teleios* is synonymous with *pneumatikos*. In *teleiōsis* the Gnostic becomes wholly *pneuma, doxa, dunamis*. One must recognize that our passage is formulated in sharp antithesis to this Gnostic thesis. The *teleiōsis* and permeation with divine *dunamis* comes about not in the sphere of the heavenly *pneuma* which is experienced in the visions of vs. 1, but precisely in the sphere of the earthly weakness.[12]

Prior to Güttgemanns, Ulrich Wilckens had detected in the use of *teleitai* "clearly one of the sharpest anti-Gnostic sallies which we find anywhere in Paul."[13] In support of his interpretation Wilckens draws attention to the use of *dunamis* and *astheneia* within Gnosis. The terms were opposed both logically and ontologically, the first indicating the heavenly, "pneumatic" sphere and the second the earthly, "fleshly" sphere.[14]

This interpretation supposes not only that Paul (1) continues in verses 9–10 the polemical argumentation that seems present in verses 1–7, but also that he (2) adopts the terminology of his opponents and

(3) does so in a way that enables us to draw conclusions about their position. Moreover, to make anti-Gnostic polemic our assured point of entry for the exegesis of verses 9–10 would be to ignore the serious alternative that Dieter Georgi and others have offered in arguing that Paul's opponents in 2 Corinthians were Jewish-Christian missionaries.[15] In any case there is no need to credit supposed Gnostics with having monopolized the insight that *dunamis* and *astheneia* seem mutually exclusive. We hardly weaken the paradox that Paul wishes to assert if we take ordinary usage—and not more or less elaborate Gnostic hypotheses—as the background for his statement.

Clearly, *he dunamis* (v. 9a), as well as "the power of Christ" (v. 9b), is used here synonymously with *he charis mou* (which according to v. 9a is already communicated to Paul). The "grace" or "power" of Christ reaches fulfillment "in weakness." Paul almost personifies "power" here. One recalls his name for Christ as the *Theou dunamis* (1 Cor 1:24). Does Paul mean that "the powerful (risen) Christ" reaches fulfillment in "the weak apostle"? Windisch refers us to Galatians 2:20, where Christ is said to "live in Paul."[16] But that assertion of Christ's existence "in" the apostle remains highly unusual. Normally Paul speaks of believers existing "in Christ," who functions as an inclusive personality into whom they are incorporated.[17]

The notion of "weakness" in noun or verb form occurs four times in verses 9 and 10. In verse 10 Paul lists four classes of "weaknesses" he experiences: "insults, hardships, persecutions, and calamities." He has already mentioned the "thorn in the flesh" that afflicted him (v. 7), apparently some physical ailment known to the Corinthians, the nature of which the description leaves obscure.[18] Beyond question, Paul understands his "weakness" christologically; its various forms are endured "for the sake of Christ" (v. 10a). The apostle professes himself perfectly willing to "boast" of his "weaknesses," so that the power of Christ (perhaps "the powerful Christ") may shelter him (v. 9; see v. 5).

In 2 Corinthians (where the question of weakness and power bulks large),[19] Paul lists in a unique series the "weaknesses" that characterize his apostolic existence (4:8–12; 6:4–10; 11:23–33; 12:10). Dieter Georgi has drawn attention to the fact that apart from 12:10 all these lists include the notion of *diakonia*. (In the case of 4:8–12 the idea is carried over from 4:1.)[20] "Weakness" constitutes a special mark of apostolic "service." Paul's work of preaching the gospel must not, of course, be interpreted apart from his Christology. The understanding of the crucifixion as the event in which Christ proved radically "weak" forms the background to Paul's whole discussion.[21] In the case of the crucifixion and resurrection, weakness and power constitute an inseparable unity. By raising Christ, God's power was effective and manifested in the face of that ultimate "weakness" that the crucifixion meant. In its turn the apostolic ministry undertaken on Christ's behalf involves participation in this weakness and power of Calvary and Easter, respectively.

Paul is far from wishing to compose a treatise on his apostolic office. His remarks occur in a letter in which among other things he confronts the self-portrayals of opponents. Apparently, these men proclaimed their "spiritual" power and boasted of their ecstatic experiences (5:12–13). Paul reluctantly takes up the theme of visions and revelations and lays claim to a high degree of such experiences (12:1–7), even though he declines to justify his apostolic authority on that basis. In chapters 10, 11, and 12, he explains his view of "boasting." He is ready—paradoxically—to boast of that "weakness" that, by aligning him with Christ's death, brings him to experience the power of the resurrection. The "thorn in his flesh" and further "weaknesses" (whether physical or otherwise) fail then to serve as evidence that he is powerlessly under the dominion of Satan's angel (12:7) and cannot count as a true apostle.[22]

Some words of summary are now in order. Our passage may be paraphrased as follows: the power that is both effective and manifested in the resurrection of the crucified Christ reaches its fulfillment for the apostle (not in ecstatic experiences but) in diverse "weaknesses." When in this sense Paul becomes and appears weak, he is in fact strong and effective in his ministry (see 10:4).

III

We are now in a position to take up the three questions posed at the start of this chapter. If we plan to arrive at conclusions by merely counting heads, then we would agree with Bultmann that Paul intends to state a general principle in the words "power is made perfect in weakness." According to Wilckens, the apostle formulates here a "thesis" that expresses the experience of "the Christian" as such.[23] Schmithals suggests that in 2 Corinthians 12:5–10 Paul "wants to be understood only as a type of correct Christian existence."[24] Windisch speaks of "the law" by which "divine power if it is to enjoy its greatest effect requires an organ afflicted by weakness."[25] Karl Prümm describes as a "universally valid law" the statement that "power passes only through weakness."[26] Heinz-Dietrich Wendland agrees,[27] as does Käsemann, who writes, "Every kind of service to Christ is governed by the law formulated by Paul in 2 Corinthians 12:9, namely, that God's power manifests itself only in the experience of temptation and in those who undergo it."[28]

In the face of this widespread agreement, it may appear brave or perhaps foolhardy to deny that Paul wishes to enunciate a general principle of divine law valid for all Christians. But the following reasons convince me that his affirmation of power in weakness bear first and foremost on his own situation. The primary meeting intended is, "my power is made perfect in your [second-person singular] weakness." (This is not, of course, to deny our right to *apply* the apostle's words to the lives of other Christians.)

In 2 Corinthians 12:1–10 and subsequently Paul consistently speaks of himself—his visions, his "thorn in the flesh," his prayer to the Lord, the reply he received, his "boasting" about the "weaknesses" he endures, his being forced to play the fool (v. 11), and the signs that accompanied his stay in Corinth (v. 12). The "general law" view supposes that in the midst of such autobiographical reflections Paul throws in a principle about the life of Christians as such, a principle that he (confusingly) repeats in the first-person singular ("whenever I am weak, then I am strong"). Windisch, who explains these words, along with the previous enunciation ("power is brought to fulfillment in weakness"), as generally valid gnomic principles, point to the use of "the present tense as well as the lack of a *mou* with *dunamis*."[29] There is, however, no real cause to read some "gnomic" value into the present tense of *teleitai*. It would be surprising to find another tense in the explanatory statement that follows the words "my grace is sufficient for you." The absence of a *mou* with *dunamis* (at least in the better reading) can scarcely prove significant, since "power" functions here synonymously with "my grace" and will be used personally in the second half of the verse ("that the power of Christ may dwell in me," v. 9b).

Furthermore, verse 9a exhibits a chiastic structure (ABC, CBA) which presumably operates to tie the second half more closely with the first half and thus render its meaning personal: A (*arkei*), B (*soi*), C (*he charis mou*); C (*he gar dunamis*), B (*en astheneia*), A (*teleitai*). "My grace" must be understood with respect to Paul's own person, especially if we accept Käsemann's suggestion that *charis* is here used in the particular sense of Paul's *charisma* as an apostle, that specific grace calling Paul to his ministry.[30] What concerns Paul in 12:9a is his own apostleship, not other *charismata*. Elsewhere he lists and reflects on various *charismata*; in 2 Corinthians he lists the "weaknesses" that mark his own apostolic existence.

Finally, we can appeal to Betz's conclusion that in 12:9a we find not "an oracle" directed to a community but "an oracle of healing directed to his [Paul's] person."[31] This conclusion would seem to rule out the "general law" interpretation of the verse.

If we move out of the immediate context in chapter 12, does this interpretation find support elsewhere in the Corinthian correspondence? Windisch refers us to 2 Corinthians 4:7 and 1 Corinthians 1:25-27.[32] When setting out in 2 Corinthians 4:7-12 the forms of "weakness" that affect his apostolic ministry, Paul contrasts himself with other Christians. "Death works" in him to the spiritual gain of the community (4:12). In 1 Corinthians 1:25-27 those who believed at Paul's preaching are styled the "weak in the world" (v. 27), but not in the sense of "weakness" in 2 Corinthians 12 (the sufferings of the apostolic ministry). In 1 Corinthians 1:26-28 "weakness" indicates the social unimportance that attaches to lowly born, ignorant nobodies (vv. 26-28). Power belongs to God's (apparent) weakness (v. 25) and to Paul's message delivered in "weakness" (1 Cor 2:3-4). In 1 Corinthians 1:25-28 we do not find Paul stating, "When you were (are) weak, then you were (are) strong."

Our second question touches the link Paul supposes to exist between weakness and power. What kind of logic governs this connection? Some exegetes join Windisch in maintaining that the existence of weakness along with the humble confession of this weakness provides the necessary *condition* for the bestowal of divine strength. Thus Plummer comments on 2 Corinthians 12:9, "The Lord's reply convinced the apostle that this grievous affliction would not hinder his work; he may even have been convinced that it was a condition of success."[33] Hans Lietzmann's paraphrase shows close agreement with this interpretation: "Through this word of the Lord I have received the comforting assurance that my weaknesses are a pre-condition for my success."[34] Robert C. Tannehill explains that the weakness contributes by preventing "man" (!) from confusing the divine strength with his own strength and attempting to rely on his own resources:

"Power Made Perfect in Weakness"

> The continuing weakness is necessary so that man might not confuse the power of God with his own power and lose God's power by attempting to rely on himself. Through 12:7–10 we see that Paul views the participation in Christ's weakness mentioned in 13:4 not only as contrasting with participation in the power of his resurrection, but also as contributing to participation in that power.[35]

Those who favor such an explanation of apostolic weakness almost inevitably slip into psychological considerations and the theme of Paul's moral education. He is taught by experience and learns the lesson of patience. Windisch reflects that "according to vs. 10a being strong is the patience with which he [Paul] bears all suffering, the energy with which in spite of all obstacles he performs his work."[36]

How do we evaluate this view that Paul is in effect saying, "When I am weak, that is the precondition of my becoming strong"? This view may command some respect, but it merits dissent. Paul's words both in 2 Corinthians 12:9–10 and elsewhere indicate the *simultaneity* of weakness and power. When he was with the Corinthians "in weakness and in much fear and trembling," his "message" was characterized by "the Spirit and…power" (1 Cor 2:3–4). As his statements stand, Paul simply asserts the coincidence of weakness and power, not that one element occurs as a precondition to the other. The psychological trend in interpretation can distract us from the christological setting in which Paul sees his ministry. Far more important than any moral education he undergoes is the fact that his apostolic activity involves participation in the weakness and power of Calvary and Easter.

Third and last, we reach the question, Do Paul's statements about power and weakness concern primarily the role of "ontological" reality? Or perhaps he wishes first to assert something about the revelatory function of "weakness": "when I am weak, then I am aware of being strong and others are aware of my being strong." We have already noted that Plummer and Bultmann favor such a "revelatory" explanation for 2 Corinthians 12:9–10. So too does Güttgemans, who repeatedly chooses the word *epiphany* in his reflections on this passage. The "apostolic weakness," he explains, should be understood as the "epiphany of the divine power of the Crucified One." Commenting on *episkēnōsē*, Güttgemans declares, "The motif conveyed by this rare word has its origin in the Jewish language of revelation and meant there the epiphany of the divine glory."[37]

Betz likewise describes Paul's "weakness" as "an epiphany of the crucified *Kyrios*."[38]

However, it seems to me that such an interpretation of our passage can be reached only by tampering with the text. Various "weaknesses" intervene to cause suffering in his apostolic activity. The risen Christ reassures his servant that his triumphant power reaches its perfection in the situation of "weakness." Power is given (in fullness) even as "a thorn in the flesh" comes to change Paul's situation. The upshot is something in the order of revelation. The divine coming with power leads to the "epiphany" of this powerful presence. This point emerges clearly in chapter 4 of 2 Corinthians, where Paul explains that his sufferings occur "so that the life of Jesus may also be visible in our bodies" (v. 10). The apostle's "boasting" serves to bring to the notice of others the victorious power at work in his sufferings: "on my behalf I will not boast, except of my weaknesses" (2 Cor 12:5; see 11:30). Ultimately what I am suggesting is the reverse of Werner Kümmel's position: "human weakness is precisely the place where Christ's glory reveals itself, and where it alone is visible and effective."[39] Paul's weakness remains first of all a transaction between himself and his risen Lord, and then plays a role in the apostolic transmission of revelation. Christ's triumphant power is "effective" in the concrete circumstances of Paul's life, and hence it is visibly revealed.

18

POWER IN WEAKNESS

The Fate of a First Love (2 Cor 12:9–10)

The Second Letter of Paul to the Corinthians arguably reaches its highpoint with the words,

> But he [the Lord] said to me, "My grace is sufficient for you, for [my] power is made perfect in weakness." So, I will boast all the more gladly of my weaknesses, so that the power of Christ may dwell in me. Therefore I am content with weaknesses, insults, hardships, persecutions, and calamities for the sake of Christ; for whenever I am weak, then I am strong. (2 Cor 12:9–10)

For five years after finishing my doctorate at the University of Cambridge in 1968, I lectured on the letters of St. Paul and taught fundamental theology as well. It was then that I published "Power Made Perfect in Weakness: 2 Cor 12:9–10."[1] My central argument could be summarized as follows. Various "weaknesses" have intervened to make Paul suffer in his apostolic activity. But then the risen Christ reassures the apostle that his triumphant power reaches its perfection in Paul's very experience of "weakness." Power has been given in fullness even as a mysterious "thorn in the flesh" has changed Paul's situation. The divine coming with power results in an "epiphany" of this powerful presence. The apostle's "boasting" brings to the notice of others what is victoriously at work in his sufferings. Christ's grace, defined as power, is effective right in Paul's "weakness" and hence can be revealed.[2]

From 1973, departmental requirements required that I confine myself to lecturing in fundamental and systematic theology. After retiring from full-time teaching, I have been freed to return even more to my first love, the inspired Scriptures, on which I had in any rate continued to publish. As an Italian proverb states, *Il primo amore non si scorda mai* (One's first love never comes apart). I have been enabled to publish scriptural articles in *Biblica*, *The Expository Times*, and other journals. Now, fifty years later, I would like to revisit what I wrote about Christ's power in Paul's weakness back in 1971.

I am encouraged to do so by recalling what Hans-Georg Gadamer and others have proposed about texts gaining a life of their own. Once published, they distance themselves from their authors and have a life of their own as they gain readers and interpreters.[3] How has my 1971 article been read and evaluated? Some writers have done so, albeit briefly; others have commented at greater length.

Minimal References

The minimum achievement we might expect for one of our publications is that it will make its way into the appropriate bibliographies. My 1971 article found its place in the pericope list, themes list, and alphabetical list published in *2 Corinthians: A Bibliography*.[4] In *2 Corinthians: Baker Exegetical Commentary on the New Testament*, George H. Guthrie included the article under "Works Cited,"[5] but it was not in fact cited, let alone discussed, in the course of his commentary.

Jerome Murphy-O'Connor introduces my article in a minimal fashion. After making a useful remark about "grace" being "defined as power" in 2 Corinthians 12:9a, he simply recalls in general terms how I wrote about the relationship between power and weakness being "diversely interpreted." He himself makes a useful suggestion about the relationship: "Weakness is the condition that the power shown" in Paul's ministry "may be recognized as of divine origin."[6] This correctly implies that, if Paul's ministry had shown power but not a power revealing itself in the midst of "weaknesses," we would remain uncertain about the divine origin of the power that Paul displayed. The power at work in the apostle's ministry could have been ascribed to a merely human origin in his natural endowments.

Michael L. Barré (1980)

As far as I can establish, the earliest scholar to discuss my article was Michael Barré in an article published by the same journal in 1980. He accepted my proposal about detecting a chiasm in the original Greek of 2 Corinthians 12:9a.[7] This meant recognizing that "my grace" and "power" function synonymously; "power" means "my power"[8]—that is to say, the risen Lord's power rather than God's power, although, of course, they can only be distinguished and never separated.

I had joined many others in reading *teleitai* (rather than *teleioutai*)[9] and translating the verb as "is made perfect." While *teleioutai* frequently means "is made perfect," *teleitai* can also have this meaning, as the *Greek-English Lexicon of the New Testament and Other Early Christian Literature* proposes: "Power finds its consummation or reaches perfection in (the presence of) weakness."[10] Barré made the interesting observation, however, that we "cannot properly speak of his [God's] power being made perfect." He suggested the translation "is accomplished."[11] This resembles the translation offered by Ralph P. Martin (see below), "is fulfilled."[12] All these translations ("is made perfect," "reaches perfection," "is accomplished," and "is fulfilled") allow the priority of Christ's power to emerge: that power is effectively deployed in situations of "weakness" and, then, this paradoxical situation is revealed as such through Paul's "boasting."

Victor Paul Furnish (1984)

The jacket drawing for Victor Furnish's *II Corinthians: A New Translation with Introduction and Commentary* features 2 Corinthians 12:9—a way of drawing attention at once to the centrality of the power-in-weakness theme.[13] Commenting on that verse, Furnish refers to my article as if it supports understanding that Paul "calls attention to his weaknesses *in order that* Christ's power can become effective" and not "just recognized."[14] In fact, I argued the opposite sequence: Paul calls attention to his "weaknesses," in which Christ's power, *already* at work and effective in these sufferings of the apostle's life and ministry, can be revealed and recognized.

Curiously, Furnish himself seems to have already said just that: first the operation of powerful grace and then its revelation and recognition. He has rightly observed that the oracle of Christ (which he translates as "my grace is enough for you, for power is made fully present in weakness") has directed the apostle "to understand his affliction as part of that weakness in and through which God's powerful grace is operative." As a result, Paul's "weaknesses" have become 'a means by which the incomparable power of God is revealed.'"[15]

Then Furnish makes the unconvincing claim that Paul "boasts of his weaknesses," including "the thorn in the flesh," "because now he understands them not as Satan's work but as the operation of the grace of the crucified Christ." Furnish concludes the section by repeating this interpretation: "The weaknesses which continue to characterize his life as an apostle...represent the effective working of the power of the crucified Christ in his ministry."[16] Rather, that grace that constitutes the power of Christ, while victoriously operating right in the sphere of Paul's sufferings, is not aimed at causing them. Others, including "an angel of Satan" (2 Cor 12:7), are responsible for bringing those hardships into Paul's life and ministry.

To be sure, Paul has written, "A thorn was given [*edothē*] me in the flesh" (2 Cor 12:7), which seems to be a divine passive and imply "given to me by God." Martin is more circumspect in describing this divine causality: "God has given Paul something to keep him weak."[17] "Has given" should be understood here as the divine permissive will: God has allowed this to happen.

Or else the passive (*edothē*), as happens commonly with the passive voice, is aimed at maintaining the focus on a subject who has already been named: here, Paul himself.[18] In that case any question about the agent ("given" by whom?) recedes further into the background.

Jan Lambrecht (1986)

Two years after Furnish's commentary appeared, Jan Lambrecht took up my contribution in the course of an article, which he originally published in 1986 and reprinted in 1994: "The *Nekrōsis* of Jesus: Ministry and Suffering in 2 Corinthians 4:7–15."[19]

Lambrecht quotes approvingly my summary conclusion on 2 Corinthians 12:9: "Christ's triumphant power is effective in the concrete circumstances of Paul's life and hence it is visibly revealed."[20] This leads Lambrecht to detect a paradoxical relation between divine power and human weakness. But "the paradox is not absolute," since Paul did not claim that weakness *is* power but rather that this power is effective in human weakness.[21] While I wrote of the paradox involved in associating "weakness" and "power,"[22] I recognize now that the words used by Paul could be rightly described as proposing what might be called a nonabsolute paradox.

Ulrich Heckel (1993)

In a study that appeared in *Wissenschaftliche Untersuchungen zum Neuem Testament* (*WUNT*), Ulrich Heckel cited my article in support of what he stated at the start of the introduction: "Nowhere in the Pauline letters do we meet the association of power and weakness so pointed as in the Lord's word in 2 Corinthians 12:9a."[23] Heckel went on to recognize the chiastic structure of this verse, without noting that I had already drawn attention to this chiasm and its significance.[24] Let me cite three of the passages in which Heckel picked up points made in my article.

First, he joins me in rejecting any notion that Paul is saying that weakness "is the precondition of my becoming strong."[25] Heckel dismisses this view as a "misunderstanding" and makes the point even more firmly: weakness "cannot be an indispensable presupposition for the power of Christ to be become effective."[26] The exercise of Christ's power does not presuppose any such indispensable precondition.

Second, Heckel approves of my confronting the revelatory function of weakness with an ontological understanding of the situation. "In the Pauline theology, without acknowledging at the same time their own weakness, human beings cannot recognize the effectiveness of Christ's power."[27] Acknowledging weakness goes hand in hand with that power being revealed effectively at work and recognized as such.

Third, while he missed in my article any treatment of the problematic nature of the paradox found in 2 Corinthians 12:9–10, Heckel praised me for raising "the decisive question about the logical relation of power and weakness." "He [O'Collins] rightly emphasizes the simultaneous coincidence [of weakness and power] and weakness as the place and concrete situation in which the power of Christ is effective."[28]

Margaret E. Thrall (2000)

In her International Critical Commentary on 2 Corinthians, Margaret Thrall, apropos of "the correlation of weakness and divine power," queries my speaking of "a simultaneous experience" and proposes rather a certain "consequence." The apostle Paul understands the weaknesses "to allow the power of Christ to rest upon me." Thus the sequence would be weaknesses, power of Christ, and Paul's revelatory "boasting," which "is the cause, not of the indwelling of Christ's power in itself, but of its *being seen* to reside in him."[29] Thus "it is the visibility of Christ's power that is the purpose or the consequence of Paul's boasting."[30] Thrall's way of interpreting 2 Corinthians 12:9–10, despite Heckel's endorsement of my original proposal, may give it greater precision.

Before leaving Thrall's commentary, I am grateful for Thrall's support when holding (against Rudolf Bultmann and others, including Ralph Martin) that "the first person singular" in our two verses is "the apostolic 'I.'" Paul's "personal weakness" "commends him as a proven apostle." In short, "he is not concerned with the application to all believers of his own claim to be strong in conditions of weakness."[31]

In a footnote Thrall defends my article against Martin's criticism that, unless 2 Corinthians 12:9a and 10b are "intended to be related to all Christians," "Paul would be nurturing an 'elitist idea' of himself." Thrall insists that "Paul does suppose himself to possess unique authority in relation to the church in Corinth, whether or not that is 'elitist' in modern terms."[32]

Martin believes that I "undercut" my position by admitting "that Christians have the right to apply Paul's words of 2 Corinthians 12:9 to their lives."[33] But I had made it quite clear what remains "the primary meaning": Christ's power is made perfect in the weakness of one individual, Paul. I added (in brackets) that I did not want to deny anyone's right to apply the verse to their own lives.[34] It is hard to see this as undercutting my position on the primary meaning.

Murray J. Harris (2005)

Just over twenty years after Furnish's commentary appeared and five years after Thrall's commentary, Murray J. Harris proved both accurate and also creative in what he gleaned from my 1971 article for another large commentary, *The Second Epistle to the Corinthians*.[35] Let me select and discuss two issues.

First, he quotes me over what he agrees to term the "simultaneity" of power and weakness. Power and weakness are "related not only by succession—first weakness, then power"—"but also by simultaneity." It is "in the midst of weakness that Christ's power reaches its plenitude." Consequently "weakness" is "the sphere where his power is revealed. It is precisely when or whenever Paul is weak that he experiences Christ's power (v. 10b)." Harris concludes that weakness "is both a prerequisite and a concomitant of Christ's power."[36] I had written of a "coincidence" between the apostle's weakness and Christ's power.[37]

But then Harris imposes *without qualification* a condition that I do not find in Paul: "His [Christ's] enabling strength cannot operate without a prior confession of weakness and need. If self-sufficiency is claimed, his power will be neither sought and granted."[38] To begin with, we face here what is more or less a tautology: those who claim to be self-sufficient, almost by definition will not seek the power of Christ. Then—and this is much more important—in what the Lord says to Paul ("my power[39] is made perfect in your weakness"), we do *not* find the Lord saying, "My power can operate and be made perfect in your weakness, *only if* you have previously confessed your weakness and need." Yet Harris introduces the notion that "the acknowledgment of 'weakness' is a precondition for the exercise of Christ's power."[40] Such a comment does not concur with Paul's widely attested insistence on the priority that belongs to the action of Christ's (or God's) powerful grace and not to our acknowledging weakness or anything else (e.g., Gal 1:15–16).

In a footnote[41] Harris suggests a certain "proportionality": "the greater the acknowledged weakness, the more evident Christ's power." This is close to a tautology. The more Paul acknowledges his weakness and Christ's power operating in it, the more evident to others will that human weakness and divine power become. In short, if the weakness and power are acknowledged, then they will become evident. I would be reluctant to attribute such a quasi-tautology to the apostle.

In his text Harris turns from highlighting as primary what is a matter of divine *revelation* and human knowledge (becoming "more evident") to recognizing the primacy of what is a matter of action: Christ's power "*operates* at the same time as the weakness" and "finds *unhindered scope* in the presence of that weakness." Harris imagines the risen Lord saying to Paul, "My risen power finds its *full scope* and potency in your acknowledged weakness." Weakness can become "the place where Christ's power realizes its *full potential*."[42] We might allow for a certain "proportionality" in the action of the risen Lord—a "being made perfect" that admits of degrees. By confessing, accepting, and even "boasting" of his "weakness," Paul allows Christ's power, *already* at work in "the sphere" of the apostle's weakness, to operate with full scope and potency, "reach its plenitude," and "realize its full potential."

Second, Harris not only accepted my proposal to detect a chiasm in the original Greek of 2 Corinthians 12:9a[43] but also, ignoring Plummer, Heckel, and others, apparently credited me with being the only[44] commentator to make that observation. He also concurred with my comment that "'power' functions here synonymously with 'my grace.'"[45] Hence, in his words, "power" and "grace" are "essentially synonymous" in this chiasm.[46]

Harris goes further by recognizing how both power and grace are "renewable endowments, not once-and-for-all acquisitions; the constancy of the supply of *charis* and *dunamis* is implied by the presents of *arkei* [is sufficient] and *teleitai* [reaches perfection]."[47] Wallace would categorize such examples of the present tense among the large class of the "broad-band presents," in particular, "iterative presents" or events that can or do repeatedly happen.[48] The Lord has already acted to supply divine grace and power to Paul in his situation of "weakness," and that action can continue to occur.

Ralph P. Martin (1986, 2014)

Although its first edition appeared in 1986, Ralph Martin's *2 Corinthians* appeared in 2014 in a second edition that incorporated some significant changes and additions.[49] When recognizing in 1 Corinthians 12:9a the presence of "a chiastic structure," he duly refers to what had already been published on this by Plummer, myself, and another, Josef

Zmijewski.[50] Martin paid more detailed attention to my article than other biblical scholars. He did so in seven different ways.

First, he questioned my observation that 2 Corinthians 12:9 constitutes "the only words of the risen Christ we find in Paul's letters,"[51] by referring to the Lord's words from the Last Supper cited in 1 Corinthians 11:23–26. But we are dealing in that latter passage with a tradition the apostle received, and Martin accepts that, unlike 2 Corinthians 12:9, we are not dealing with "direct speech."[52]

Second, he agrees with me and others that "the power" in 2 Corinthians 12:9b is "the power of Christ" and accepts, accordingly, the translation "for [my] power is fulfilled in weakness."[53] This means that, along with others, I am also correct in understanding in this context as synonyms "grace" and "power."[54]

Third, as we saw above when presenting Thrall's reflections, Martin notes that I disagree with Bultmann and others by denying that 2 Corinthians 12:9 contains "a general principle for Christians concerning weakness," a "law regarding Christian service."[55] The "oracle" reported by that verse "was directed at Paul and not the community." Martin wonders, however, "whether Paul would want to be understood like this. More likely he would not accept this exclusivist interpretation, for it would make him out as somebody special."[56] Nevertheless, we may not argue that Paul would never make himself "out as somebody special." He does just that when claiming a special role as an apostolic witness to the risen Lord: "Am I not an apostle? Have I not seen Jesus our Lord?" (1 Cor 9:1; see 15:8). As I argued, the primary reference of the oracle (2 Cor 12:9) is to Paul alone; readers may want to "apply" to themselves what the Lord says to Paul about power being made perfect in weakness.

Fourth, at the time when I wrote my article, some scholars were still overready to bring in Gnostic explanations, interpreting, for instance, Paul's choice of *teleitai* as a "deliberate anti-Gnostic polemic." I spent a page arguing against such an interpretation and showed a preference for the view developed by Dieter Georgi and others: "Paul's opponents in 2 Cor were Jewish-Christian missionaries." I added, "There is no need to credit supposed Gnostics with having monopolized the insight that *dunamis* and *astheneia* seem mutually exclusive. We hardly weaken the paradox which Paul wishes to assert if we take ordinary usage—and not more or less elaborate Gnostic hypotheses—as the background to his statement."[57] Martin agrees and adds a further argument: "Paul was not consciously responding to the Gnostics in this emotional and intimate passage under study. What can be said is that the fulfillment of God's power comes not in heavenly visions and ecstatic demonstrations, but in earthly weakness."[58]

Fifth, I had pointed out firmly that "Paul understands his 'weakness' Christologically."[59] Martin agrees and presses the ontological and revelatory (my adjectives) case for interpreting christologically what has been "done," "fulfilled," and "completed," on the one hand, and "seen," "manifested," and "displayed," on the other.[60]

Sixth, I had spotted a certain "Pelagian" tendency in what two commentators (Hans Windisch and R. H. Strahan) said about "the humble confession of weakness" constituting "a pre-condition for the communication of the divine power."[61] Martin believes that I "may be right in spotting a Pelagian tendency."[62] Both of us spoke of a "tendency," not straight-out Pelagianism.

Seventh, Martin summarizes accurately my central argument about the sequence in what the Lord does and reveals: "The ontological reality of the gift of power leads to an 'epiphany' of this presence. Possibly O'Collins sums up best the role that weakness played in Paul's life."[63]

Obviously, it is gratifying to find this measure of agreement between what I wrote in 1971 and what the latest substantial commentary on 2 Corinthians (Martin's revised edition of 2014) proposes. How might we sum up the fate of my article after its initial publication in 1971? What lessons might we draw from the life it led on its own for nearly fifty years?

Conclusions

To a degree, my 1971 article has served to assess those who responded to it. The various ways in which major commentators reacted to my article illustrates the superiority of Thrall, Harris, and Martin over Furnish. But many scholars would already make such a judgment on other grounds. They do not depend on my article to do so.

I welcome such additions as the reminder from Martin that Plummer had long ago remarked on the chiastic structure of 2 Corinthians 12:9. Furthermore, Furnish and Martin recalled the need to clarify the force of the passive in 2 Corinthians 12:7, "I was given." Harris added the significance of the use of the present tense in "my grace is sufficient for you" and "[my] power is made perfect in weakness." On both these issues, I have been able to bring into play the magisterial observations on Greek grammar made by Daniel Wallace.

A firm endorsement of my article came from Ulrich Heckel. This may have been partly due to the fact that, although I wrote in English, I engaged in dialogue with ten books and one article that had appeared in German (which were familiar territory to him) and with only four books that had appeared in English.

It was satisfying to have Thrall on my side in maintaining, against Martin and others, that Paul does not propose "power in weakness" as a general "law regarding Christian service." Paul cites not some "general principle," but an oracle of the Lord concerned with his own apostolic mission.

At the same time, I am grateful to Martin for putting so clearly the issue my article faced: "Did Paul see weakness as a means of revealing a power already present in him, or is weakness the door through which comes the power of Christ?"[64] The significance of this and related questions raised by 2 Corinthians 12:9–10 has made it personally worthwhile revisiting my "first love."

EPILOGUE

The eighteen chapters that make up this book have aimed at throwing light on New Testament passages concerned with four areas: the nativity of Jesus Christ; the proclamation of the divine kingdom embodied in his ministry of preaching and miracles; his death, burial, resurrection appearances, and impact of his risen existence; and three central themes found in Paul's preaching of salvation.

First, chapter 7 explored Luke's account of the annunciation to Mary and the meaningful links the evangelist made to Simeon's welcoming the Christ child when presented in the temple. Chapter 8 examined ways in which Luke's nativity story prefigures what was to come at Jesus's death and resurrection. Christian painters and spiritual writers have led the way by appreciating the shadow that Calvary cast over the birth in Bethlehem.

Second, chapters 1—3 took up themes from the ministry of Jesus, illustrating the full significance of the healing of Peter's mother-in-law and images that Jesus drew from farming and domestic activities. His miraculous deeds and preaching revealed his identity and role in the divine kingdom that was coming into the world.

Third, chapters 4—6, 9—13, and 16 moved to questions concerned with the burial of Jesus, the discovery of his empty tomb, his postresurrection appearances, the Easter witness of Mary Magdalene and Peter, and the experience of the risen Lord in Christian life and proclamation. These chapters set themselves to answer such questions as the following: Did Joseph of Arimathea bury Jesus (all four Gospels)? What led the three women to flee in silent terror from the tomb of Jesus (Mark 16:8)? Did the Easter appearances involve some kind of seeing on the part of the witnesses (1 Cor 15:5–8)? What meaning was conveyed by the risen Christ eating some fish (Luke 24:42–43)?

A final cluster of chapters (14, 15, and 17—18) investigate the message of Paul about our reconciliation with God, the love at the heart of Christian existence, and the "power made perfect in the weakness" of Paul. These chapters establish the need to be alert to different nuances in the language of reconciliation, the verbal nature of love, and the priority of the divine grace in the apostle's ministry.

It is my hope that this exposition of passages from the Gospels, the Acts of the Apostles, and the letters of Paul will serve an attentive reading of the New Testament and promote a richer appropriation of its good news.

NOTES

Preface

1. F. Bovon, *Luke*, vol. 3, trans. J. E. Crouch (Grand Rapids: Fortress Press, 2012), 355.

1. From the Weather to Mustard Seeds

1. On *tektōn*, see Walter Bauer, Frederick W. Danker, William F. Arndt, and F. Wilbur Gingrich, *Greek-English Lexicon of the New Testament and Other Early Christian Literature*, 3rd ed. (Chicago: University of Chicago Press, 2000), 995; hereafter *BDAG*.

2. *BDAG*, 429.

3. S. Freyne, *Jesus, A Jewish Galilean: A New Reading of the Jesus Story* (London: T&T Clark, 2004), 59.

4. On *ombros* (rainstorm or thunderstorm), *votos*, and *kausōn*, see *BDAG*, 705, 679, and 536, respectively.

5. On reasons for holding the verses in square brackets to be a later gloss, see Ulrich Luz, *Matthew 8—20*, trans. James E. Crouch (Minneapolis: Fortress Press, 2001), 347. F. Bovon, however, accepts these verses as authentic; see *Luke: A Commentary*, vol. 1, trans. Donald S. Deer (Minneapolis: Fortress Press, 2013), 256. The United Bible Societies' Greek New Testament (4th rev. ed.) retains Matthew 16:2–3 but encloses the verses within square brackets: see Bruce M. Metzger, *A Textual Commentary on the Greek New Testament* (Stuttgart: Deutsche Bibelgesellschaft, 1994), 33.

6. Matthew and, before him, Jesus are both echoed by popular wisdom: "Red sky at night, sailors' delight; red sky at morning, sailors

take warning." An alternate, also popular, version offers the wisdom gleaned, not from traveling by sea, but from sheep farming: "Red sky at night, shepherds' delight; red sky at morning, shepherds take warning."

    7. Bovon offers plausible reasons for recognizing how Luke adapted the saying as he received it from the tradition (*Luke*, vol. 2, trans. Christine M. Thomas [Minneapolis: Fortress Press, 2013], 256).

    8. Bovon, *Luke*, 2:248.

    9. Luz, *Matthew 8—20*, 103.

    10. Bovon, *Luke*, 2:181.

    11. On *epilanthanomai* (forget), see *BDAG*, 374, which puts Luke 12:6 under the heading of "to be inattentive to, neglect, overlook, care nothing about," and proposes the translation "not one of them has escaped God's notice."

    12. Bovon, *Luke*, 2:181.

    13. Luz, *Matthew 8—20*, 103.

    14. Luz, *Matthew 8—20*, 103.

    15. Some ancient texts read "donkey" rather than "child." But this seems a later alteration to make the verse conform to Luke 13:15 ("Does not each of you on the sabbath untie his ox or his donkey from the manger and lead it away to give it water?"). Or, as Metzger proposes, copyists found it "somewhat incongruous" to link "son" and "ox," and altered "son" to "donkey" or to "sheep" (as in Matt 12:11): *Textual Commentary on the Greek New Testament*, 138–39. The two cases (of an ox and a son) may have arisen from an original saying of Jesus (in Aramaic) that spoke only of a single "beast of burden"; see Bovon, *Luke* 2:346n49.

    16. Bovon, *Luke*, 2:345-46. In Matthew's version, the "only one sheep" that falls into a pit suggests something particularly precious to a poor farmer; on Matt 12:11, see Luz, *Matthew 8—20*, 187-88.

    17. Bovon, *Luke*, 2:346.

    18. Bovon, *Luke*, 2:288-89.

    19. Bovon, *Luke*, 2:294. In the words of Jesus from Luke 13:18-19, "What is the kingdom of God like? And to what should I compare it? It is like a mustard seed that someone took and sowed in the garden; it grew and became a tree, and the birds of the air took shelter in its branches" (NRSV corrected). Bovon thinks that Luke (and Matthew) draw this parable from Q, rather than from Mark, with Luke preserving "the wording better than Matthew," except for the seed being "sowed in his garden." That can give the impression of a town or village; Matthew's "in the field" seems original and corresponds to the way mustard bushes

grew in fields, not gardens (*Luke*, 2:295). Like Bovon, Luz agrees that Jesus chose and presented the image of the mustard seed to his "original hearers," but argues that the black mustard (the one in question) was "probably planted in the garden" (*Matthew 8—20*, 261).

20. See *BDAG*, "*kataskēnoō*," 527, which prefers "to nest" rather than "to take shelter in."

21. Luz, *Matthew 8—20*, 261.

22. Bovon, *Luke*, 2:298–99.

23. Luz, *Matthew 8—20*, 261. The version of the parable found in Mark and then in Matthew suggests that the "mustard plant was chosen as the central image for the parable not because it was not a cedar but because it was so well adapted to the contrast between small beginnings and large outcomes." The "mustard plant, with its large branches, is bigger than all the other shrubs, and immensely larger than the tiny seed from which it starts" (Joel Marcus, *Mark 1—8* [New York: Doubleday, 2000], 324).

2. Peter's Mother-in-Law

1. D. E. Nineham, *Saint Mark* (London: Penguin, 1992; orig. 1963), 80–81. Nineham distinguishes between exorcism and other forms of sickness as relevant to Peter's mother-in-law being healed. This distinction has been challenged by John G. Cook, "In Defense of Ambiguity: Is There a Hidden Demon in Mark 1:29–31?" who shows how Mark and/or his audience could have assigned demonic as well as other causes to illness: *New Testament Studies* 43 (1997): 184–208.

2. Nineham, *Saint Mark*, 80–81.

3. Significantly it is in relation to Peter that a young *paidiskē* of the high priest is brought into the story at the end, just as an older, also anonymous, woman enters the story as Peter's mother-in-law at the beginning.

4. Is she a widow? There is no reference to her husband, Peter's father-in-law. She lives in a house seemingly owned by the two brothers, Simon Peter and Andrew; there is no reference to their parents (dead or living) here or elsewhere. Peter's mother-in-law appears to run the household and would be expected to show hospitality to any guests. The silence about Peter's wife has led some to imagine that at this point he was a widower and married again later (see 1 Cor 9:5).

5. S. Miller, *Women in Mark's Gospel* (London: T&T Clark, 2004), 2.

6. M. E. Boring notes that "now restored to the fullness of life," she "can serve guests in her own home, which she had been prevented from doing by the devastating fever" (*Mark: A Commentary* [Louisville, KY: Westminster John Knox Press, 2006], 66). This observation stops short of noting how she is the only person cured by Jesus in Mark's Gospel who then does something for him (and his disciples). As Miller writes, "It is the only narrative in which a human being responds to Jesus' healing with service" (*Women in Mark's Gospel*, 22; see 30). Bartimaeus is a kind of exception here; after he is cured, he does something for Jesus by following him "on the road" to crucifixion and resurrection (Mark 10:52). He differs, of course, from Peter's mother-in-law in that it is he who informs Jesus of his situation (blindness) and asks for healing.

7. Miller, *Women in Mark's Gospel*, 29.

8. Mary Ann Tolbert comments, "The author of Mark, by using the same word for the action of angels and the action of the healed woman, obviously equated their level of service to Jesus" ("Mark," in Carol A. Newsom and Sharon H. Ringe, eds., *The Women's Bible Commentary* [Louisville, KY: Westminster John Knox Press, 1992], 263–74, at 267). Tolbert also notes how Peter's mother-in-law is "the first women to appear in the Gospel of Mark" (267) but does not acknowledge how she is the only person cured by Jesus in that Gospel who then does something for him.

9. To relate the use of "serve" in various contexts does not entail assigning it a monolithic meaning but rather noting similar, overlapping usages and meanings.

10. J. R. Donahue and D. J. Harrington, *The Gospel of Mark* (Collegeville, MN: Liturgical Press, 2002), 85.

11. Boring, *Mark*, 66.

12. Nineham, *Saint Mark*, 81.

13. C. Focant, *The Gospel according to Mark*, trans. Leslie Robert Keylock (Eugene, OR: Pickwick Publications, 2012), 72.

14. The word order in Nineham's translation also parallels a general rule in Greek: "the aorist participle is normally, though by no means always, *antecedent* in time to the action of the main verb" (Daniel B. Wallace, *Greek Grammar beyond the Basics: An Exegetical Syntax of the New Testament* [Grand Rapids: Zondervan, 1996], 624; my italics).

15. Focant, *Gospel according to Mark*, 71, 72. Focant does not specify the adverbial function of the aorist participle *kratēsas* (here indicating

Notes

the means, "by grasping"), but such specification would not affect his argument, which is concerned with word order, not function; see Wallace, *Greek Grammar*, 614–15.

16. Foçant observes more accurately that "there is no explicit request for healing, contrary to the usual practice in the miracle narratives. There is at the very most a secret hope, an indirect request that is translated by speaking to Jesus about the ill person" (*Gospel according to Mark*, 72). Boring even thinks that the disciples "tell Jesus of her malady more likely to excuse her conduct than as a request for healing—Jesus has as yet performed no healings in Mark" (*Mark*, 66).

17. F. J. Moloney, *The Gospel of Mark: A Commentary* (Peabody, MA: Hendrickson, 2002), 55.

18. Moloney, *Gospel of Mark*, 55.

19. M. D. Hooker, *The Gospel according to Mark* (London: Continuum, 2001), 70.

20. At least as old as the eighth-century BC epic poet Homer, *inclusio* is a technique for linking (for various purposes) the beginning and the end of a poem, historical work, drama, prayer, biography, or some other written work—not to mention its role in spoken performances. *Inclusio* may be used for an entire work or simply for a section of a work. We detect the presence of *inclusio* by observing the similar or even identical material (and language) found at the beginning and the end of the work or section in question.

21. Moloney, *Gospel of Mark*, 56n46.

22. Hooker, *Gospel according to Mark*, 70.

23. J. Marcus, *Mark 1—8* (New York: Doubleday, 2000), 199. Hence, while contexts differ, the "raising" of Peter's mother-in-law and the "raising" of Jesus justify associating Mark 1:41 and 16:6 and using this association as *part* of the argument for recognizing an *inclusio* (see later).

24. Marcus, *Mark 1—8*, 199.

25. Marcus, *Mark 1—8*, 73–75.

26. In other places Paul uses *diakonein* and related forms to speak of the new life of the baptized as a life of service (see, e.g., 2 Cor 3:3; 6:4; 11:8, 23).

27. D. Krause, "Simon Peter's Mother-in-Law—Disciple or Domestic Servant," in *A Feminist Companion to Mark*, ed. Amy-Jill Levine (Sheffield, UK: Sheffield Academic Press, 2001), 37–53, at 39. Krause fails to note either that Peter's mother-in-law is the first woman

to be mentioned in Mark's Gospel or that she is (with the possible exception of Bartimaeus) the only person in that Gospel who is cured by Jesus and then does something for him.

28. Krause, "Simon Peter's Mother-in-Law," 50. Peter-Ben Smit has taken issue with Krause's article: performing household tasks does not exhaust the meaning of *diakonein* in Mark 1:29–31. He finds "a very special feature of the healing" in the fact that "the story is the only one in which the healing of an ill person is followed by [a] concrete and positive response towards Jesus" ("Simon Peter's Mother-in-Law Revisited," *Lectio difficilior* 1 [2003]: 1–12). Smit sees nothing special, however, in the fact that Peter's mother-in-law is the first woman to be mentioned in Mark's Gospel.

29. See E. Schüssler Fiorenza, *In Memory of Her: A Feminist Reconstruction of Christian Origins*, rev ed. (London: SCM Press, 1994), 320–21.

30. Other commentators on Mark's Gospel (James R. Edwards, Robert T. France, Joachim Gnilka, Rudolf Pesch, Eduard Schweizer, Robert H. Stein, Mark L. Strauss, and Vincent Taylor) also fail to make any reference to her being the first woman named in the Gospel. Nor do they raise the possibility of her featuring in a significant *inclusio* between the opening and conclusion of that Gospel.

31. Adela Yarbro Collins, *Mark: A Commentary* (Minneapolis: Fortress Press, 2007), 174–75.

32. Apropos of Mark 1:31 and 15:41, Miller remarks that "Jesus' mission is framed by two references to the service of women" (*Women in Mark's Gospel*, 23), and that "the conclusion of the Gospel draws Mark's audience back to the beginning" (199). But she does not speak explicitly of an *inclusio*.

33. R. Bauckham, *Jesus and the Eyewitnesses: The Gospels as Eyewitness Testimony* (Grand Rapids: Eerdmans, 2006), 155–81.

34. Apropos of Mark 15:41, Adela Yarbro Collins comments, "The only woman that Mark portrays earlier in the narrative as serving Jesus is the mother-in-law of Simon (1:31)" (*Mark*, 774–75). This comment ignores the anonymous woman of Mark 14:3–9, who does something remarkable for Jesus even if her action is not literally called "service" and takes place in Bethany (near Jerusalem), not in Galilee. She is, however, found portrayed "earlier" in Mark's narrative.

Notes

3. Unshrunk Cloth and New Wineskins

1. In correcting the NRSV here, I follow M. Eugene Boring in translating both *neos* and *kainos* as "new"; see his *Mark: A Commentary* (Louisville, KY: Westminster John Knox Press, 2006), 83, 87n14.

2. Boring, *Mark*, 85; D. E. Nineham, *The Gospel of Mark* (London: Penguin, 1969), 104. Joel Marcus writes of a "pair of parables" (*Mark 1—8* [New York: Doubleday, 2000], 235, see 238). Francis J. Moloney, *The Gospel of Mark: A Commentary* (Peabody, MA: Hendrickson, 2002), 67, takes Mark 2:21–22 as one parable. Bas M. F. van Iersel, however, describes these two verses as "metaphors" (*Mark: A Reader-Response Commentary* [Sheffield, UK: Sheffield Academic Press, 1998], 156); Adela Yarbro Collins speaks of "metaphorical sayings" (*Mark: Commentary* [Minneapolis: Fortress Press, 2007], 197). Arland J. Hultgren leaves the parabolic status of the verses "an open question" (*The Parables of Jesus: A Commentary* [Grand Rapids: Eerdmans, 2000], 3). I follow Marcus and others in identifying here a pair of parables, but such classifying of the two verses does not affect conclusions about their background and origin.

3. U. Luz, *Matthew 8—20*, trans. James E. Crouch (Minneapolis: Fortress Press, 2001), 37–38.

4. Moloney, *Gospel of Mark*, 67. Van Iersel writes, "That the new stands no chance whenever an attempt is made to combine it with the old is a common *empirical* fact, but the two pronouncements say in addition that not only the new but also the old is destroyed. Neither of the two can withstand combination with the other" (*Mark*, 156; my italics). That neither of the two can withstand combination with the other holds true of the wine parable, but not of old/new cloth. Here an unwise combination and subsequent washing bring damage and only partial, not complete, destruction.

5. Moloney, *Gospel of Mark*, 67.

6. E. Schweizer, *The Good News according to Mark*, trans. Donald H. Madvig (London: SPCK, 1971), 67. Schweizer, rather than understanding these two verses to contain parables fashioned by Jesus, proposes that they "may consist of proverbs which Jesus appropriated or of metaphors formulated by him." But Schweizer fails to cite (from wisdom literature or elsewhere) any such proverbs. Moreover, unlike the

words of Jesus to Simon and Andrew in Mark 1:17 ("I will make you fish for people"), Mark 2:21-22 does not contain metaphors—that is to say, language used in an extended sense that is false in the literal sense. In fact, these two verses make their point precisely because their language about cloth and wineskins is used in a literal sense.

7. Marcus, *Mark 1—8*, 235.

8. Yarbro Collins, *Mark*, 200.

9. Schweizer, *Good News*, 67, 68, 69; my italics.

10. Boring, *Mark*, 86.

11. C. Focant, *The Gospel according to Mark*, trans. Leslie Robert Keylock (Eugene, OR: Pickwick Publications, 2012), 110.

12. Focant, *Gospel according to Mark*, 87.

13. See Matt 6:16-18; Luke 2:37; Acts 10:30; 13:2-3; 14:23; 27:9; 1 Cor 9:25-27; 2 Cor 6:5; 11:27; on fasting, see Boring, *Mark*, 84-85. From the late first-century Didache, we learn that Christians fasted on Wednesdays and Fridays (8.1, see 1.3).

14. On Jewish and Christian fasting, see Marcus, *Mark 1—8*, 236; Yarbro Collins, *Mark*, 197-98; and François Bovon, *Luke: A Commentary*, vol. 2, trans. Christine M. Thomas (Minneapolis: Fortress Press, 2013), 192-93.

15. Boring, *Mark*, 87.

16. Nineham, *Gospel of Saint Mark*, 101, 102.

17. Moloney, *Gospel of Mark*, 67.

18. Unlike Moloney, Focant does not cite the time of salvation but proposes a different reference for the wine image: "The image of wine to speak of teaching is not unknown." He recalls a later, rabbinic saying that connects teaching with new and old wine (*Gospel according to Mark*, 110). Yarbro Collins also links the new wine with teaching, albeit Jesus's own "new teaching" with "authority" (Mark 1:22, 27), and she locates this new teaching within the "qualitatively new situation" in which the divine kingdom has drawn near (*Mark*, 199-200).

19. See n. 4 above.

20. Were these activities gender specific, with wives, daughters, and female servants engaged in mending torn clothes, and husbands, sons, and male servants engaged in the storage of new wine? Classic commentators like Roland de Vaux do not raise and answer these questions: see, e.g., his account of "Family Institutions," *Ancient Israel: Its Life and Institutions*, trans. John McHugh (London: Darton, Longman & Todd, 1974), 19-61. Tradition supplied the evangelists with pairs of

brief parables—one involving a man (the lost sheep in Luke 15:3-7) and the second involving a woman (the lost coin in Luke 15:8-10); the mustard seed (presumably involving a man) in Luke 13:18-19 parr. and the leaven (involving a woman) in Luke 13:20-21 parr. Can we presume the same in Mark 2:21-22 parr., except that in this case the first parable (of mending clothes) implies the activity of a woman and the second (of storing wine) implies the activity of a man?

    21. See G. O'Collins, *The Beauty of Jesus Christ* (Oxford: Oxford University Press, 2020), 56-64.

4. Did Joseph of Arimathea Exist and Bury Jesus?

    1. John Dominic Crossan, who rejected, as we shall see, the historicity of the burial story in Mark, also rejected the historicity of the discovery of the empty tomb (16:1-8), claiming that Mark created the tradition of the empty tomb: see Crossan, "Empty Tomb and Absent Lord," in *The Passion in Mark: Studies on Mark 14—16*, ed. Werner H. Kelber (Philadelphia: Fortress Press, 1976), 135-52.

    2. U. Luz, *Matthew 21—28*, trans. James E. Crouch (Minneapolis: Fortress Press, 2005), 580. Adela Yarbro Collins unconvincingly suggests that followers of Jesus created this tradition: they "may have emphasized that he was buried because of the belief, current at the time [but where? in Greece?], that the shades of those who were unburied could not enter Hades but wandered the earth....They also probably wanted to minimize the dishonor and shame associated with death by crucifixion" (*Mark: A Commentary* [Philadelphia: Fortress Press, 2007], 775).

    3. R. Bultmann, *The History of the Synoptic Tradition*, trans. John Marsh (Oxford: Basil Blackwell, 1963), 274.

    4. J. A. Fitzmyer, *The Gospel according to Luke (X—XXIV)* (New York: Doubleday, 1985), 1526. Luz echoed Fitzmyer when he admitted that he did not "find it understandable that the Christian church should have invented the name of an otherwise unknown, pious Jew who buried Jesus" (*Matthew 21—28*, 580).

    5. S. E. Porter, "Joseph of Arimathea," in *Anchor Bible Dictionary*, vol. 3, ed. D. N. Freedman (New York: Doubleday, 1992), 971-72; see

also Pierre Benoit, *The Passion and Resurrection of Jesus Christ*, trans. Benet Weatherhead (New York: Herder and Herder, 1969), 227–30; Joachim Gnilka, *Das Evangelium nach Markus*, vol. 2 (Zurich: Benziger, 1979), 336; Morna Hooker, *The Gospel according to Mark* (London: A. & C. Black, 1991), 380.

6. R. E. Brown, *The Death of the Messiah*, vol. 2 (New York: Doubleday, 1994), 1340–41.

7. (Grand Rapids: Eerdmans, 2002), 286–88.

8. Luz, *Matthew 21—28*, 580.

9. J. D. Crossan, *Four Other Gospels: Shadows on the Contours of the Canon* (Minneapolis: Winston Press, 1985), 152–57; *The Cross that Spoke: The Origins of the Passion Narrative* (San Francisco: Harper & Row, 1988), 234–48; *The Historical Jesus: The Life of a Mediterranean Jewish Peasant* (San Francisco: HarperSanFrancisco, 1991), 391–94.

10. Crossan, *Four Other Gospels*, 145.

11. Crossan, *Four Other Gospels*, 145, 160–61, 164.

12. Crossan, *The Cross that Spoke*, xiii.

13. *Four Other Gospels*, 160–61, sec. 16A. For parallel claims, see *The Cross that Spoke*, 237, and *The Historical Jesus*, 392–93.

14. Crossan, *The Cross that Spoke*, 248.

15. Crossan, *The Historical Jesus*, 394.

16. R. E. Brown, "The Gospel of Peter and Canonical Gospel Priority," *New Testament Studies* 33 (1987): 321–43. Brown repeated, implicitly, his criticism of Crossan by expanding his account of the Gospel of Peter, its date, and its dependence on Matthew's passion narrative in *Death of the Messiah*, 1317–49.

17. Brown, "The Gospel of Peter," 339. Luz likewise rejects Crossan's thesis, right from its basic move: "a 'Cross Gospel' extrapolated from the later Gospel of Peter is methodologically untenable" (*Matthew 21—28*, 580).

18. J. P. Meier, review of *The Historical Jesus*, *America*, March 7, 1992, 198–99.

19. See P. A. Mirecki, "Peter, Gospel of," *Anchor Bible Dictionary*, 5:278–81, at 280.

20. C. C. Black, *Journal of Religion* 69 (1989): 398–99; R. H. Fuller, *Interpretation* 45 (1991): 71–72; J. B. Green, *Journal of Biblical Literature* 109 (1990): 356–58; F. J. Matera, *Worship* 63 (1989): 269–70; J. P. Meier, *Horizons* 16 (1989): 378–79; W. Wink, *The Christian Century*, December 14, 1988, 1159–60.

Notes

21. J. Marcus, *Mark 8—16* (New Haven, CT: Yale University Press, 2009), 927. For a discussion of Crossan's thesis about the Gospel of Peter, see also N. T. Wright, *The Resurrection of the Son of God* (Minneapolis: Fortress Press, 2003), 592-56.

22. Marcus, *Mark 8—16*, 925; see R. E. Brown, *Death of the Messiah*, vol. 1 (New York: Doubleday, 1994), 46-57.

23. Luz, *Matthew 21—28*, 304-5.

24. Crossan, *Four Other Gospels*, 147.

25. Crossan, *Four Other Gospels*, 138, 147, 148.

26. Crossan, *Four Other Gospels*, 164; see 153-54.

27. Crossan, *The Historical Jesus*, 389.

28. Green, *Journal of Biblical Literature*, 357-58; for the reviews of Black and Fuller, see n. 20 above.

29. Fitzmyer, *Luke*, 2:1501.

30. Fitzmyer, *Luke*, 1368.

31. Hooker, *The Gospel according to Mark*, 380.

32. Marcus, *Mark 8—16*, 927-28.

33. Marcus, *Mark 8—16*, 928-29.

34. Crossan, *The Historical Jesus*, 390.

35. J. Marcus, *Mark 1—8* (New York: Doubleday, 2000), 62.

36. Crossan, *The Historical Jesus*, 389-91.

37. A. Schweitzer, *The Quest of the Historical Jesus*, trans. W. Montgomery (New York: Macmillan, 1964), 4.

38. G. Tyrrell, *Christianity at the Cross-Roads* (London: Longman, Green & Co, 1909), 44.

39. Crossan, *Four Other Gospels*, 156, 161; see also *The Cross that Spoke*, 237-48, and *The Historical Jesus*, 393-94.

40. Crossan, *The Cross that Spoke*, 238-99.

41. Mark's language about Joseph does not make it quite clear that he belonged to the Jerusalem Sanhedrin (as Luke 23:51 seems to suppose); it may indicate a rich property owner and member of some local council. Hence Matthew may be interpreting Mark's text rather than changing it.

42. Fitzmyer, *Luke*, 2:1525.

43. See Fitzmyer, *Luke*, 1523-30; Porter, "Joseph of Arimathea," 972.

44. Crossan, *The Cross that Spoke*, 17-20.

45. Crossan, *The Historical Jesus*, 393. Here Crossan at once exaggerates when describing this Joseph of Arimathea created by Mark as

enjoying a "powerful foot in both camps." Joseph obviously lacked sufficient power needed in the Jewish court to prevent the condemnation of Jesus. His lack of "power" in the Christian camp may be gauged by the fact that, outside the burial story in the Gospels, the New Testament nowhere mentioned him.

46. J. Ernst, *Das Evangelium nach Markus* (Regensburg: Pustet, 1981), 479.

47. D. E. Nineham, *Saint Mark* (London: Penguin, 1963), 433.

48. R. Pesch, *Das Markusevangelium*, vol. 2 (Freiburg im Breisgau: Herder, 1977), 57.

49. E. Schweizer, *The Good News according to Mark*, trans. Donald H. Madvig (London: SPCK, 1970), 361.

50. V. Taylor, *The Gospel according to St. Mark*, 2nd ed. (London: Macmillan, 1966), 599.

51. D. C. Allison, *Resurrecting Jesus: The Earliest Christian Tradition and Its Interpreters* (New York: T&T Clark, 2005), 352–63; on Allison's rebuttal of Crossan's dismissal of the burial story's historicity, see G. O'Collins, *Believing in the Resurrection* (Mahwah, NJ: Paulist Press, 2012), 13–14.

52. J. R. Edwards, *The Gospel according to Luke* (Grand Rapids: Eerdmans, 2015), 701–4.

53. C. Foçant, *The Gospel according to Mark: A Commentary*, trans. Leslie Robert Keylock (Eugene, OR: Pickwick Publications, 2012), 651–52.

54. R. H. Stein, *Mark* (Grand Rapids: Baker Academic, 2008), 722–26.

55. *Theological Studies* 26 (1965): 189–214.

56. "Anti-Semitism in the Gospel," *Theological Studies* 26 (1965): 663–66; in the same issue of *Theological Studies*, Joseph Fitzmyer drew attention to one, crucial New Testament text (Matt 27:25) that Crossan had failed to consider: "Anti-Semitism and 'the Cry of All the People,'" 667–71.

Notes

5. The Terrified Silence of Three Women

1. On variant endings (and theories of lost endings) of Mark, see Joel Marcus, *Mark 8—16* (Newhaven, CT: Yale University Press, 2009), 1088-96.

2. R. H. Lightfoot, *The Gospel Message of St. Mark* (Oxford: Oxford University Press, 1950), 88.

3. Lightfoot, *Gospel Message of St. Mark*, 90-91.

4. D. E. Nineham, *Saint Mark* (London: Penguin, 1963), 447-48.

5. R. Pesch, *Das Markusevangelium*, vol. 2 (Freiburg im Breisgau: Herder, 1977), 536 (trans. mine); see also 522.

6. Lightfoot, *Gospel Message*, 87.

7. Pesch, *Markusevangelium*, 2:528; my italics.

8. Pesch, *Markusevangelium*, 535.

9. R. Otto, *The Idea of the Holy*, trans. John W. Harvey (London: Penguin, 1959).

10. Pesch, *Markusevangelium*, 2:541; my italics.

11. N. Perrin, *The Resurrection Narratives: A New Approach* (London: SCM Press, 1977), 31-32.

12. Perrin, *The Resurrection Narratives*, 32-33.

13. M. D. Hooker, *The Gospel according to St. Mark* (London: Continuum, 2001; orig. 1981), 392. It is worth remarking that the evangelist does *not* state that the women "disobeyed" and were "culpable," but only that, after receiving the message from the angel about the resurrection and a rendezvous in Galilee, "they said nothing to anyone" (Mark 16:8)—a silence that is to be explained and not a silence on which the text has already passed a (negative) judgement.

14. Hooker, *St. Mark*, 387.

15. Hooker, *St. Mark*, 393. But do the male disciples' flight from arrest and the women's flight from the tomb stand in parallel? The men flee from danger at the hands of human beings; the women flee when "confronted with the power of God." Faced with "the mightiest act of

all," they flee. This is "precisely how many other characters in the story [of Mark] have reacted when confronted" with the divine power (387). Here Hooker herself recognizes that the flight of the men and that of the women are differently motivated; they should not be explained in the same way.

16. F. J. Moloney, *The Gospel of Mark: A Commentary* (Peabody, MA: Hendrickson, 2002), 348.

17. Moloney, *Gospel of Mark*, 348–52.

18. Moloney, *The Gospel of Mark*, 352. James R. Edwards agrees with Hooker and Moloney by attributing a disobedience and failure in faith to the three women (*The Gospel according to Mark* [Grand Rapids: Eerdmans, 2002], 495–96).

19. Private communication from Moloney.

20. See, e.g., J. Marcus, *Mark 1—8* (New York: Doubleday, 2000), 73–75.

21. J. Marcus, *Mark 8—16* (New Haven, CT: Yale University Press, 2009), 1081–82.

22. Marcus, *Mark 8—16*, 1087.

23. Marcus, *Mark 8—16*, 1087.

24. Marcus, *Mark 8—16*, 1093.

25. Marcus, *Mark 8—16*, 1095.

26. M. E. Boring, *Mark: A Commentary* (Louisville, KY: Westminster John Knox), 449n16. Boring attends here to the requirements of the *narrative*. Those requirements must be distinguished from plausible guesses about the *historical* sequence of events: for instance, given the danger in Jerusalem, Peter and the other Galilean (male) disciples would presumably have been well on the way to Galilee by mid-morning on Easter Sunday. It was there that the risen Jesus historically appeared to them. What was a historical event or series of historical events was narrated as fulfilling a divine command (Mark 16:7; see 14:28).

27. T. Dwyer, *The Motif of Wonder in the Gospel of Mark* (Sheffield, UK: Sheffield Academic Press, 1996), 189.

28. Dwyer, *The Motif of Wonder*, 191–92.

29. J. Lee Magness, *Sense and Absence: Structure and Suspension in the Ending of Mark's Gospel* (Atlanta: Scholars Press, 1986), 100.

30. G. O'Collins, *Easter Faith: Believing in the Risen Jesus* (London: Darton, Longman & Todd, 2003), 72–73.

31. Marcus, *Mark 8—16*, 1082.

32. G. O'Collins, *Interpreting the Resurrection* (Mahwah, NJ: Paulist Press, 1988), 53–58; O'Collins, *Easter Faith*, 66–71; O'Collins, *Believing in the Resurrection* (Mahwah, NJ: Paulist Press, 2012), 80–91.

33. Magness, *Sense and Absence*, 102.

34. C. Foçant, *The Gospel according to Mark: A Commentary*, trans. Leslie Robert Keylock (Eugene, OR: Pickwick Publications, 2012), 661.

35. Foçant, *The Gospel according to Mark*, 662.

6. Thomas Torrance and Mark 16:19–20

1. See "Ascension of Christ," in *The Oxford Dictionary of the Christian Church*, 3rd ed. rev., ed. F. L. Cross and E. A. Livingstone (Oxford: Oxford University Press, 2005), 114; James D. G. Dunn et al., "Ascension of Christ," *Encyclopedia of the Bible and Its Reception*, vol. 2 (New York: Walter de Gruyter, 2009), 908–30; Douglas Farrow, *Ascension and Ecclesia: On the Significance of the Doctrine of the Ascension for Ecclesiology and Christian Cosmology* (Edinburgh: T&T Clark, 1999); Farrow, *Ascension Theology* (London: T&T Clark, 2011); Alfons Weiser et al., "Himmelfahrt Christi," *Theologische Realenzylopädie*, vol. 15 (Berlin: Walter de Gruyter, 1986), 330–41.

2. T. F. Torrance, *Space, Time and Resurrection* (Edinburgh: Handsel Press,1976), 106–58.

3. Torrance, *Space, Time and Resurrection*, 119–20; my italics.

4. Torrance, *Space, Time and Resurrection*, 119.

5. On Mark 15:9–20, see Joseph Hug, *Le finale de l'Évangile de Marc* (Paris: J. Gabalda, 1978); Joel Marcus, *Mark 8—16* (New Haven, CT: Yale University Press, 2009), 1088–96.

6. Andrew T. Lincoln summarizes the growing use in the New Testament of *Logos* as a title for Christ (*The Gospel according to John* [London: Continuum, 2005], 94–98), but fails to mention how Luke uses the term/title in Acts. "The word of the Lord" or "the word of God" throughout Acts "represents most often the good news about Christ" (Craig S. Keener, *Acts: An Exegetical Commentary*, vol 1 [Grand Rapids: Baker Academic, 2012], 524).

7. See G. O'Collins, "Vatican II on the Liturgical Presence of Christ," *The Second Vatican Council: Message and Meaning* (Collegeville,

MN: Liturgical Press, 2014), 89–104. On Christ as the supreme moral exemplar, see St. Irenaeus, *Adversus Haereses* 5.1.1: "There is no other way to learn than to see our Master and hear his voice with our own ears. It is by becoming imitators of his actions and doers of his words—that we may have communion with him" (trans. mine); Adelin Rousseau et al., *Sources Chrétiennes* 153 (Paris: Cerf, 1969), 15–16.

    8. Marcus, *Mark 8—16*, 1090.

    9. The NRSV presumes here to add "the good news," even though the Greek text leaves unspecified the object of the proclamation.

    10. Where the risen Christ in Matt 28:20 simply promises "I will be with you," Mark 16:20 specifies two ways in which he will be with those he commissions: he "worked with them" and "confirmed" their message with signs.

    11. Joachim Gnilka comments that the missionaries themselves experienced the cooperation of the risen and ascended Lord (*Das Evangelium nach Markus* [Neukirchen-Vluyn/Mannheim: Neukirchener Verlag/Patmos Verlag, 2010; orig. ed., 1977], 358).

    12. M. D. Hooker, *The Gospel according to Saint Mark* (London: Continuum, 2005), 591. Eduard Schweizer agrees: "What Luke does in Acts may be seen in embryo here" (*The Good News according to Mark*, trans. H. Madvig [London: SPCK, 1970], 378). Rudolf Pesch sees Mark 16:20 as summarizing Acts "in nuce" (*Das Markusevangelium*, vol. 2 [Freiburg: Herder, 1977], 555). This observation calls for modification, inasmuch as neither Mark 16:20 nor the entire, second-century addition (16:9–20) refers to the Holy Spirit, unlike Acts, which contains nearly one-quarter of all the references to the Spirit in the New Testament (Keener, *Acts*, 1:520).

    13. On the Holy Spirit in Acts, see Keener, *Acts*, 1:519–28.

    14. V. Taylor, *The Gospel according to Mark* (London: Macmillan, 1966; 1st ed., 1952), 613.

    15. T. F. Torrance, *Theology in Reconciliation* (London: Geoffrey Chapman, 1975).

    16. Torrance, *Theology in Reconciliation*, 107.

    17. Rev 5:6 gets close to such a vision, with its apocalyptic picture of the Lamb of God standing near the throne of God; see G. K. Beale, *The Book of Revelation* (Grand Rapids: Eerdmans, 1999), 350–55.

    18. See Keener, *Acts*, 2:1440–43.

    19. D. E. Nineham, *Saint Mark* (London: Penguin, 1963, reprinted 1992), 452.

20. Taylor, *The Gospel according to Mark*, 613.
21. Schweizer, *The Good News according to Mark*, 378.
22. F. J. Moloney, *The Gospel of Mark: A Commentary* (Peabody, MA: Hendrickson, 2002), 359.
23. Moloney, *Gospel of Mark*, 361.
24. Moloney, *Gospel of Mark*, 361.
25. Torrance, *Space, Time and Resurrection*, 122.
26. Torrance, *Space, Time and Resurrection*, 122. On the same page, Torrance also explains how the risen Christ, in his kingly/shepherding role, governs the church.
27. T. F. Torrance, *The Mediation of Christ* (Edinburgh: T&T Clark, 1992). For an account of Torrance's presentation of Christ's priesthood, see G. O'Collins and M. K. Jones, *Jesus Our Priest: A Christian Approach to the Priesthood of Christ* (Oxford: Oxford University Press, 2010), 224–29.

7. Mary and Simeon

1. R. C. Tannehill, *The Narrative Unity of Luke–Acts: A Literary Interpretation*, vol. 1 (Philadelphia: Fortress Press, 1986), 39.
2. L. T. Johnson, *The Gospel of Luke* (Collegeville, MN: Liturgical Press, 1991), 55.
3. F. Bovon, *Luke*, vol. 1, trans. Christine M. Thomas (Minneapolis: Fortress Press, 2002); this commentary will be quoted within my text.
4. See Raymond E. Brown, *The Birth of the Messiah: A Commentary on the Infancy Narratives in the Gospels of Matthew and Luke*, new ed. (New York: Doubleday, 1993), 684–87.
5. Raymond Brown, but without commenting on its meaning, provides statistics for the use of *kai idou* in the Lukan infancy narratives (ten occurrences) as well as in the Matthean infancy narratives (six occurrences) (*The Birth of the Messiah*, 263).
6. Brown offers less than convincing reasons for the softer translation of "servant" and "handmaid" (*The Birth of the Messiah*, 439).
7. Tannehill, *Narrative Unity of Luke–Acts*, 17. As John Nolland comments, "Mary is given the last word and in a statement of faith… declares her unreserved readiness for God's purposes" (*Luke 1—9:20* [Dallas, TX: Word Books, 1989], 59).

8. Tannehill, *Narrative Unity of Luke–Acts*, 18.
9. Johnson, *Gospel of Luke*, 14.
10. Johnson, *Gospel of Luke*, 38–39.
11. Tannehill, *Narrative Unity of Luke–Acts*, 16, 17.
12. Tannehill, *Narrative Unity of Luke–Acts*, 15.
13. Tannehill, *Narrative Unity of Luke–Acts*, 15–16, 23–26.
14. *Birth of the Messiah*, 292–98.
15. The *nun* "marks the decisive turning point in Simeon's life. This patient slave is now being released by his Master from his duty as watchman"; the "goal of his watching is now accomplished." "As God has promised, his release comes *before* death. The slave is now 'in peace' because the time of messianic salvation has come" (Nolland, *Luke*, 1:119).
16. On unconvincing attempts to identify Simeon with and/or relate him to some known and famous person, see Brown, *Birth of the Messiah*, 437–38.
17. Tannehill, *Narrative Unity of Luke–Acts*, 19.
18. Tannehill, *Narrative Unity of Luke–Acts*, 20.

8. The Nativity in View of the Cross and Resurrection

1. F. Bovon, *Luke: A Commentary*, 3 vols. (Minneapolis: Fortress Press, 2002–12), 1:82; hereafter references to Bovon will be cited within my text. His commentary has appeared at least in English, French, German, Italian, and Spanish—a striking witness to its status. While attending to texts in Luke's Gospel, this chapter will also draw on their reception history in the work of various artists, Martin Luther (d. 1545), and Ignatius Loyola (d. 1556).

2. Here and subsequently the translation is taken from Joseph A. Munitiz and Philip Endean, *Saint Ignatius of Loyola: Personal Writings* (London: Penguin, 2004).

3. Munitiz and Endean, *Saint Ignatius of Loyola*, 33–35.

4. Bovon allows that *phatnē* might mean here a "stable" or a "half-open feeding place, sometimes located in a cave." But he opts for "manger" and suggests that "the manger was probably made of stone

Notes

(perhaps chiseled into the wall of a cave or the face of a rock) or of mud; wood was too expensive" (1:90).

5. See Walter Bauer, Frederick W. Danker, William F. Arndt, and F. Wilbur Gingrich, eds., *Greek-English Lexicon of the New Testament and Other Early Christian Literature*, 3rd ed. (Chicago: University of Chicago Press, 2000), 1050; hereafter *BDAG*.

6. "An ox knows its owner, and a donkey its master's stall" (Isa 1:3; Revised English Bible).

7. *BDAG*, 1050.

8. Joseph A. Fitzmyer, *The Gospel according to Luke I—IX* (New York: Doubleday, 1981), 408.

9. Roman A. Siebenrock, "Jesus Christ: Life as Passion for the Kingdom of God," in *"Godhead Here in Hiding": Incarnation and the History of Human Suffering*, ed. Terrence Merrigan and Frederik Glorieux (Leuven: Peeters, 2012), 37.

10. I have not found any commentator on the *Spiritual Exercises* who remarks on the way, apropos of Christ's nativity, Ignatius's notes for the mysteries of Christ's life differ partially from what has been stated in the contemplation on the nativity in *SpEx* 110–17.

11. At least as old as the eighth-century epic poet Homer, *inclusio* is a technique for linking the beginning and end of some short or long piece of writing. We detect an *inclusio* by noting the similar or even identical material found at the beginning and the end of the work or section in question; see further ch. 2, n. 20 above.

12. Bovon (3:144–45) argues convincingly against introducing hard "furniture" like couches; what Luke has in mind are soft objects like carpets or even blankets.

13. *BDAG*, 521. Fitzmyer prefers to translate *kataluma* in Luke 2:7 as "lodge." But this choice carries a distracting burden of modern meanings, as in "the local Masonic lodge," "the president's hunting lodge," "the porter's lodge," and "a motor lodge" or motel, for instance. Fitzmyer himself goes on to suggest "a public caravansary or khan, where groups of travelers would spend the night under one roof" (*The Gospel according to Luke I—IX*, 391, 394, 408).

14. *BDAG*, 753.

15. Raymond Brown joins others in questioning "the image of the hard-hearted innkeeper turning Joseph and Mary away from the door. Rather, all that Luke is saying is that because travelers were sheltered in one crowded room," the inn was not a fitting place for the birth. The

innkeeper was "correct rather than hard-hearted. He refused accommodation to (the obviously pregnant) Mary because if she went into labor and gave birth in the place where people were lodged, the other guests would have been inconvenienced by having to go out from it." Nevertheless, Brown shows himself at least open to the notion of "rejection." It fits "the larger Lucan picture," by anticipating "the career of the Son of Man who will be rejected" (*The Birth of the Messiah: A Commentary on the Infancy Narratives in the Gospels of Matthew and Luke*, rev. ed. [New York: Doubleday, 1993], 670).

16. Bovon, 2:56n24. Bovon lists here "example stories" that Luke has drawn from L, his special source: the rich farmer (12:16–21), the rich man and the poor Lazarus (16:19–31), and the Pharisee and the tax collector (18:10–14).

17. Martin Luther identified Christ as the Good Samaritan and made the inn a kind of field hospital (Erwin Mülhaupt, *D. Martin Luthers Evangelien-Auslegung*, vol. 3 [Göttingen: Vandenhoeck & Ruprecht, 1968], 152–56).

18. Here Peter and John act as servants; after the resurrection and Pentecost they will be twinned as the church's first leaders; on Peter and John leading together, see Acts 3:1, 11; 4:3, 19; and 8:14.

19. St. Bonaventure, as cited by Bovon (3:146).

20. On this see more fully G. O'Collins, *Salvation for All: God's Other Peoples* (Oxford: Oxford University Press, 2008), 100–120.

9. Peter as Neglected Witness to Easter

1. Martin Hengel, *Der unterschäzte Petrus. Zwei Studien* (Tübingen: Mohr Siebeck, 2006); *Saint Peter: The Underestimated Apostle*, trans. Thomas H. Trapp (Grand Rapids: Eerdmans, 2010).

2. Oscar Cullmann, *Peter: Disciple, Apostle, Martyr: A Historical and Theological Study*, trans. Floyd V. Filson (London: SCM Press, 1962); Raymond E. Brown, Karl P. Donfried, and John Reumann, eds., *Peter in the New Testament: A Collaborative Assessment by Protestant and Roman Catholic Scholars* (Minneapolis: Augsburg, 1973).

3. Christian Grappe, *Images de Pierre aux deux premiers siècles* (Paris: Presses Universitaires de France, 1995); Rudolf Pesch, *Die bib-

lischen Grundlagen des Primats, Quaestiones Disputatae 187 (Freiburg im Breisgau: Herder, 2001).

4. Hengel, *Saint Peter*, 32, 36, 45, 53.

5. Hengel, *Saint Peter*, 30–31.

6. In "Peter as Easter Witness," *Heythrop Journal* 22 (1981): 1–18, I showed how earlier scholars had widely neglected the priority of Peter's witness to the resurrection. This situation has hardly changed over the last forty years. In *The Remembered Peter: In Ancient Reception and Modern Debate* (Tübingen: Mohr Siebeck, 2010), Markus Bockmuehl treats in a balanced fashion various Petrine themes, but does not discuss Peter's witness to the resurrection. See, however, William Thomas Kessler, *Peter as the First Witness of the Risen Lord: An Historical and Theological Investigation* (Rome: Editrice Pontificia Università Gregoriana, 1998).

7. Hengel, *Saint Peter*, 20–25.

8. Hengel, *Saint Peter*, 25–28.

9. Hengel, *Saint Peter*, 28–36.

10. Hengel, *Saint Peter*, 36–48.

11. Hengel, *Saint Peter*, 48.

12. Hengel, *Saint Peter*, 82; see also 99.

13. Hengel, *Saint Peter*, 43.

14. Hengel, *Saint Peter*, 44.

15. Hengel, *Saint Peter*, 22.

16. Hengel, *Saint Peter*, 29; see also 34, 44, 66 (n215), 88, 100. Hengel notes, however, the claim expressed in the Gospel of the Hebrews that the first appearance of the risen Jesus was to his "brother" James (*Saint Peter*, 9).

17. See Gerald O'Collins and Daniel Kendall, "Mary Magdalene as Major Witness to Jesus' Resurrection," *Theological Studies* 48 (1987): 22–38; revised as ch. 11 in this book.

18. Richard Bauckham, *Gospel Women: A Study of the Named Women in the Gospels* (Grand Rapids: Eerdmans, 2002); see Hengel, *Saint Peter*, 108–10, 122.

19. Hengel, *Saint Peter*, 100.

20. Hengel, *Saint Peter*, 99. The key "appearance-to-Peter" texts (Luke 24:34; 1 Cor 15:5), which we will examine below, are notable for their absence in St. Peter's Basilica. Obviously, popes have not been very interested in linking their primacy to Peter *precisely* in his function as "first witness to the resurrection."

21. Pesch, *Die biblischen Grundlagen*, 60.

22. Pesch, *Die biblischen Grundlagen*, 21–26, 31–39.

23. See, e.g., Richard Bauckham, *Jesus and the Eyewitnesses: The Gospels as Eyewitness Testimony* (Grand Rapids: Eerdmans, 2006).

24. Pesch, *Die biblischen Grundlagen*, 39–41, 48.

25. Pesch, *Die biblischen Grundlagen*, 79.

26. Pesch, *Die biblischen Grundlagen*, 40, 41–42, 63, 79, 80, 87.

27. Pesch, *Die biblischen Grundlagen*, 85–91.

28. Pesch, *Die biblischen Grundlagen*, 87–88.

29. Pesch, *Die biblischen Grundlagen*, 57. Apropos of the origin of Christian faith in Jesus's resurrection, over the years Pesch changed his position in important aspects but continued to differ from my analysis of the emergence of Easter faith; see G. O'Collins, *Jesus Risen: An Historical, Fundamental, and Systematic Examination of Christ's Resurrection* (Mahwah, NJ: Paulist Press, 1987), 110, 120; O'Collins, *Believing in the Resurrection: The Meaning and Promise of the Risen Jesus* (Mahwah, NJ: Paulist Press, 2012), 77, 83–85.

30. In *Peter: Apostle for the Whole Church* (Columbia: University of South Carolina Press, 1994), Pheme Perkins refers to Peter as witness to the risen Christ only rarely (3, 8, 33); and, somewhat like Grappe, she presents Peter much more in such roles as exemplary disciple (who eventually suffers martyrdom), founder, universal apostle, and shepherd.

31. Brown, Donfried, and Reumann, *Peter in the New Testament*, 162–68. We should note that Peter as Easter witness does *not* explicitly feature among the seven images that conclude and summarize the study, even though the work has already examined the three key texts that concern Peter's witness to Christ's resurrection: 1 Cor 15:5 (33–36); Luke 24:34 (125–28); and Mark 16:7 (69–73).

32. Brown, Donfried, and Reumann, *Peter in the New Testament*, 21n47.

33. Grappe, *Images de Pierre*, 152, 201–5.

34. Grappe, *Images de Pierre*, 275.

35. Grappe, *Images de Pierre*, 155. Willi Marxsen and some others have understood Mark 16:7, along with 14:28, to refer, not to postresurrection appearances, but to the Parousia that will occur in Galilee. For references and a convincing list of reasons for rejecting this explanation, see Christopher Bryan, *The Resurrection of the Messiah* (New York:

Notes

Oxford University Press, 2011), 285; and Joel Marcus, *Mark 8—16* (New Haven, CT: Yale University Press, 2009), 1081.

36. *Origins*, 8, no. 19 (October 26, 1978): 292.

37. Heinrich Denzinger and Peter Hünermann, eds., *Enchiridion Symbolorum, Definitionum et Declarationum* (Freiburg im Breisgau: Herder, 37th ed., 1991), no. 3053; hereafter DzH. See also Josef Neuner and Jacques Dupuis, eds, *The Christian Faith in the Doctrinal Documents of the Catholic Church* (Bangalore: Theological Publications in India, 7th Ed., 2001), no. 819; hereafter ND.

38. DzH 3070; ND 836.

39. Anglican Roman-Catholic International Commission (ARCIC), *The Final Report* (London: SPCK, 1982), 64.

40. ARCIC, *The Final Report*, 81–85.

41. *Origins* 25, no. 4 (June 8, 1995): 69.

42. ARCIC, *Final Report*, 82.

43. Jean-Marie-Roger Tillard, *The Bishop of Rome*, trans. John de Satgé (London: SPCK, 1983), 112–13.

44. John Michael Miller, *The Shepherd and the Rock: Origins, Development, and Mission of the Papacy* (Huntington, IN: Our Sunday Visitor, 1995), 12–49, 31–33.

45. Miller, *Shepherd and the Rock*, 346–70, at 363 and 365.

46. As regards the Petrine Epistles, 1 Peter may have been written by Peter; 2 Peter almost certainly did not come directly from Peter. While mentioning Jesus's resurrection (1 Pet 1:3, 21; 3:21) and echoing the language of shepherding and martyrdom found in John 21:15–19 (see 1 Pet 5:1–4), 1 Peter has nothing clearly to say about any appearance of the risen Christ to Peter. The reference to Peter as one who "shares" in Christ's "glory" (1 Pet 5:1) seems to refer to what will be revealed in the future, rather than to Peter having been the first (male) disciple to meet and witness to the risen Jesus. 2 Peter 1:16–18 recalls Peter's experiencing, not the Christ's resurrection, but his transfiguration—a passage that second-century Gnostics took up and developed (see Grappe, *Images de Pierre*, passim).

47. On 1 Cor 15:1–11, see Joseph A. Fitzmyer, *First Corinthians* (New Haven, CT: Yale University Press, 2008), 539–57.

48. Bryan, *Resurrection of the Messiah*, 263.

49. On the empty tomb, see Bryan, *Resurrection of the Messiah*, 50–51, 264; and my *Believing in the Resurrection*, 80–99.

50. On Peter's visit and preaching in Corinth, see Hengel, *Saint Peter*, 66–78.

51. For examples, see Adela Yarbro Collins, *Mark: A Commentary* (Minneapolis: Fortress Press, 2007), 797, 801; and Francis J. Moloney, *The Gospel of Mark: A Commentary* (Peabody, MA: Hendrickson, 2002), 347n34. In *Peter in the New Testament,* Brown, Donfried, and Reumann remarked that "many scholars have concluded from this verse [16:7] that Mark was aware of the tradition that Jesus had appeared first to Peter" (71).

52. Marcus, *Mark 8—16*, 1086.

53. F. Lapham, *Peter: The Myth, the Man and the Writings* (London: Sheffield Academic Press, 2003), 9; see 239. Despite this flat denial, curiously he then recognizes that "Luke does in fact record, in the Emmaus story, that the Lord had appeared to Simon (24:34)" (9n22).

54. On this verse, which current scholarship recognizes as belonging to the original text of Luke's Gospel, see François Bovon, *Luke: A Commentary*, vol. 3, trans. James E. Crouch (Minneapolis: Fortress Press, 2012), 353–55; Joseph A. Fitzmyer, *The Gospel according to Luke X—XXIV* (New York: Doubleday, 1985), 1547–48. Andrew T. Lincoln shows how, by adding the figure of the Beloved Disciple, John 20:3-10 elaborated on the tradition of Peter running to the tomb in Luke 24:12: *The Gospel according to St. John* (London: Continuum, 2005), 489, 491, 495.

55. On Luke 24:34, see Bovon, *Luke*, 3:375–76; and Fitzmyer, *Gospel according to Luke X—XXIV*, 1569.

56. On Luke 22:31-34, see Bovon, *Luke*, 3:176–81.

57. Robert C. Tannehill, *The Narrative Unity of Luke-Acts: A Literary Interpretation*, vol. 1 (Philadelphia: Fortress Press, 1986), 293.

58. Lincoln, *The Gospel according to St. John*, 514–15. On Luke 5:1-11 containing elements of the "lost" appearance to Peter, see Brendan Byrne, "Peter as Resurrection Witness in the Lukan Narrative," in *The Convergence of Theology*, ed. Daniel Kendall and Stephen T. Davis (Mahwah, NJ: Paulist Press, 2001), 19–33, at 24–29.

59. Raymond E. Brown, *The Gospel according to John XIII—XXI* (New York: Doubleday, 1970), 1085–92, 1110–12. See also Brown, "John 21 and the First Appearance of the Risen Jesus to Peter," in *Resurrexit*, ed. Eduard Dhanis (Rome: Libreria Editrice Vaticana, 1974), 246–65.

60. Brown, *Gospel according to John XIII—XXI*, 1087.

61. Brown, *Gospel according to John XIII—XXI*, 1097.

Notes

62. Brown, *Gospel according to John XIII—XXI*, 1087-92. On possible postresurrection elements in Matt 14:28-33, see Ulrich Luz, *Matthew 8—20*, trans. James E. Crouch (Minneapolis: Fortress Press, 2001), 317-23, at 318; and John Nolland, *The Gospel of Matthew* (Grand Rapids: Eerdmans, 2005), 595-603. On such postresurrection elements in Matt 16:16b-19, see Luz, *Matthew 8—20*, 353-77, at 356, 358; Nolland, *Gospel of Matthew*, 661-82. On probable postresurrection elements in Luke 5:1-11, see François Bovon, *Luke 1: A Commentary*, trans. Christine M. Thomas (Minneapolis: Fortress Press, 2002), 166-72; and Joseph A. Fitzmyer, *The Gospel according to Luke I—IX* (New York: Doubleday, 1981), 559-70, at 560-62.

63. Matthew possibly knew this longer tradition about an appearance to Mary Magdalene but abbreviated it (Matt 28:9-10); see Bryan, *Resurrection of the Messiah*, 329n82. Her prestige is hinted at: Matt 28:9 is the only text in the New Testament that speaks of Jesus "meeting" someone else.

64. On these texts, see (in Matthew) Ulrich Luz, *Matthew 21—28*, trans. James E. Crouch (Minneapolis: Fortress Press, 2005), 590-608; Nolland, *Gospel of Matthew*, 1240-54; (in Mark) Yarbro Collins, *Mark*, 779- 801; Marcus, *Mark 8—16*, 1079-87; (in Luke) Bovon, *Luke*, 3:341-60; Fitzmyer, *The Gospel according to Luke X—XXIV*, 1532-53; (in John) Lincoln, *The Gospel according to St. John*, 488-89, 491-96.

65. On Mark 16:9, see Yarbro Collins, *Mark*, 808.

66. Some translate this phrase as "distinguished in the eyes of the apostles." See Joseph A. Fitzmyer, *Romans* (New York: Doubleday, 1993), 739-40.

67. On the qualifications and functions for "apostles" in the early church, see Joseph A. Fitzmyer, *The Acts of the Apostles* (New York: Doubleday, 1998), 196-97.

68. See Luz, *Matthew 21—28*, 606.

69. In John's Gospel, when Mary Magdalene discovers the tomb of Jesus to be open, she goes at once to inform "Simon Peter and the other disciple, the one whom Jesus loved." Then they both run to inspect the tomb (John 20:2-10). This episode suggests closeness rather than conflict between Mary and Peter (and other male disciples).

70. Among these later apocryphal works, see, e.g., *The Gospel of Mary*, in *The Nag Hammadi Library in English*, ed. James M. Robinson (Leiden: Brill, 3rd ed., 1988), 523-27.

71. Philip Jenkins, *Hidden Gospels: How the Search for Jesus Lost Its Way* (New York: Oxford University Press, 2001), 133–43.

72. Hippolytus, *De Cantico* 24–26 (Corpus Scriptorum Christianorum Orientalium 264, 43–49); Leo, *De ascensione Domini sermo*, 2.4 (*Sources Chrétiennes* 74, 280–81); Gregory, *De apparitione Christi Magdalenae facta*, *homilia* 25.6 (*Sources Chrétiennes* 522, 120–21).

73. On these passages about Peter's witness to the resurrection, see Charles Kingsley Barrett, *The Acts of the Apostles*, vol. 1 (Edinburgh: T&T Clark, 1994); Joseph A. Fitzmyer, *The Acts of the Apostles* (New York: Doubleday, 1998); C. S. Keener, *Acts: An Exegetical Commentary* (Grand Rapids: Baker Academic, 2012).

74. See, e.g., the order in which the 1964 Dogmatic Constitution on the Church, *Lumen Gentium*, expresses the triple *munus*, or office of bishops: first, the teaching/prophetic role of the bishops, and then their priestly role in worship and their pastoral/kingly role in leadership (nos. 25–27).

75. Brown, Donfried and Reumann, *Peter in the New Testament*, 165.

76. Charles Kingsley Barrett finds a reference to Peter's death by crucifixion in John 21:18–19: *The Gospel according to John* (London: SPCK, 2nd ed., 1978), 585; so too does Lincoln, *The Gospel according to St. John*, 318–19.

77. For the data, the debates, and bibliographies about Paul, Peter, and their martyrdom in Rome, see Frank Leslie Cross and Elizabeth Anne Livingstone, eds., "Paul, St." and "Peter, St.," in *The Oxford Dictionary of the Christian Church*, 3rd rev. ed. (Oxford: Oxford University Press, 2005), 1243–46, 1269–70.

78. Among many publications on the Bishop of Rome, see Tillard, *The Bishop of Rome*; and James F. Puglisi, ed., *How Can the Petrine Ministry Be of Service to the Unity of the Universal Church?* (Grand Rapids: Eerdmans, 2010).

79. On Paul's conflict with Peter at Antioch, see Hengel, *Saint Peter*, 57–65.

80. Brown, Donfried and Reumann, eds, *Peter in the New Testament*, 8.

81. See further William Henn, "The Church as Easter Witness in the Thought of Gerald O'Collins, S.J.," in Kendall and Davis, *The Convergence of Theology*, 208–20.

Notes

10. Did Jesus Eat the Fish?

1. Some versions (e.g., the NRSV) translate *sunalizomenos* as "staying with" or as "being in the company of" the disciples (NEB). But the majority of commentators and translators favor "eating with" or "being at table with": e.g., Ernst Haenchen, *The Acts of the Apostles: A Commentary*, trans. Bernard Noble and Gerald Shinn (Philadelphia: Westminster Press, 1971), 141.

2. In *The Gospel according to Luke*, 5th ed. (Edinburgh: T&T Clark, 1922), Alfred Plummer commented on Luke 24:43: "Nothing is said here or in the meal at Emmaus about drinking, but are we to infer that nothing was drunk?" (561). Plummer, who wrote before form and redaction criticism affected Gospel exegesis, may have nursed the presupposition "you cannot have a proper meal unless there is also something to drink."

3. J. A. Fitzmyer, *The Gospel according to Luke X—XXIV* (New York: Doubleday, 1985), 1574, 1576.

4. Fitzmyer, *Gospel according to Luke X—XXIV*, 1577.

5. I. H. Marshall, *The Gospel of Luke* (Exeter: Paternoster Press, 1978), 903.

6. C. F. Evans, *Saint Luke* (London: SCM Press, 1990), 920.

7. Evans, *Saint Luke*, 920.

8. Evans, *Saint Luke*, 900–901.

9. Plummer, *Gospel according to Luke*, 560.

10. François Bovon, *Luke: A Commentary*, vol. 3, trans. James E. Crouch (Minneapolis: Fortress Press, 2012), 392.

11. L. Morris, *The Gospel according to Luke* (London: InterVarsity Press, 1974), 342.

12. F. F. Bruce, *The Book of Acts*, rev. ed. (Grand Rapids: Eerdmans, 1988), 34. James R. Edwards says something similar about Jesus eating to show that he was no "angel or ghost" (*The Gospel according to Luke* [Grand Rapids, MI: Eerdmans, 2015], 731–32).

13. Bovon remarks that, while "Luke does not yet ask the question," it "will be asked in the second century: did the Risen One digest this food and, if so, how did he do it? The Christians will find the answer in the Jewish tradition that had to solve the same problem about the angels who had accepted the invitation of Abraham and Sarah (Gen 18:6–8). Instead of saying that Christ only pretended to eat, the ancient

authors preferred to imagine that the resurrected or angelic bodies did indeed eat, but that they did not digest the food as did human bodies" (*Luke*, 3:393).

14. J. Schmid, *Das Evangelium nach Lukas* (Regensburg: Friedrich Pustet, 1955), 360; trans. mine.

15. P. Benoit, *The Passion and Resurrection of Jesus Christ*, trans. Benet Weatherhead (New York: Herder and Herder, 1969), 285.

16. Fitzmyer, *Luke*, 2:1573, 1574.

17. Fitzmyer, *Luke*, 2:1576–77.

18. Edwards, *Gospel according to Luke*, 732.

19. Fitzmyer, *Luke*, 2:1574, 1575.

20. W. Grundmann, *Das Evangelium nach Lukas* (Berlin: Evangelische Verlagsanstalt, 1971), 449, 451; trans. mine.

21. J. Ernst, *Das Evangelium nach Lukas* (Regensburg: Friedrich Pustet, 1977), 668; trans. mine. Bovon also points out the "apologetic" involved in the fish-eating episode (*Luke*, 3:303).

22. Ernst, *Das Evangelium nach Lukas*, 666–67; Grundmann, *Das Evangelium nach Lukas*, 449. Bovon writes of Luke's "argument for the physical resurrection directed against Docetism" (*Luke*, vol. 3:303n43).

23. Marshall, *The Gospel of Luke*, 900.

24. Grundmann, *Das Evangelium nach Lukas*, 449.

25. Ernst, *Das Evangelium nach Lukas*, 666.

26. Raymond E. Brown, *The Birth of the Messiah*, new ed. (New York: Doubleday, 1993).

27. See Bovon, *Luke*, 3:361–81; Bovon argues that in the Emmaus story Luke "reworks" the tradition he has received and does not "create" a completely new episode (369).

28. G. Lohfink, *Die Himmelfahrt Jesu: Untersuchungen zu den Himmelfahrts—und Erhohungstexten bei Lukas* (Munich: Kosel-Verlag, 1971), 247.

29. In "Paul's Conversion/Call: A Comparative Analysis of the Three Reports in Acts," Charles W. Hedrick shows how in Luke's literary technique the three narratives from chs. 9, 22, and 26, respectively, "are composed so as to supplement, complement and *correct* one another" (*Journal of Biblical Literature* 100 [1981]: 415–32, at 432; my italics).

30. Bovon, *Luke*, 3:393.

31. Marshall, *Gospel of Luke*, 900.

32. Jean-Marie Guillaume, *Luc interprète des anciennes traditions sur la résurrection de Jésus* (Paris: Lecoffre/Gabalda, 1979), 136.

Notes

33. Bovon, *Luke*, 3:393.
34. Guillaume, *Luc interprète*, 158n1.
35. Bovon, *Luke*, 3:392.
36. Bovon, *Luke*, 3:392–93.
37. E. LaVerdière, *Luke* (Wilmington, DE: Michael Glazier, 1980), 290.
38. R. Dillon, *From Eye-Witnesses to Ministers of the Word: Tradition and Composition in Luke 24* (Rome: Biblical Institute Press, 1978), 187.
39. Dillon, *From Eye-Witnesses to Ministers of the Word*, 188; see Bovon's questioning of Dillon's interpretation (*Luke*, 3:390n23; 393n43).

11. Mary Magdalene as Major Witness to Jesus's Resurrection

1. On the confusion of Mary Magdalene with the sinful woman and with Mary of Bethany, see Susan Haskins, *Mary Magdalen: Myth and Metaphor* (London: HarperCollins, 1993).
2. Flavius Josephus, *Antiquities*, 4.219; only in rare and urgent cases were women admitted as witnesses; see Haim Cohn and Yuval Sinai, "Witness," *Encyclopedia Judaica*, vol. 21, 2nd ed. (Detroit: Macmillan, 2007), 115–25, esp. 115–16.
3. From Celsus's *True Discourse*, cited by Origen, *Contra Celsum*, 2.70; trans. Henry Chadwick (Cambridge: Cambridge University Press, 1953), 109.
4. E. Renan, *Life of Jesus*, no translator indicated (Buffalo, NY: Prometheus Books, 1991; French orig. 1863), 215.
5. Ricciotti argued that the early church was reluctant to appeal to the Easter witness of Mary Magdalene and other women, so as not to let Jews and others have the impression that too much credence was being placed in overimaginative women given to spreading tales; see his *The Life of Christ*, trans. Alba I. Zizzamia (Milwaukee: Bruce, 1947), 650–51.
6. F. Spadafora, *La risurrezione di Gesù* (Rovigo: Istituto Padano, 1978), 204.
7. Leo the Great, *De Ascensione Domini*, sermo 2.4 (*Sources Chrétiennes* 74, 141–42).

8. Gregory the Great, *De apparitione Christi Magdalenae facta, homilia* 25.6 (*Sources Chrétiennes*, 522, 120-21). Gregory is often recalled (e.g., by Ann Graham Brock, *Mary Magdalene, The First Apostle: The Struggle for Authority* [Cambridge, MA: Harvard University Press, 2003], 168-69) for another sermon (*homilia* 33), in which he wrongly conflated Mary Magdalene with the sinful woman in Luke 7:36-50 (*SC*, 522, 293-319). But Brock and others regularly ignore what Gregory said about Mary Magdalene in *homilia* 25.

9. U. Luz, *Matthew 21—28*, trans. James E. Crouch (Minneapolis: Fortress Press, 2005), 608.

10. Hippolytus of Rome, *De Cantico*, 24-26 (*Corpus Scriptorum Christianorum Orientalium* 264, 43-49).

11. See C. A. J. Coady, *Testimony: A Philosophical Study* (Oxford: Clarendon Press, 1992).

12. J. A. Fitzmyer, *The Gospel according to Luke X—XXIV* (New York: Doubleday, 1985), 1535-37.

13. On Mark 16:1-8, see Joel Marcus, *Mark 8—16* (New Haven, CT: Yale University Press, 2009), 1079-87.

14. On Matthew 28, see Luz, *Matthew 21—28*, 590-636.

15. On Luke 24, see François Bovon, *Luke: A Commentary*, vol. 3, trans. James E. Crouch (Minneapolis: Fortress Press, 2012), 341-421.

16. R. Schnackenburg, *The Gospel according to John*, vol. 3, trans. David Smith and G. A. Kon (New York: Crossroad, 1982), 321.

17. Bovon, *Luke*, 3:352.

18. "The Women and the Empty Tomb," *Bibliotheca Sacra* 13 (1966): 301-09, at 309.

19. See Andrew Lincoln, *The Gospel according to St. John* (London: Continuum, 2005), 487-508.

20. On the Markan appendix, see Marcus, *Mark 8—16*, 1088-96.

21. Luz, *Matthew 21—28*, 606.

22. Bovon, *Luke*, 3:352.

23. R. E. Brown, *The Gospel according to St. John (XIII—XXI)* (New York: Doubleday, 1970), 988.

24. R. Bultmann, *The Gospel of John*, trans. John Marsh (Oxford: Blackwell, 1963), 686.

25. Bultmann, *The Gospel of John*, 687.

26. E. Hoskyns, *The Fourth Gospel*, ed. Francis N. Davey, 2nd. ed. (London: Faber and Faber, 1947), 542.

27. Hoskyns, *The Fourth Gospel*, 543.

Notes

28. C. H. Dodd, *The Interpretation of the Fourth Gospel* (Cambridge: Cambridge University Press, 1953), 440.

29. Dodd, *Interpretation of the Fourth Gospel*, 440.

30. Dodd, *Interpretation of the Fourth Gospel*, 442–43.

31. C. K. Barrett, *The Gospel according to St. John* (London: SPCK, 1955), 466.

32. Schnackenburg, *Gospel according to John*, 3:301.

33. Schnackenburg, *Gospel according to John*, 3:308.

34. Schnackenburg, *Gospel according to John*, 3:315.

35. This claim was challenged by Hodges on the obvious grounds that all four Gospels report Jesus's tomb to have been found empty by one (John) or more women (the Synoptics): "The Women and the Empty Tomb," 101–9.

36. Schnackenburg, *Gospel according to John*, 3:321.

37. F. Bovon, "Le privilege pascal de Marie-Madeleine," *New Testament Studies* 30 (1984): 50–62, at 51.

38. Bovon, "Le privilege pascal de Marie-Madeleine," 51–52.

39. Bovon, "Le privilege pascal de Marie-Madeleine," 51–52.

40. E. Schüssler Fiorenza, *In Memory of Her: A Feminist Reconstruction of Christian Origins* (New York: Crossroad, 1983), 322.

41. R. E. Brown, *The Community of the Beloved Disciple* (New York: Paulist Press, 1979).

42. E. Schüssler Fiorenza, *In Memory of Her*, 326.

43. Schüssler Fiorenza, *In Memory of Her*, 332.

44. Schüssler Fiorenza, *In Memory of Her*, 304–5.

45. Schüssler Fiorenza, *In Memory of Her*, 306.

46. In *Miriam's Child: Sophia's Prophet* (New York: Continuum, 1994), 125, Schüssler Fiorenza takes up this issue of geographical location.

47. Schüssler Fiorenza, *Miriam's Child*, 304.

48. Joseph Hug dates Mark 16:9–20 to the second third of the second century (*Le finale de l'Evangile de Marc* [Paris: J. Gabalda, 1978], 214). Elsewhere he concludes that Mark 16:9–11 does not depend either on John 20:14–18 or on Matt 28:9–10, but comes from a common tradition (165).

49. Bovon, "Le privilege pascal," 50. On Gnosticism, see Kurt Rudolph, "Gnosticism," *Anchor Bible Dictionary*, vol. 2 (New York: Doubleday, 1992), 1033–40.

50. Pheme Perkins's *The Gnostic Dialogue* (New York: Paulist Press, 1980).

51. E. Pagels, *The Gnostic Gospels* (New York: Random House, 1979).

52. Perkins, *The Gnostic Dialogue*, 205.

53. Perkins, *The Gnostic Dialogue*, 205.

54. P. Perkins, *Resurrection: New Testament Witness and Contemporary Reflection* (New York: Doubleday, 1984), 167.

55. Reviewing Schüssler Fiorenza's *In Memory of Her*, Robert Grant called it "a wholehearted attempt to rewrite traditional Christian history in favor of a feminist version" (*Journal of Religion* 65 [1985]: 83).

56. Perkins, *Resurrection*, 129.

57. Perkins, *Resurrection*, 131–32. Perkins should have talked of scholars holding that Peter's primacy is *"largely but not exclusively"* based on his rallying the others after his vision of the risen Lord; see Luke 22:32; 24:34 and chap. 9 in this book.

58. Perkins, *Resurrection*, 137.

59. Perkins, *Resurrection*, 167.

60. Perkins, *Resurrection*, 177.

61. Lincoln, *The Gospel according to St. John*, 494–95.

62. Brock, *Mary Magdalene, The First Apostle*, 174–75.

12. "His Life Rose with Him"

1. H. S. Holland, "Criticism and the Resurrection," in *On Behalf of Belief: Sermons Preached in St. Paul's Cathedral*, 2nd ed. (London: Longman, Green, & Co., 1892), 1–24, at 12.

2. R. A. Culpepper, *Anatomy of the Fourth Gospel: A Study in Literary Design* (Philadelphia: Fortress Press, 1983). Over twenty years later, in "Designs for the Church in the Imagery of John 21: 1–14," in *Imagery in the Gospel of John*, ed. J. Frey et al. (Tübingen: Mohr Siebeck, 2006), 369–402, at 369–71, Culpepper declared himself "even more convinced that John 1—21 forms a literary unity," and listed Richard Bauckham and others who agreed with him and rejected the "once-dominant view that John 21 is a later appendix." On the literary unity of John 21 with John 1—20, see M. Hasitschka, "The Significance of the Resurrection Appearance in John 21," in *The Resurrection of Jesus in the Gospel*

of John, ed. C. R. Koester and R. Bieringer (Tübingen: Mohr Siebeck, 2008), 311–28.

3. Many older commentators considered John 21 an appendix added by a later hand, even though we lack evidence for the Fourth Gospel ever circulating without that chapter. It seems more like an epilogue added by the original author; see R. Bauckham, *The Testimony of the Beloved Disciple* (Grand Rapids: Baker Academic, 2007), 271–84; C. S. Keener, *The Gospel of John: A Commentary*, vol. 1 (Peabody, MA: Hendrickson, 2003), 1217–22; and F. J. Moloney, "John 21 and the Johannine Story," in *Johannine Studies 1975—2017* (Tübingen: Mohr Siebeck, 2017), 521–37.

4. M. Marcheselli, *Studi sul vangelo di Giovanni: Testi, temi e contesto storico* (Rome: Gregorian and Biblicum Press, 2016), 131–56, at 131; trans. mine. See also J. Zumstein, *Kreative Erinnerung: Relecture und Auslegung im Johannesevangelium* (Zürich: Pano, 1999), 15–30.

5. Marcheselli, *Studi zum vangelo di Giovanni*,142–56; see also 95–118. In this later book he summarizes and slightly modifies what he had argued in *"Avete qualcosa da mangiare?": Un pasto, il Risorto, la comunità* (Bologna: Edizioni Dehoniane, 2006).

6. Keener, *The Gospel of John*, 1217.

7. On the Logos, see A. T. Lincoln, *The Gospel according to John* (London: Continuum, 2005), 93–109.

8. Brendan Byrne comments that "a reference to crucifixion" is "more or less inescapable" (*Life Abounding: A Reading of John's Gospel* [Collegeville, MN: Liturgical Press, 2012], 351n78); he agrees with Lincoln (*The Gospel according to St. John*, 318–19). C. K. Barrett in *The Gospel according to St. John*, 2nd ed. (London: SPCK, 1978), when commenting on the words "you will stretch out your hands," writes, "This passage must be taken as comparatively early and good evidence for the martyrdom of Peter by crucifixion" (585). M. M. Thompson also recognizes a reference to Peter's death by crucifixion (*John: A Commentary* [Louisville, KY: Westminster John Knox, 2015], 443).

9. Unlike the Synoptic Gospels, where we find Jesus sometimes employing "the single Amen in a striking position," John alone uses "the double Amen formula" (Lincoln, *The Gospel according to John*, 122).

10. This translation is preferable to "the true light enlightening everyone who was coming into the world"; see Lincoln, *The Gospel according to John*, 101.

11. See Lincoln, *The Gospel according to John*, 225–38, about this discourse on the bread of life.

12. Greek and Latin zoologists, according to Jerome, classified 153 different kinds of fish; the catch in John 21 symbolizes that, with the help of Jesus, the disciples have caught "all kinds" of people. Since 153 is the sum of the numbers from one to seventeen and so the sum of the numbers seven and ten (both of which represent completeness), Augustine proposed a symbolic explanation of perfection. See Barrett, *Gospel according to John*, 581; Culpepper, "Designs for the Church," 383–94; Keener, *The Gospel according to John*, 1231–33; C. Marucci, "Il significato del numero 153 in Gv 21: 11," *Rivista Biblica* 52 (2004): 403–40; M. Rastoin, "Encore un fois les 153 poissons (Jn 21,11)," *Biblica* 90 (2009): 84–92; and Thompson, *John*, 437–39. Luke knew of a (somewhat different) miracle involving Peter and a great catch of fish (Luke 5:1–11) but inserted it in the context of Peter and other disciples being called; see ch. 9 above and Y. Mathieu, *La figure de Pierre dans l'oeuvre de Luc* (Paris: Gabalda, 2004), 65–78.

13. Hasitschka points out how "by bringing Thomas and Nathanael together, the evangelist invites us to think about these two disciples, who in the Gospel of John express a first [1.49] and the last [20.28] great confession of faith in Jesus" ("The Significance of the Resurrection Appearance in John 21," 314).

14. See M.-E. Boismard, "Le disciple que Jésus aimait d'après Jn 21:1ss et 1:35ss," *Revue Biblique* 105 (1998): 76–80.

15. John 21:3 presupposes that Peter has at his disposition a boat big enough for seven fishermen, at least one large net, and other tackle needed for a serious fishing expedition; it also implies that the other six disciples already knew something about fishing, since they all spontaneously join Peter. Marcheselli illustrates how no other section of John's Gospel shows such contacts with the Synoptic traditions as does John 21. Its use of a catch of fish to convey mission, for instance, is nowhere else to be found in John's Gospel but is familiar from Mark 1:17 (= Matt 4:19) and Luke 5:1–11. It is only in John 21 that we hear of the sons of Zebedee, who enjoy a considerable role in the Synoptic Gospels (*Studi sul vangelo di Giovanni*, 94–96, and 144n49). On the relationship of John to the other Gospels, see A. Denaux, ed., *John and the Synoptics* (Leuven: Leuven University Press, 1992).

Notes

16. "The most obvious reading of the passage is that he [the Beloved Disciple] is one of 'two others of his disciples,' listed as part of the fishing group" (Lincoln, *The Gospel according to John*, 22).

17. As Lincoln suggests, the *seven* disciples, "with that number's connotation of completeness, may suggest that the group is meant" to represent all Jesus's followers (*The Gospel according to John*, 510).

18. Unlike John 20:11–29, where the account of the Easter appearances uses *theōreō* (see), *erchomai* (come), and *horaō* (see), "manifest" should alert the attentive reader to much earlier episodes in John's Gospel, as we shall see. "By the Sea of Tiberias" could also be translated "on the Sea of Tiberias." In that case the text would recall the appearance of Jesus walking on the sea (John 6:19); an Easter appearance resurrects that dramatic episode.

19. In John 21:1, the NRSV translates *ephanerōsen* twice as "showed" himself; in John 21:14, another form of the same verb is rendered "appeared." Back in John 1:31 and 2:11, the very same verb is translated "revealed," and in John 17:6 as "made known." Those who lack Greek have no way of knowing that in all five places it is the same verb that recurs (*phaneroō*).

20. Marcheselli points out how the choice of *phaneroō* in John 21 serves to "re-read" not only John 20:11–29 but also John 1:19—2:12. No part of the Fourth Gospel re-presents "in such an analytic and articulated way the process of Jesus' manifestation and reception" as does John 21, by reproposing in the postresurrection setting what has been "narrated at the beginning of Jesus' ministry": *Studi sul vangelo di Giovanni*, 103–5. In the context of the Church's post-Easter mission to the world, John 21 reactualizes the Messiah's original manifestation to Israel (144–46).

21. Lincoln, *The Gospel according to John*, 21; see 119–24.

22. This is suggested by Jesus moving from "you will see" in the singular (John 1:50) to "you will see" in the plural (John 1:51).

23. William Loader refers the "greater things" to "the outcome of Jesus' death, exaltation and glorification" (*Jesus in John's Gospel: Structure and Issues in Johannine Christology* [Grand Rapids: Eerdmans, 2017], 258; see 266–72, 280–81).

24. On the marriage in Cana, see Lincoln, *The Gospel according to John*, 125–31.

25. See Paul D. Duke, *Irony in the Fourth Gospel* (Atlanta: John Knox, 1985).

26. Byrne, *Life Abounding*, 345.

27. On the Beloved Disciple, see Lincoln, *The Gospel according to John*, 17–26.

28. Byrne, *Life Abounding*, 257.

29. The verb *agapaō* occurs in John 13:1, 23, 34; 14:15, 21 (four times), 23 (twice), 28, 31; 15:9 (twice), 12 (twice), 17; 17:23 (twice), 24, 26. The noun *agapē* occurs in John 13:35; 15:9, 10 (twice), 13; and 17:26. The verb *phileō* occurs in 15:19; 16:27 (twice); the noun *philos* occurs in 15:13, 14, 15.

30. See in John 11:3 (*phileō*) and 11:5 (*agapaō*) Jesus's love for Lazarus; in John 5:20 (*phileō*) and 3:35; 10:17 (*agapaō*) the Father's love for Jesus; in John 16:27 (*phileō*) and 14:21 (*agapaō*) the Father's love for the disciples; and in John 20:2 (*phileō*) and 13:23 (*agapaō*) the disciple whom Jesus loved. For some current discussion of the two verbs, see Marcheselli, *Studi sul vangelo di Giovanni*, 139.

31. Just as "the boy" in John 6 brings food (fish and bread) to Jesus, so the "boys/children" of John 21 will also bring him some food (fish).

32. Thompson, *John*, 437.

33. Byrne, *Life Abounding*, 346.

34. See Loader, *Jesus in John's Gospel*, 379–80.

35. Hasitschka comments that the disciples contribute something "they have caught themselves, albeit with the assistance of the Lord" ("The Significance of the Resurrection Appearance in John 21," 317).

36. On this theme of "hauling," see Marcheselli, *Studi sul vangelo di Giovanni*, 106–7.

37. Keener, *The Gospel of John*, 1234.

38. Marcheselli, *Studi sul vangelo di Giovanni*, 103. Yet the sign of the great catch may still be compared with the changing of water into wine (John 2:1–11) and the feeding of the five thousand (6:1–15). In all three cases there is shortage; Jesus remedies the situation abundantly; all three signs happen in Galilee and in the context of a meal.

39. Marcheselli, *Studi sul vangelo di Giovanni*, 105–6.

40. Since at the breakfast in John 21 there is no "breaking of bread," drinking of wine, and "giving thanks" (see John 6:11) and since the theme of fish dominates over that of bread, Keener argues that the "eucharistic overtones" are not "clear" (*The Gospel of John*, 1231). It might be more accurate to say that those eucharistic overtones are not "complete." Nevertheless, Jesus's taking and giving bread in the context

Notes

of a postresurrection meal provide the needed overtones. As Barrett puts matters, the meal has "evidently *some* Eucharistic significance," and points out that "fish occurs" with bread "in some early representations of the Eucharist" (*The Gospel according to St. John*, 578; my italics). By evoking John 6, John 21 necessarily moves readers toward the theme of the Eucharist; see Marcheselli, *Studi sul vangelo di Giovanni*, 148-50.

41. Marcheselli rightly insists on the full meaning of food in John 6 and 21: it indicates "the totality of the person of Jesus, his word of revelation, and the Eucharist, the gift of his existence as a fountain of life for the world" (*Studi sul vangelo di Giovanni*, 150).

42. Thompson, *John*, 433, 434; my italics.

43. This is, in fact, the only *explicit* recall in John 21 of something that has happened during the earthly life of Jesus; the chapter, as we have seen and will see, teems with implicit recalls of things said and done during his earthly life.

44. See Culpepper, "Design for the Church," 395-402; M. Wallraff et al., "Fish, Fishing," in *The Encyclopedia of the Bible and Its Reception*, vol. 9 (Berlin: De Gruyter, 2014), 120-34, esp. 124-25, 129-33.

45. Lincoln, *The Gospel according to John*, 23.

46. Lincoln, *The Gospel according to John*, 512.

47. See J. S. Sturtevant, "The Centrality of Discipleship in the Johannine Portrayal of Peter," in Bond and Hurtado, *Peter in Early Christianity*, 109-20.

48. Significantly it is only after Peter has been fed by the risen Jesus (John 21:15) that he is commissioned to feed others (John 21:15-17).

49. Byrne, *Life Abounding*, 349. In "The (Not So) Good Shepherd: The Use of Shepherd Imagery in the Characterization of Peter in the Fourth Gospel," François Tolmie writes, "Peter will 'shepherd' Jesus' sheep by doing himself what is expected of the sheep of the Good Shepherd: *following* the Good Shepherd" (in Frey et al., *Imagery in the Gospel of John*, 352-67, at 367; my italics).

50. See Keener, *The Gospel of John*, 1237-38, and n. 8 above.

51. Barrett, *The Gospel according to St. John*, 583.

52. Loader, *Jesus in John's Gospel*, 214, 215; on glorification in John's Gospel, see 213-40.

53. Lincoln writes, "As the witness in 19:35, the Beloved Disciple testifies to the pronouncement of God's positive verdict of life through the death of Jesus. The function of his witness here is the same as that of

his witness in the Gospel as a whole (cf. 20:31); it is in order that readers may believe" (*The Gospel according to John*, 25; see 479–81). The witness role of the Beloved Disciple distinguishes him from the role of Peter as "the great pastor" (Barrett, *The Gospel according to St. John*, 583).

54. Keener, *The Gospel according to John*, 1238.

55. Lincoln, *The Gospel according to John*, 522. See R. Bauckham, "The Fourth Gospel as the Testimony of the Beloved Disciple," in *The Gospel of John and Christian Theology*, ed. R. Bauckham and Carl Mosser (Grand Rapids: Eerdmans, 2008), 120–39.

56. Byrne, *Life Abounding*, 353.

57. Culpepper doubts, however, that "the ecclesial emphasis of John 21 surpasses that of the rest of the Gospel" ("Designs for the Church," 371–72; see 402). However, judging between his view and that of Marcheselli would require a separate study.

13. Buried by His Enemies?

1. J. A. Fitzmyer, *The Acts of the Apostles* (New York: Doubleday, 1998), 515.

2. C. R. Holladay, *Acts: A Commentary* (Louisville, KY: Westminster John Knox, 2011), 270.

3. D. L. Bock, *Acts* (Grand Rapids: Baker Academic, 2007), 454–55.

4. R. I. Pervo, *Acts: A Commentary* (Minneapolis: Fortress Press, 2009), 338.

5. C. S. Keener, *Acts: An Exegetical Commentary*, vol. 2 (Grand Rapids: Baker Academic, 2013), 2068.

6. Keener, *Acts*, 2068.

7. F. Bovon, *Luke*, vol. 3, trans. J. E. Crouch (Grand Rapids: Fortress Press, 2012), 355. Although he did not mention Maurice Goguel, Bovon agreed with Goguel's thesis that Jewish opponents buried Jesus: *The Birth of Christianity*, trans. H. C. Snape (London: Allen and Unwin, 1953), 30–33.

8. Bovon, *Luke*, 3:355. Here we should recall Raymond Brown's warning that "apologetics and historicity" are not necessarily "incompatible" (*The Death of the Messiah*, vol. 2 [New York: Doubleday, 1994], 1310). Things that truly happened are often used for apologetical purposes.

9. On the day of Pentecost, Peter's speech contrasts two known tombs, that of David whose body was corrupted and that of Jesus (in which "his flesh did not experience corruption"); see Fitzmyer, *Acts*, 255–56.

10. H. Conzelmann, *Acts of the Apostles*, trans. J. Limburg et al. (Philadelphia: Fortress Press, 1987), 105.

11. J. Calvin, *The Acts of the Apostles*, trans. J. W. Fraser and W. J. G. McDonald, vol. 1 (Edinburgh: Oliver & Boyd, 1965), 642.

12. For serious arguments against the historicity (but not the theological value) of the guard story, see R. E. Brown, *The Death of the Messiah*, vol. 2 (New York: Doubleday, 1994), 1310–13. According to Ulrich Luz, "there is no way to salvage the historicity" either of the appointment of the guard (Matt 27:62–66) or of their subsequent collaboration in deception (Matt 28:11–15): *Matthew 21—28*, trans. W. C. Linss (Minneapolis: Augsburg Fortress, 2005), 587.

13. On the identity and role of Joseph of Arimathea, see Brown, *The Death of the Messiah*, 2:1213–19. On the significance of his being a Sanhedrinist for attributing Jesus's burial to his enemies in Acts 13:29, see Keener, *Acts*, 2068.

14. C. K. Barrett, *The Acts of the Apostles*, vol. 1 (Edinburgh: T&T Clark, 1994), 641.

15. Barrett, *Acts of the Apostles*, 1:642.

16. E. Haenchen, *The Acts of the Apostles: A Commentary*, trans. B. Noble and G. Shinn (Philadelphia: Westminster Press, 1971), 410.

17. J. Jervell, *Die Apostelgeschichte* (Göttingen: Vandenhoeck & Ruprecht, 1998), 358: "…but we have here a shortened report. The burial is the background, the contrast scheme for God's saving deed [the resurrection]"; trans. mine.

14. The Language of Reconciliation

1. I wrote the original version of this chapter with T. Michael McNulty, SJ ("St. Paul and the Language of Reconciliation," *Colloquium* 6 [1973]: 3–8).

2. See "*katallagē, katallassō*," in Walter Bauer, Frederick W. Danker, William F. Arndt, and F. Wilbur Gingrich, *Greek-English Lexicon of the New Testament and Other Early Christian Literature*, 3rd ed. (Chicago: University of Chicago Press, 2000), 521; hereafter *BDAG*. In

the words of Brendan Byrne, Paul "was taking an image from the world of diplomacy" and "applying it to God's work in Christ" (*Romans* [Collegeville, MN: Liturgical Press, 1996], 172). See the seminal study by Cilliers Breytenbach, *Versöhnung: Eine Studie zur paulinischen Soteriologie* (Neukirchen-Vluyn: Neukirchener Verlag, 1989), 107–43.

3. L. Wittgenstein, *Philosophical Investigations*, trans. G. E. M. Anscombe, 3rd ed. (New York: Macmillan, 1971), par. 109.

4. Jan Lambrecht, *Second Corinthians* (Collegeville, MN: Liturgical Press, 1999), 100.

5. G. D. Kaufman, *Systematic Theology: A Historicist Perspective* (New York: Charles Scribner's Sons, 1968), 389n1.

6. As Margaret E. Thrall comments, with the Christ event "what has changed is not God's fundamental disposition [of love] towards mankind, but rather his means of dealing with the sinfulness which has caused the state of estrangement" (*The Second Epistle to the Corinthians*, vol. 1 [Edinburgh: T&T Clark, 1994], 431).

7. J. D. G. Dunn, *The Theology of Paul the Apostle* (Grand Rapids: Eerdmans, 1998), 229.

8. Thrall, *The Second Epistle to the Corinthians*, 1:430.

9. *BDAG*, 521; emphasis original. On reconciliation in Rom 5:8–11, see Douglas J. Moo, *The Epistle to the Romans* (Grand Rapids: Eerdmans, 1996), 297, 309–14. Moo presumes only two stages and so avoids any inaccurate presupposition by presenting reconciliation simply as bringing together or making peace "between two estranged or hostile parties" (311). He does the same when commenting on "reconciliation" in Rom 11:15: "Reconciliation...refers to God's act of bringing sinners into a peaceful relationship with himself" (693). Dunn, like Moo, also correctly names only two stages when calling reconciliation "the bringing together of two parties at enmity with each other into new peace and cooperation" (*The Theology of Paul the Apostle*, 328).

10. J. A. Fitzmyer, "Pauline Theology," in *The Jerome Biblical Commentary*, ed. R. E. Brown, J. A. Fitzmyer, and R. E. Murphy (Englewood Cliffs, NJ: Prentice-Hall, 1968), 814. Fitzmyer dropped this language in the corresponding section on "reconciliation" in Brown, Fitzmyer, and Murphy, *The New Jerome Biblical Commentary* (Englewood Cliffs, NJ: Prentice-Hall, 1990), 1398–99; there he recognized only two stages: "God through Christ brings it about that human beings are brought from a status of enmity to friendship" (1398–99).

Notes

11. Thrall, *The Second Epistle to the Corinthians*, 1:429; my italics. But like Fitzmyer, who later silently abandoned the language of "return," Thrall appears to switch in her account of "reconciliation," albeit in the same commentary, from speaking of "restoration" (three stages) to that of "removal" of estrangement (two stages): "it is through sinfulness that they [men and women] have become estranged and hostile," and "reconciliation must entail the removal of this barrier to friendly relations" (435).

12. See *BDAG*, 521.

13. Thrall, *The Second Epistle to the Corinthians*, 431.

14. Thrall, *The Second Epistle to the Corinthians*, 97.

15. See Jean-Noël Aletti, "'God Made Christ to Be Sin' (2 Cor 5:21): Reflections on a Pauline Paradox," in *The Redemption: An Interdisciplinary Symposium on Christ as Redeemer*, ed. Stephen T. Davis, Daniel Kendall, and Gerald O'Collins (Oxford: Oxford University Press, 2004), 101–20, esp. 102–9; see also J. T. Fitzgerald, "Paul and Paradigm Shifts: Reconciliation and its Linkage Group," in *Paul beyond the Judaism/Hellenism Divide*, ed. T. Engberg-Pedersen (Louisville, KY: John Knox Press, 2001), 241–62. On 2 Cor 5:21, see George Hunsinger, *Philippians* (Grand Rapids: Brazos Press, 2020), 204–13.

16. Thrall, *The Second Epistle to the Corinthians*, 1:437–38.

17. J. P. Sampley, "The Second Letter to the Corinthians," *The New Interpreter's Bible*, vol. 11 (Nashville: Abingdon Press, 2000), 95.

18. Sampley distinguishes the explicit call to be "reconciled to God" from the "encoded message": the Corinthians should "be reconciled to Paul, the ambassador who has brought the reconciliation gospel to them in the first place and thereby been the occasion for the end of their enmity with God (cf. Rom 5:1, 10)" (Sampley, "The Second Letter to the Corinthians," 95).

19. Thrall, *The Second Epistle to the Corinthians*, 437.

20. J. A. Fitzmyer, *Romans* (New York: Doubleday, 1993), 612; Dunn also takes *kosmos* here in the sense of cosmic reconciliation (*The Theology of Paul the Apostle*, 229n128). On the meanings of *kosmos*, see *BDAG*, 561–63. Moo convincingly interprets *kosmos* in Rom 11:15 as referring to the Gentiles, and not to the whole created world: *Epistle to the Romans*, 694.

21. Thrall, *The Second Epistle to the Corinthians*, 434.

22. Victor P. Furnish, *II Corinthians* (New York: Doubleday, 1984), 319. Sampley understands 2 Cor 5:19 to state that "God's work in Christ

was cosmic in scope" ("Second Letter to the Corinthians," 95). But Jan Lambrecht avoids "a cosmological understanding of "world"; it "means sinful humankind" (*Second Corinthians*, 99).

23. Col 1:20 does not use *katallassō* but the related verb *apokatallassō*, which also means "reconcile": see *BDAG*, 112.

24. E. Käsemann, "Some Thoughts on the Theme 'The Doctrine of Reconciliation in the New Testament,'" in *The Future of Our Religious Past*, ed. James M. Robinson (London: SCM Press, 1971), 451–64.

25. A. T. Lincoln, "The Letter to the Colossians," in *The New Interpreter's Bible*, vol. 11 (Nashville: Abingdon Press, 2000), 600.

26. E. Lohse, *Colossians and Philemon*, trans. William R. Poehlmann and Robert J. Karris (Philadelphia: Fortress Press, 1971), 59.

15. Love as a Verb

1. J. A. Fitzmyer, *First Corinthians* (New Haven, CT: Yale University Press, 2008), 488. One of these verbs (*chrēsteuetai*) is middle in voice but active in meaning. Daniel B. Wallace explains, "In the middle voice the subject *performs* or *experiences the action* expressed by the verb in such a way that *emphasizes the subject's participation*" (*Greek Grammar: Beyond the Basics* [Grand Rapids: Zondervan, 1996], 414; my italics; see also 428). Two other verbs used by Paul (*phusioutai* and *paroxunetai*) are likewise active in meaning, whether we understand them to be middle or passive in voice.

2. Fitzmyer, *First Corinthians*, 487–507, at 487.

3. Fitzmyer, *First Corinthians*, 489, 495.

4. Fitzmyer, *First Corinthians*, 487.

5. Fitzmyer, *First Corinthians*, 488–90.

6. C. K. Barrett, *The First Epistle to the Corinthians* (London: A. & C. Black, 1971), 303.

7. G. D. Fee, *The First Epistle to the Corinthians* (Grand Rapids: Eerdmans, 1987), 637, 641.

8. C. Spicq, *Agapē dans le nouveau testament*, vol. 2 (Paris: Gabalda, 1959), 77, 80, 93.

9. C. L. Craig, *The First Epistle to the Corinthians*, in *The Interpreter's Bible*, vol. 10 (Nashville: Abingdon Press, 1953), 172.

Notes

10. A. C. Thiselton, *The First Epistle to the Corinthians* (Grand Rapids: Eerdmans, 2000), 1046–48.

11. Thiselton, *The First Epistle to the Corinthians*, 1046–61. In the case of two verbs, *phusioutai* and *zētei*, his translation, however, uses "is" followed by a participle ("not inflated" and "not preoccupied," respectively).

12. Fitzmyer, *First Corinthians*, 487.

13. Thiselton, *First Epistle to the Corinthians*, 1026.

14. This translation also draws slightly on Archibald Robertson and Alfred Plummer, *The First Epistle of Paul to the Corinthians* (Edinburgh: T&T Clark 1929), 292–96.

15. Wallace, *Greek Grammar*, 410; his italics. Wallace adds and defines another, much less frequent form of the active voice, the "stative active": "the subject exists in the state indicated by the verb." A stative active, he adds, can be identified as "one that in translation uses *am* + a predicate adjective"; Wallace offers a convincing example: *plouteō* (I am rich). He cites as another example 1 Cor 13:4: "love is patient, love is kind" (412–13); many versions agree with this translation. But the question remains: does this translation correspond appropriately to the "verbal" quality of the whole passage, 1 Cor 13:4–8a? Are we truly dealing here with a "stative active"? Without citing 1 Cor 13:4–8a, Kenneth L. McKay, in *A New Syntax of the Verb in New Testament Greek: An Aspectival Approach* (New York: Peter Lang, 1994), writes, "The present tense is so named because one of its main uses is to describe a process taking place in present time." He adds at once a reference to the related, "timeless present": "an equally common use of the present tense Is to describe an activity as generally or customarily occurring" (40). In 1 Cor 13:4, two activities are occurring.

16. Wallace, *Greek Grammar*, 514.

17. Two examples: on 1 Cor 13:4–8a, see, e.g., Raymond F. Collins, *First Corinthians* (Collegeville, MN: Liturgical Press, 1999), 478–93; and Wolfgang Schrage, *Die erste Brief an die Korinther (1 Kor 11,17—14,40)* (Zürich/Neukirchen-Vluyn: Benziger Verlag/Neukirchener Verlag, 1999), 293–305.

18. These statistics do not include the biblical passages Paul quotes in these verses.

16. The Appearances of the Risen Christ

1. Curiously, after translating *ōphthē* in 1 Cor 15:5, 6, 7 as "he was seen by," in v. 8 Phillips translates the same word as "he appeared." Somewhat surprisingly, 1 Cor 15:6 (the only example selected from the four occurrences of *ōphthē* in these verses) is translated by Johannes P. Louw and Eugene A. Nida, eds., as Christ "was seen by more than 500 faithful, even though they have just explained" the subdomain of seeing as "coming into the range of vision" or "appearing": *Greek-English Lexicon of the New Testament Based on Semantic Domains*, vol. 1 (New York: United Bible Societies, 1988), 277.

2. With the aim of elucidating Paul's language about seeing the risen Lord and the Lord's appearing, this paragraph has introduced examples from other (later) New Testament authors using various forms of *horaō*. The next paragraph will recall relevant passages from the (much earlier) LXX. We must examine later and earlier usage when investigating Paul's possible meaning(s).

3. Joseph A. Fitzmyer, *First Corinthians* (New Haven, CT: Yale University Press, 2008), 549.

4. In this and other Old Testament theophanies what God *says* is regularly to the fore rather than any details about the divine "appearance."

5. Normal Hellenistic language shows up in the appendix to Mark: Christ "appeared [*ephanē*] first to Mary Magdalene" (Mark 16:9; see also 16:12 and 14, which use the form *ephanerōthē*).

6. Fitzmyer, *First Corinthians*, 549; in a partial list, Fitzmyer cites eighteen examples of this usage in the LXX.

7. J. Jeremias, *Eucharistic Words*, trans. Norman Perrin (London: SCM Press, 1966), 101–3. F. F. Bruce, clearly respectful of Jeremias's scholarship, translated *ōphthē* in 1 Cor 15 as "he let himself be seen"; *1 and 2 Corinthians* (London: Oliphants, 1971), 140.

8. Joseph H. Thayer, *Greek-English Lexicon of the New Testament* (Peabody, MA: Hendrickson, 1999; reprint of 4th ed. of 1896), 452.

9. Fitzmyer, *First Corinthians*, 542.

10. Raymond F. Collins, *First Corinthians* (Collegeville, MN: Liturgical Press, 1999), 528, 535.

Notes

11. A. Thiselton, *The First Epistle to the Corinthians* (Grand Rapids: Eerdmans, 2000), 1198.

12. W. Schrage, *Der erste Brief an die Korinther*, vol. 4 (Düsseldorf: Benziger Verlag, and Neukirchen-Vluyn: Neukirchener Verlag, 2001), 47.

13. D. B. Wallace, *Greek Grammar beyond the Basics: An Exegetical Syntax of the New Testament* (Grand Rapids: Zondervan, 1996), 165n72; he refers not only to the four occurrences in 1 Cor 15 but also to Matt 17:3; Mark 9:4; Luke 1:11; 22:43; 24:34; Acts 7:2, 26, 30; 13:31; 16:9; 1 Tim 3:16. Besides the use of *ōphthē*, we should also recall the participle *ophtheis* (Acts 9:17), and the verbs *ōphthēn* (Acts 26:16) and *ophthēsomai* (Acts 26:16). In all three cases the subject initiates the manifestation; the person mentioned in the dative—in all three cases Paul—is the recipient.

14. Friedrich Blass and Albert Debrunner, *A Greek Grammar of the New Testament and Other Early Christian Literature*, trans. and rev. Robert W. Funk (Cambridge: Cambridge University Press, 1961), no. 313; see also no. 101.

15. Walter Bauer, Frederick W. Danker, William F. Arndt, and F. Wilbur Gingrich, *A Greek-English Lexicon of the New Testament and other Early Christian Literature*, 3rd ed. (Chicago: University of Chicago Press, 2000), 719; hereafter *BDAG*.

16. Acts 10:40, however, not only uses Hellenistic language (*emphanē*) rather than a Hebraism or what Fitzmyer (see above) calls "a semitized Greek verb" (*ōphthē*), but also names God as subject of the verb rather than Christ, as in 1 Cor 15. Thus Acts 10:40, while yielding a valid theological comment on 1 Cor 15:5–8, does not directly guide its translation. Similar Hellenistic language turns up in an apocalyptic addition in Matt 27:52–53, which speaks of "holy ones" emerging from tombs and "appearing [*enphanisthēsan*] to many people after his [Jesus's] resurrection."

17. Schrage, *Der erste Brief an die Korinther*, 4:47–48.

18. Jacob Kremer, who also examines the possibility of understanding *ōphthē* to be a divine passive, rejects it even more emphatically on the grounds that Christ is the subject of the verb: "Interpreting this phrase as a theological passive 'God caused him to be visible' founders on the fact that Christ is the subject": J. Kremer, "*horaō*," in *Exegetical Dictionary of the New Testament*, vol. 2, ed. Horst Balz and Gerhard Schneider (Grand Rapids: Eerdmans, 1991), 528.

19. When discussing 1 Cor 15:5–8, N. T. Wright also adopts the same translation, "he appeared": *The Resurrection of the Son of God* (Minneapolis: Fortress Press, 2003), 322–28.

20. Fitzmyer, *First Corinthians*, 550; Schrage, *Der erste Brief an die Korinther*, 54, 61.

21. Fitzmyer, *First Corinthians*, 550.

22. For example, Bruce, *1 and 2 Corinthians*, 140; Richard B. Hays, *1 Corinthians* (Louisville, KY: Knox, 1997), 257; Michael R. Licona, *The Resurrection of Jesus: A New Historiographical Approach* (Downers Grove, IL: IVP Academic, 2010), 323, 337, 349–55.

23. Thiselton, *The First Epistle to the Corinthians*, 668. Commentaries on 1 Cor 9:1 (in particular, Bruce, Collins, Fitzmyer, Schrage, and Thiselton) understand the verse to refer to the risen Jesus's appearance claimed by Paul in 1 Cor 15:8. As Collins says, the question ("Have I not seen Jesus our Lord?") "clearly makes reference to the event to which Paul alludes in 15:8" (*First Corinthians*, 334).

24. Collins, *First Corinthians*, 329. As Collins later states, "That Paul has seen the Lord has permanently established him as an apostle" (335).

25. In 2 Cor 4:6, Paul, although speaking in the plural ("our hearts"), may refer to his Damascus road encounter. But, while introducing "light," "shining," "glory," and "knowledge," he does not speak of his "seeing" the risen Christ: "It is the God who said, 'Let light shine out of darkness,' who has shone in our hearts to give the light of the knowledge of the glory of God on the face of Jesus Christ."

26. Daniel Kendall and Gerald O'Collins, "The Uniqueness of the Easter Appearances," *Catholic Biblical Quarterly* 54 (1991): 287–307, at 295–97.

27. Wilhelm Michaelis attempted to explain the Easter encounters simply as episodes of revelation, reducing the Easter encounters to a revelation by word (that we find repeatedly in the Jewish Scriptures) and playing down their eyewitness quality. But unlike the formula "the Lord appeared *and said*" (Gen 12:7; 17:1; 26:2, 24; 35:9), the postresurrection encounters echo only the first part of the formula ("he appeared"): 1 Cor 15:5–8 (4 examples); Luke 24:34; Acts 13:31; there is no revelation by word in these six cases. Such revelation by word predominates with the great prophets, but in the case of these six New Testament appearances, we never read that "the Lord appeared and said to them." The Old Testament background to which Michaelis appealed does not support

Notes

his case. For full details and a complete rebuttal of his view, see Kendall and O'Collins, "The Uniqueness of the Easter Appearances," 289–92.

28. Here this article moves its focus beyond Paul to examine the use (and possible meanings) of *ōphthē* and related forms of *horaō* in other New Testament texts.

29. *BDAG*, 719.

30. Stephen (as reported by Luke in Acts 7:2) speaks of God "appearing," whereas the relevant LXX passage (Gen 12:1) simply says that God "spoke" to Abraham.

31. Collins, *First Corinthians*, 334.

32. Wallace detects here hymnic material: *Greek Grammar*, 340–42.

33. Luke Timothy Johnson, *The First and Second Letters to Timothy* (New York: Doubleday, 2001), 233; Jerome D. Quinn and William C. Wacker, *The First and Second Letters to Timothy* (Grand Rapids: Eerdmans, 2000), 297, 315–48. Philip H. Towner, *The Letters to Timothy and Titus* (Grand Rapids: Eerdmans, 2006), 281–82, considers a "reference to human messengers" possible but prefers to translate "angels." I. Howard Marshall, *The Pastoral Epistles* (London: T&T Clark, 1999), 526–27, likewise notes the possibility of human "messengers," but prefers to translate *aggeloi* as "angels."

34. Kremer, "*horaō*," 528.

35. For a complete account of the (visual) vocabulary used to express the risen Christ's appearances, see Joseph Hug, *La finale de l'Évangile de Marc* (Paris: Gabalda, 1978), 53–61.

36. Kremer, "*horaō*," 528; see n. 22 above.

37. The New Testament endorses this transcendence by characterizing God as invisible: John 1:18; 5:37; 6:46; Col 1:15; 1 Tim 1:17, Heb 11:27; 1 John 4:12. While affirming that no one "can see" God (1 Tim 6:16), the New Testament also says paradoxically that Moses "persevered because he saw him [God] who is invisible" (Heb 11:27). This could also be translated, "persevered as though he saw him [God] who is invisible" (NRSV).

38. Collins, *First Corinthians*, 535. As regards "the traditional Jewish understanding of divine transcendence," there could be exceptions: e.g., in his vision of the heavenly throne room Isaiah says, "My eyes have seen the King, the LORD of hosts" (Isa 6:5).

39. I say "immediately," so as not to deny what was quoted from Schrage (see n. 17 above): "Ultimately it is God himself who brings about the appearances of Christ."

40. Kremer, "*horaō*," 528.

41. Collins, *First Corinthians*, 535.

42. To be sure, in 1 Cor 15:42–44 Paul writes about the resurrection of the dead (in the plural). However, he moves at once to speak of Christ "the last Adam," who first had a "physical" and then a "spiritual" existence (15:45–49). Paul has already called the risen Christ "the first fruits of those who have fallen asleep" (15:20), thus implying some real analogy between the "spiritual body" of Christ and that of those who would be resurrected. See further G. O'Collins, *Jesus Our Redeemer: A Christian Approach to Salvation* (Oxford: Oxford University Press, 2007), 242–62.

43. G. O'Collins, *The Easter Jesus*, new ed. (London: Darton, Longman & Todd, 1980), 72; see also G. O'Collins, *Believing in the Resurrection: The Meaning and Promise of the Risen Jesus* (Mahwah, NJ: Paulist Press, 2012), 78–79, which also reflects on Mary Magdalene turning twice ("physically" and "spiritually," respectively).

44. Thiselton, *The First Epistle to the Corinthians*, 1199.

45. Against this view see G. O'Collins, *Interpreting the Resurrection* (Mahwah, NJ: Paulist Press, 1988), 59–61; Schrage, *Der erste Brief an die Korinther*, 4:47n159.

46. Notice how, when citing the foundational appearance to him of the risen Jesus, Paul speaks of "Jesus our *Lord*" (1 Cor 9:1); this encounter also brought Paul a revelation of the *Son of God* (Gal 1:16).

47. To justify the claim that these appearances were unique and not repeatable, see Kendall and O'Collins, "The Uniqueness of the Easter Appearances," 287–307.

48. Origen, *Contra Celsum*, trans. Henry Chadwick (Cambridge: Cambridge University Press, 1953; reprinted 1978), 2.65, p. 116.

49. *Summa Theologiae*, 3a, 55, 2, ad primum. This laconic phrase might also be translated as "eyes/sight working through faith," or "with the eyes/sight of faith," or "with a faith that has eyes/sight."

50. On this view, see Kremer, "*horaō*," 528; Licona, *The Resurrection of Jesus*, 339–43; Schrage, *Der erste Brief an die Korinther*, vol. 4, 49–51; Wright, *The Resurrection of the Son of God*, 677–78.

51. See ch. 11 of this book; Wright, *The Resurrection of the Son of God*, 677–78.

52. On 2 Cor 12:1–4, see Licona, *The Resurrection of Jesus*, 381–82.

53. See further G. O'Collins, *Jesus Risen: An Historical, Fundamental and Systematic Examination of Christ's Resurrection* (Mahwah,

NJ: Paulist Press, 1987), 210–16; O'Collins, *Interpreting the Resurrection*, 13–15; Wright, *The Resurrection of the Son of God*, 324–25.

54. Quinn and Wacker, *The First and Second Letters to Timothy*, 297.

55. J. H. Moulton and G. Milligan, *The Vocabulary of the Greek Testament* (London: Hodder and Stoughton, 1930), 455.

56. *BDAG*, 719–20.

57. Various translations (e.g., NAB, NRSV, REB, and RSV) simply leave "see" here without an object. The NJB follows Bauer-Danker in translating "will see him."

58. R. E. Brown, *The Epistles of John* (New York: Doubleday, 1982), 403, 427–28, 720–21, 748.

59. A fuller lexical treatment would need to examine the related nouns: *horama* ("vision," used six times in the NT), *horasis* ("vision," "appearance," used three times in the NT), and *optasia* ("vision," used four times in the NT). With all three nouns the "visions" are somehow "objective" and not mere figments of the imagination. In Acts 26:19, Luke uses *optasia* of Paul's encounter with the risen Christ on the Damascus road, describing it as a "heavenly vision" or "vision from heaven."

17. "Power Made Perfect in Weakness"

1. Hans Dieter Betz, "Eine Christus-Aretalogie bei Paulus (2 Kor 12:7–10)," *Zeitschrift für Theologie und Kirche* 66 (1969): 288–305. Since the next and final chapter of this book examines the reception of my article as published in the *Catholic Biblical Quarterly* 33 (1971): 528–37, I do not rewrite the article but reproduce it here in its original form.

2. *A Critical and Exegetical Commentary on the Second Epistle of St. Paul to the Corinthians* (Edinburgh: T&T Clark, 1915), 354, 356; my italics.

3. R. Bultmann, *Theology of the New Testament*, vol. 1, trans. Kenneth Grobel (London: SCM Press, 1952), 285.

4. Bultmann, *Theology of the New Testament*, 351.

5. Bultmann, *Theology of the New Testament*, 349.

6. Ernst Käsemann, "God's Righteousness in Paul," *Journal for Theology and Church* 1 (1965): 104.

7. Hans Windisch, *Der zweite Korintherbrief* (Göttingen: Vandenhoeck & Ruprecht, 1924), 392; trans. mine.

8. Hans Windisch, *Paulus und Christus* (Leipzig: Hinrichs, 1934), 234.

9. Windisch, *Paulus und Christus*, 192–93.

10. R. H. Strachan, *The Second Epistle of Paul to the Corinthians* (London: Hodder & Stoughton, 1965), 33.

11. See Betz, "Eine Christus-Aretalogie," 203–4. Betz classifies the logion as an "oracle of healing" (*Heilungsorakel*) presented in the style of an "aretalogy." But there remain serious differences from contemporary forms of such "aretalogies," which Betz himself recognizes: the revelation is stated in the indicative (rather than in the usual imperative for the command of healing); there is in fact no (miraculous) healing; hence the usual offering after the healing is lacking (297, 303).

12. E. Güttgemanns, *Der leidende Apostel und sein Herr* (Göttingen: Vandenhoeck & Ruprecht, 1966), 168.

13. U. Wilckens, *Weisheit und Torheit. Eine exegetisch-religionsgeschichtliche Untersuchung zu 1 Kor. und 2 Kor.* (Tübingen: J. C. B. Mohr, 1959), 218n2; see also Ernst Käsemann, *Das wandernde Gottesvolk* (Göttingen: Vandenhoeck & Ruprecht, 1957), 82–90; Walter Schmithals, *Gnosticism in Corinth*, trans. John E. Steely (Nashville: Abingdon Press, 1971), 166–217.

14. Wilckens, *Weisheit und Torheit*, 150–51.

15. For details, see Betz, "Eine Christus-Aretalogie," 304.

16. Windisch, *Der zweite Korintherbrief*, 393.

17. C. F. D. Moule, *The Phenomenon of the New Testament* (Naperville: Allenson, 1967), 22–27.

18. Güttgemanns, *Der leidende Apostel*, 162–65.

19. 1 Cor 1:8; 4:7; 6:7; 10:4, 10, etc.

20. D. Georgi, *Dei Gegner des Paulus im 2. Korintherbrief* (Tübingen: J. C. B. Mohr, 1964), 244.

21. See 2 Cor 13:4; Wilckens, *Weisheit und Torheit*, 48.

22. Wilckens, *Weisheit und Torheit*, 218.

23. Wilckens, *Weisheit und Torheit*, 218–19.

24. Schmithals, *Die Gnosis in Korinth*, 154.

25. Windisch, *Der zweite Korintherbrief*, 391.

26. K. Prümm, *Diakonia Pneumatos*, vol. 2 (Freiburg im Breisgau: Herder, 1960), 90.

Notes

27. H.-D. Wendland, *Die Briefer an die Korinther*, 8th ed. (Göttingen: Vandenhoeck & Ruprecht, 1962), 164.

28. Käsemann, *Studies in Biblical Theology*, 41; Käsemann, *Essays in New Testament Themes* (London: SCM Press, 1964), 84. In an earlier essay ("Die Legitimität des Apostels"), he stated this law as follows: "Clearly Paul recognizes here a 'divine law' that goes beyond his personal experience....God gives his grace to the earth only in, with and through weakness" (*Zeitschrift für neutestamentliche Wissenschaft* 41 [1942]: 54).

29. Windisch, *Der zweite Korintherbrief*, 391.

30. Käsemann, "Die Legitimität des Apostels": "In this place 'grace' means concretely the power which proves the apostle as representative of Christ. This power is linked to the presupposition of 'weakness'" (53).

31. Betz, "Eine Christus-Aretalogie," 297.

32. Windisch, *Der zweite Korintherbrief*, 391.

33. Plummer, *The Second Epistle of St. Paul to the Corinthians*, 354.

34. H. Lietzmann, *Der zweite Korintherbrief* (Tübingen: J. C. B. Mohr, 1949), 155.

35. Tannehill, *Dying and Rising with Christ* (Berlin: Töpelmann, 1967), 100.

36. Windisch, *Der zweite Korintherbrief*, 394.

37. Güttgemanns, *Der leidende Apostel*, 169.

38. Betz, "Eine Christus-Aretalogie," 303.

39. W. G. Kümmel, "Anhang" to Lietzmann, *Der zweite Korintherbrief*, 212 (on 155, line 53).

18. Power in Weakness

1. G. O'Collins, "Power Made Perfect in Weakness: 2 Cor 12:9–10," *Catholic Biblical Quarterly* 33 (1971): 528–37.

2. Timothy B. Savage used "through" rather than "in" for the title of his book: *Power through Weakness: Paul's Understanding of the Christian Ministry in 2 Corinthians* (Cambridge: Cambridge University Press, 1996). Yet he writes of "Christ who is his [Paul's] sufficiency *in* weakness" (63; my italics). Both in Greek and English, "in" (*en*) and "through" (*dia*) differ in meanings and are not interchangeable: it is one thing to speak of "power in weakness" but another to speak of "power through weakness."

3. On this principle that affects the reading of both scriptural and nonscriptural texts, see G. O'Collins, *Inspiration: Towards a Christian Interpretation of Biblical Inspiration* (Oxford: Oxford University Press, 2018), 156–57.

4. Reimund Bieringer et al., eds., *2 Corinthians: A Bibliography* (Leuven: Peeters, 2008), 122, 258, 324.

5. G. H. Guthrie, *2 Corinthians* (Grand Rapids: Baker Academic, 2015), 669.

6. J. Murphy-O'Connor, "The Second Letter to the Corinthians," in *The New Jerome Biblical Commentary*, ed. Raymond E. Brown, Joseph A. Fitzmyer, and Roland E. Murphy (Englewood Cliffs, NJ: Prentice Hall, 1990), 828.

7. O'Collins, "Power Made Perfect in Weakness," 534. My article should have cited Alfred Plummer's remarks on the chiasm in 1 Cor 12:9; he also points out further places in 2 Cor where the apostle uses chiasms: *Second Epistle of St. Paul to the Corinthians* (Edinburgh: T&T Clark, 1915), 354.

8. M. L. Barré, "Qumran and the 'Weakness' of Paul," *Catholic Biblical Quarterly* 42 (1980): 216–27, at 220.

9. Bruce M. Metzger, on behalf of the editorial committee of the United Bible Societies' Greek New Testament, also prefers *teleitai* (*A Textual Commentary on the Greek New Testament*, 3rd ed. [New York: United Bible Societies, 1975], 586).

10. Walter Bauer, Frederick W. Danker, William F. Arndt, and F. Wilbur Gingrich, *Greek-English Lexicon of the New Testament and Other Early Christian Literature*, 3rd ed. (Chicago: University of Chicago Press, 2000), 997. Curiously under *astheneia*, this dictionary proposes a different rendering of 2 Cor 12:9a (which mistakenly, as I argue) gives the priority to revelation: "God's [better 'Christ's'] *dunamis* manifests itself… thus in effect converting displays of weakness into heroic performance" (142). Paul is rather saying, "The risen Lord's power converts situations of weakness into heroic performance, which is then manifested and displayed as such."

11. Barré, "Qumran and the 'Weakness' of Paul," 222.

12. R. P. Martin, *2 Corinthians*, rev. ed. (Grand Rapids: Zondervan, 2014), 579.

13. Victor Furnish, *II Corinthians: A New Translation with Introduction and Commentary* (New York: Doubleday, 1984).

14. Furnish, *II Corinthians*, 551; my italics.

Notes

15. Furnish, *II Corinthians*, 513, 550–51.
16. Furnish, *II Corinthians*, 551–52.
17. Martin, *2 Corinthians*, 585.
18. See Daniel B. Wallace, *Greek Grammar beyond the Basics: An Exegetical Syntax of the New Testament* (Grand Rapids: Zondervan, 1996), 435–38, at 436.
19. R. Bieringer and J. Lambrecht, *Studies on 2 Corinthians* (Leuven: Leuven University Press, 1994), 309–33. Lambrecht also listed my article in his *Second Corinthians* (Collegeville, MN: Liturgical Press, 1999), 209, but did not interact with any of my arguments.
20. O'Collins, "Power Made Perfect in Weakness," 537.
21. Lambrecht, *Studies on 2 Corinthians*, 320.
22. O'Collins, "Power Made Perfect in Weakness," 531.
23. U. Heckel, *Kraft in Schwachheit: Untersuchungen zu 2 Kor 10—13* (Tübingen: Mohr Siebeck, 1993), 2. The translations from Heckel are my own.
24. Heckel, *Kraft in Schwachheit*, 87.
25. O'Collins, "Power in Weakness," 536.
26. Heckel, *Kraft in Schwachheit*, 104.
27. Heckel, *Kraft in Schwachheit*, 106.
28. Heckel, *Kraft in Schwachheit*, 215.
29. M. E. Thrall, *2 Corinthians 8—13* (London: T&T Clark International, 2000), 826–27; my italics.
30. Thrall, *2 Corinthians 8—13*, 828.
31. Thrall, *2 Corinthians 8—13*, 830–31.
32. Thrall, *2 Corinthians 8—13*, 831n466.
33. Martin, *2 Corinthians*, 617n975.
34. O'Collins, "Power in Weakness," 534.
35. Murray J. Harris, *The Second Epistle to the Corinthians* (Grand Rapids: Eerdmans, 2005).
36. Harris, *Second Epistle to the Corinthians*, 864.
37. O'Collins, "Power Made Perfect in Weakness," 536.
38. Harris, *Second Epistle to the Corinthians*, 864. In *Power through Weakness* Savage endorses this problematic reading of Paul: "[The apostle's humility] became the necessary pre-condition for the indwelling power of Christ (2 Cor 12:9). In other words, *the very existence* of Christ's power in Paul was conditioned [surely conditional?] on the apostle's prior humility and weakness" (167; italics original).

39. Harris agrees with me and many others in understanding *hē dunamis* of 2 Cor 12:9a as "my power": *Second Epistle to the Corinthians*, 863n187.

40. Harris, *Second Epistle to the Corinthians*, 865.

41. Harris, *Second Epistle to the Corinthians*, 864n197.

42. Harris, *Second Epistle to the Corinthians*, 864; my italics.

43. O'Collins, "Power Made Perfect in Weakness," 234.

44. Harris, *Second Epistle to the Corinthians*, 862.

45. O'Collins, "Power Made Perfect in Weakness," 234.

46. Harris, *Second Epistle to the Corinthians*, 863.

47. Harris, *Second Epistle to the Corinthians*, 863.

48. Wallace, *Greek Grammar*, 520–21.

49. Martin, *2 Corinthians*.

50. Martin, *2 Corinthians*, 585n672.

51. O'Collins, "Power Made Perfect in Weakness," 530.

52. Martin, *2 Corinthians*, 613n924.

53. Martin, *2 Corinthians*, 614.

54. Martin, *2 Corinthians*, 614.

55. Martin, *2 Corinthians*, 614.

56. Martin, *2 Corinthians*, 617.

57. O'Collins, "Power Made Perfect in Weakness," 531.

58. Martin, *2 Corinthians*, 615.

59. O'Collins, "Power Made Perfect in Weakness," 532.

60. Martin, *2 Corinthians*, 615.

61. O'Collins, "Power Made Perfect in Weakness," 529–30.

62. Martin, *2 Corinthians*, 617.

63. Martin, *2 Corinthians*, 617. As much as anyone, Martin appreciated the need to honor Paul's sequence: the gift of divine "power" in Paul's weakness precedes its "manifestation," and not vice versa, as in the way A. E. Harvey reads 2 Cor 12:9–10 (*Renewal through Suffering* [Edinburgh: T&T Clark, 1996], 104). Savage also seems to endorse the mistaken sequence: first the manifestation of weakness and then the operation of the Lord's power (*Power through Weakness*, 177).

64. Martin, *2 Corinthians*, 616.

INDEX OF NAMES

Aguilar, E. xii, xv
Aletti, J.-N. 245
Allison, D. C. 34, 216
Anscombe, G. E. M. 244
Aquinas, St. Thomas 176
Arndt, W. F. 205, 223, 243, 249, 256
Augustine of Hippo, St. 238
Avis, Paul xv

Balz, H. 249
Barré, M. L. 193, 256
Barrett, C. K. 110-11, 116, 142-44, 160, 230, 235, 237-38, 241-43, 246
Bauckham, R. 17, 75, 210, 225-26, 236-37, 242
Bauer, W. 168, 172, 178-79, 205, 223, 243, 249, 253, 256
Beale, G. K. 220
Benoit, P. 97, 214, 232
Betz, H.-D. 181, 188, 190, 253-55
Bieringer, R. 237, 256-57
Black, C. C. 30, 214-15
Blass, F. 168, 249
Bock, D. L. 140, 144, 242
Bockmuehl, M. 225
Boismard, M.-E. 238
Bonaventure, St. 224

Bond, H. K. 241
Boring, M. E. 10, 12, 18, 20, 41, 208-9, 211-12, 218
Botticelli, Sandro 63-65
Bovon, F. *passim*
Breytenbach, C. 244
Brock, A. G. 118, 234, 236
Brown, R. E. *passim*
Bruce, F. F. 97, 231, 248, 250
Bryan, C. 226-27, 229
Bultmann, R. viii, 27, 34, 110, 116, 182-83, 186, 189, 196, 199, 213, 234, 253
Byrne, B. xii, 125, 228, 237, 240-42, 244

Calvin, J. 142, 144, 243
Catchpole, D. xii
Celsus 233
Chadwick, H. 233, 252
Clement of Alexandria 77
Clement of Rome, St. 86, 113
Coady, C. A. J. 234
Cohn, H. 233
Collins, R. F. 167-68, 170, 173, 247-48, 250-52
Conzelmann, H. 141, 143-44, 243
Cook, J. G. 207

Craig, C. L. 161, 163, 246
Crilly, D. xii
Cross, F. L. 219, 230
Crossan, J. D. viii, 27–34, 213–16
Crouch, J. E. 205, 211, 213, 228–29, 231, 234, 242
Cullmann, O. 73, 224
Culpepper, R. A. 119, 236, 238, 241–42
Cyril of Alexandria, St. 107

Danker, F. W. 168, 172, 178–79, 205, 223, 243, 249, 253, 256
Davey, F. N. 234
Davis, S. T. 228, 230, 245
Debrunner, A. 168, 249
Deer, D. S. 205
Denaux, A. 238
Denzinger, H. 227
De Vaux, R. 212
Dhanis, E. 228
Dibelius, M. 30
Dillon, R. 104, 233
Dodd, C. H. 110–11, 116, 235
Donahue, J. R. 10, 12, 208
Donfried, K. P. 224, 226, 228, 230
Duke, P. 239
Dunn, J. D. G. xii, 154, 219, 244–45
Dupuis, J. 227
Dwyer, T. 41, 218

Edwards, J. R. 27, 34, 98, 210, 216, 218, 231–32
Eliade, M. xiv
Endean, P. 222
Engberg-Pederson, T. 245
Ernst, J. 34, 98–99, 101, 103, 216, 232
Evans, C. F. 95, 231

Farrow, D. 219
Fee, G. D. 160, 246
Filson, F. V. 224
Fitzgerald, J. T. 245
Fitzmyer, J. A. *passim*
Foçant, C. 10, 13, 15, 20, 34, 42–43, 208–9, 212, 216, 219
France, R. T. 210
Francis of Assisi, St. 63
Fraser, J. W. 243
Freedman, D. N. xiv, 213
Frey, J. 236, 241
Freyne, S. 3–4, 205
Fuller, R. H. 30, 214–15
Funk, R. W. 249
Furnish, V. P. 193–94, 197, 200, 245, 256–57

Gadamer, H.-G. 192
Geertgen Tot Sint Jans 63
Georgi, D. 185, 199, 254
Gingrich, W. 205, 223, 243, 249, 256
Glorieux, F. 223
Gnilka, J. 27, 34, 210, 214, 220
Goguel, M. 242
Grant, R. 236
Grappe, C. ix, 73–74, 77, 91, 224, 226–27
Green, J. B. 30–31, 214–15
Gregersen, N. xv
Gregory the Great, St. 87, 107, 113, 117, 234
Grelot, P. 76
Grobel, K. 253
Grundmann, W. 98–99, 101, 232
Grünewald, M. 63
Guillaume, J.-M. 103, 232–33

Index of Names

Guthrie, G. H. 192, 256
Güttgemanns, E. 184, 189, 254–55

Haenchen, E. 143–44, 231, 243
Harnack, A. von 32
Harrington, D. J. 10, 12, 208
Harris, M. J. 197–98, 200, 257–58
Harvey, A. E. 258
Harvey, J. W. 217
Hasitschka, M. 236, 238, 240
Haskins, S. 233
Hayes, M. A. xv
Hays, R. B. 250
Heckel, U. 195–96, 198, 201, 257
Hedrick, C. W. 232
Hengel, M. ix, 73–77, 224–25, 228, 230
Henn, W. 230
Hilary of Poitiers, St. 107
Hippolytus of Rome, St. 87, 107, 113, 230, 234
Hodges 108, 235
Hoehner, H. W. xii
Holladay, C. R. 140, 242
Holland, H. S. 119–20, 135, 236
Homer 209, 223
Hooker, M. D. 10, 14–15, 27, 31, 34–35, 37–39, 48, 209, 214–15, 217–18, 220
Hoskyns, E. 110, 116, 234
Hug, J. 219, 235, 251
Hultgren, A. J. 211
Hünermann, P. 227
Hunsinger, G. 245
Hurtado, L. xv, 241

Ignatius Loyola, St. 61–65, 72, 222–23

Ignatius of Antioch, St. 77, 86, 113
Irenaeus, St. 77, 86, 113, 220

Jenkins, P. 86, 230
Jeremias, J. 167, 248
Jerome, St. 11, 107, 238
Jervell, J. 143–45, 243
John Chrysostom, St. 107
John Paul II, Pope St. 78–79
Johnson, L. T. 54, 57–58, 60, 221–22, 251
Jones, M. K. 221
Josephus, Flavius 106, 233
Justin Martyr, St. 62, 77, 86, 113

Karris, R. J. 246
Käsemann, E. 157, 182–83, 187–88, 246, 253–55
Kaufman, G. D. 153, 244
Keener, C. S. 120, 141, 144, 219–20, 230, 237–38, 240–43
Kelber, W. H. 213
Kendall, D. vii, xii–xiv, 225, 228, 230, 245, 250–52
Kessler, W. T. 225
Keylock, L. R. 208, 212, 216, 219
Koester, C. R. 237
Kon, G. A. 234
Krause, D. 16, 209–10
Kremer, J. 173–74, 249, 251–52
Kümmel, W. 190, 255

Lambrecht, J. 155, 194–95, 244, 246, 257
Lapham, F. 82, 228
LaVerdière, E. 104, 233
Leo the Great, St. 87, 107, 113, 230, 233

Levine, A.-J. 209
Licona, M. R. 250, 252
Lietzmann, H. 188, 255
Lightfoot, R. H. viii, 35–36, 217
Limburg, J. 243
Lincoln, A. T. 83–84, 118, 130, 157, 219, 228–30, 234, 236–42, 246
Linss, W. C. 243
Livingstone, E. A. 219, 230
Loader, W. 132, 239–41
Lohfink, G. 100, 232
Lohse, E. 157, 246
Louw, J. P. 248
Luther, M. 65, 222, 224
Luz, U. 19, 26–27, 29, 107, 109, 205–7, 211, 213–15, 229, 234, 243

Madvig, D. H. 211, 216, 220
Magness, J. L. 42–43, 218–19
Marcheselli, M. 119, 135, 237–42
Marcus, J. *passim*
Marsh, J. 213, 234
Marshall, I. H. 95–99, 101–2, 231–32, 251
Martin, R. P. 193–94, 196, 198–201, 256–58
Marucci, C. 238
Marxsen, W. 175, 226
Matera, F. J. 214
Mathieu, Y. 238
McDonald, W. J. G. 243
McHugh, J. 212
McKay, K. L. 247
McNulty, T. M. vii, xii–xiii, 243
Meier, J. P. 29, 214
Merrigan, T. 223
Metzger, B. 205–6, 256

Michaelis, W. 250
Miller, J. M. 79, 227
Miller, S. 11, 208, 210
Milligan, G. 178, 253
Mirecki, P. A. 214
Moloney, F. J. 10, 13–15, 19, 21, 35, 37, 39–40, 51–53, 209, 211–12, 218, 221, 228, 237
Morris, L. 96–97, 231
Mosser, C. 242
Moule, C. F. D. xi, 254
Moulton, J. H. 178, 253
Mülhaupt, E. 224
Munitiz, J. A. 222
Murphy, R. E. 244, 256
Murphy-O'Connor, J. 192, 256

Neuner, J. 227
Newsom, C. A. 208
Nida, E. A. 248
Nineham, D. E. 10–13, 18, 20, 34–36, 42–43, 51, 207–8, 211–12, 216–17, 220
Noble, B. 231, 243
Nolland, J. 221–22, 229

O'Connell, M. J. xiv
Origen 62, 69, 106, 175, 233, 252
Otto, R. 37, 217

Pagels, E. 114, 236
Paul VI, Pope St. 92
Perkins, P. 114–15, 117, 226, 236
Perrin, N. 35, 37–38, 217, 248
Pervo, R. I. 141, 144, 242

Index of Names

Pesch, R. ix, 34–37, 41–43, 73–74, 76–77, 210, 216–17, 220, 224, 226
Pfammatter, J. 168
Phillips, J. B. 166, 248
Plummer, A. 96–97, 99, 182, 188–89, 198, 200, 231, 247, 255–56
Poehlmann, W. R. 246
Porter, S. E. xiv, 27, 34, 213, 215
Prümm, K. 187, 254
Puglisi, J. F. 230

Quinn, J. D. 251, 253

Rastoin, M. 238
Renan, E. 106, 233
Rengstorf, K. H. 168
Reumann, J. 224, 226, 228, 230
Ricciotti, G. 107, 233
Ringe, S. H. 208
Robertson, A. 247
Robinson, J. M. 229, 246
Roloff, J. 76
Rousseau, A. 220
Rudolph, K. 235

Sampley, J. P. 156, 245
Satgé, J. de 227
Savage, T. B. 255, 257–58
Schmid, J. 97, 232
Schmithals, W. 186, 254
Schnackenburg, R. 108, 111, 116–17, 234–35
Schneider, G. 249
Schottroff, L. 16
Schrage, W. xi, 167–69, 177, 247, 249–52

Schüssler Fiorenza, E. 16, 112–14, 210, 235–36
Schweitzer, A. 32, 215
Schweizer, E. 19, 21, 34, 51–52, 210–12, 216, 220–21
Shinn, G. 231, 243
Siebenrock, R. 223
Sinai, Y. 233
Smit, P.-B. 210
Smith, D. 234
Snape, H. C. 242
Spadafora, F. 107, 233
Spicq, C. 160, 246
Stanton, G. xii
Stein, R. H. 34, 210, 216
Steely, J. E. 254
Strachan, R. H. 183, 254
Strauss, M. L. 210
Sturtevant, J. S. 241

Tannehill, R. C. ix, 54, 56–58, 60, 83, 188, 221–22, 228, 255
Taylor, V. 34, 49, 51, 210, 216, 220–21
Thayer, J. 167, 248
Thiselton, A. C. 161–63, 167–68, 175, 247, 249–50, 252
Thomas, C. M. 206, 212, 221, 229
Thompson, M. M. 237–38, 240–41
Thrall, M. 154–57, 196–97, 199–201, 244–45, 257
Tillard, J.-M.-R. 79, 227, 230
Tolbert, M. A. 16, 208
Tolmie, F. 241
Torrance, T. F. viii, 44–45, 49, 51–53, 219–21
Towner, P. H. 251

Trapp, T. H. 224
Tyler, P. xv
Tyrrell, G. 32, 215

Van Iersel, B. M. F. 24, 211

Wacker, W. C. 251, 253
Wallace, D. B. 162–64, 168, 198, 201, 208–9, 246–47, 249, 251, 257–58
Wallraff, M. 241
Weatherhead, B. 214, 232
Weiser, A. 219
Wendland, H.-D. 187, 255
Wilckens, U. 184, 186, 254

Windisch, H. 182–83, 185–89, 200, 254–55
Wink, W. 214
Wittgenstein, L. 150, 244
Woods, R. xv
Wright, N. T. 215, 250, 252–53

Yarbro Collins, A. 16, 19, 21, 210–13, 228–29
Young, F. xii

Zizzamia, A. I. 233
Zmijewski, J. 198–99
Zumstein, J. 237

BIBLICAL INDEX

Old Testament

Genesis
9:5	21
9:13	21
9:18–27	23
12:1	251
12:7	167, 169, 250
15:12	40
17:1	169, 250
18:8	98
19:3	98
26:2	250
26:24	250
27:27	21
28:20	21
35:9	250
37:29	21
37:34	21
38:14	21
38:19	21
44:13	21

Exodus
3:2	169
24:16–17	124

Leviticus
9:23	124
13:6	21
13:17	21
13:22	21
13:27	21
13:34	21
13:45	23
14:8	21
14:9	21
14:14	21
14:47	22
15:5	22
15:6	22
16:26	22
16:28	22
19:19	22
21:10	22

Numbers
16:19	124

Deuteronomy
7:12–13	23
21:22–23	26, 30

JOSHUA		DANIEL	
9:4–5	24	4:10–15	8
9:13	24	7:15	37
		7:28	36
JUDGES		8:17	37
6:12	169	8:27	37
6:15	56	10:7	37
		10:15	40
1 KINGS			
8:11	124	MICAH	
		5:2–5a	70
2 KINGS			
5:7	23	TOBIT	
		3:16—12:22	98
PSALMS		12:19	98
9:12	6		
74:19	6	WISDOM	
74:23	6	7:4–7	63
102:26	22		
104:14–15	23		
110:1	48–49		

New Testament

ISAIAH		MATTHEW	
1:3	63	1:3	11
6:5	251	1:18	100
25:6	23	4:19	238
35:6–8	11	6:3	3
37:1	23	6:16–18	212
50:9	22	7:24–27	3
51:8	22	8:14–15	11
52:15	179	9:16–17	19
59:17	22	10:29–31	vii, 3, 5
63:1–6	22	11:10	172
64:6	22	11:29–30	3
		12:11	vii, 3, 6–7, 206
EZEKIEL		13:14–15	179
16:13	22	13:31–32	vii, 3, 8
16:39	22	13:55	3
17:22–24	8	14:28–33	84, 229
31:1–18	8	16:1–4	vii, 3, 5
		16:2–3	205

Biblical Index

16:16b–19	84, 229	1:41	14, 209
16:17–19	73–74	1:44	41
16:18	89	2:1	14
16:18–19	75, 77–79	2:1–12	14, 18
17:3	171, 249	2:9	12
17:20	8	2:11	12
26:56	104	2:13–17	18
27:52–53	249	2:17	18
27:57–58	33	2:18–20	11
27:57–61	139	2:18–22	18
27:62	142	2:19–20	18
27:62–66	142, 243	2:21–22	viii, 18–19, 21, 211–13
28:1–10	84		
28:1–15	141	3:1–6	14
28:1–20	108	3:3	12
28:5	114	3:10	14
28:7	84, 115, 172–73	3:13–19	177
28:9	174, 229	3:16	81
28:9–10	75, 84–85, 107–9, 229, 235	3:31–35	11
		4:12	179
28:10	115	4:30–32	8
28:16–20	95	4:35–41	36
28:17	100, 172	4:40–41	39
		4:41	36
Mark		5:15	39
1—15	39	5:21–43	11
1:2	172	5:24–34	14
1:3	43	5:25–34	14
1:12–13	12	5:27–31	14
1:13	15	5:34	38
1:16–18	viii, 81, 89	5:41	12–14
1:16–20	122	6:3	11
1:17	212, 238	6:5	14
1:18–19	17	6:6	16
1:22	212	6:7–13	177
1:29	12	6:14	12
1:29–31	viii, 10, 13, 17, 39, 207, 210	6:14–29	11
		6:16	12
1:31	viii, 16, 210	6:52	38

267

6:56	14	15:40	38
7:24–30	11, 14	15:40–41	viii, 12, 15, 37–39
7:29	38	15:40—16:8	11, 14
7:32–33	14	15:41	13, 16–17, 210
8:14–21	38	15:42–47	viii, 26, 139
8:22–25	14	15:43	33
8:33	81	15:44–45	27
9:4	166, 168, 171, 173, 249	15:47	38–39, 141
9:6	39	16:1	38
9:9–13	39	16:1–8	26, 37, 39, 42, 84, 107, 111, 213, 234
9:14–29	14	16:2	42
9:26–27	12	16:6	12, 114, 209
9:32	39	16:6–7	40
10:33	39	16:7	viii, 17, 35, 76, 81, 100, 114–15, 172–73, 175, 178, 218, 226, 228
10:35	12		
10:35–45	12		
10:41	12	16:8	viii, 35–40, 43, 203, 217
10:43	12		
10:45	12, 15	16:9	85, 174, 229, 248
10:46–52	14	16:9–11	85, 113, 235
10:49	12	16:9–20	44–46, 51, 86, 109, 113, 220, 235
10:52	208		
12:26	12, 15	16:11	166, 174
12:36	48	16:12	174, 248
12:41–44	11, 38	16:12–20	113
13:6–27	175	16:14	100
14:3–9	11, 17, 38, 210	16:15–16	46
14:5–9	38	16:15–18	46–47
14:14	67	16:16	46
14:28	12, 218, 226	16:19	49
14:50	39, 103	16:19–20	viii, 44–45, 50–51, 53, 219
14:51–52	38		
14:52	39	16:20	45–47, 51–53, 220
14:62	48		
14:63	23	Luke	
14:66–69	11	1—2	58
14:66–72	81	1:1–4	100, 143
14:72	89	1:2	87
15:33	42		

268

Biblical Index

1:5	11	2:29	ix, 54–55, 58–59
1:5–20	173	2:30	179
1:11	166, 168, 171, 249	2:36–38	59
1:15	57	2:37	212
1:17	57	2:37–38	60
1:20	37	3:6	178
1:26–38	ix, 54, 100	3:22	100
1:27	56	4:38–39	11
1:31	55	5	83
1:32	57	5:1–11	83–84, 227–29, 238
1:33	57	5:8	91
1:35	56, 57	5:10	89
1:36	55, 57	5:36	19
1:37	56	6:14	83
1:38	ix, 54–58	7:13	70
1:45	59	7:18	20
1:48	56, 59	7:27	172
1:51–54	56	7:36–50	102, 234
1:54–55	60	7:37	106
2:1–20	61	8:4–15	68
2:1–5	61	9:10–17	99, 103
2:7	ix, 62, 64–67, 223	9:11–17	68
2:8–9	65	9:12	66
2:8–20	65	9:16	103
2:10	65	9:31	171
2:12	65	10:2–12	104
2:13–14	64–65	10:7	104
2:14	65	10:9	104
2:15	64	10:29	68
2:16	65	10:29–37	68
2:19	72	10:33	70
2:22–38	54, 58	10:34	64, 67
2:23–24	60	11:1	20
2:25	58–60	12:6	206
2:25–27	59	12:6–7	5
2:25–35	58	12:16–21	224
2:26	59	12:37	102
2:27	60	12:54–56	4
2:28	59	13:15	7, 62, 206

269

13:18–19	7, 206, 213	24:9	109
13:20–21	7, 213	24:9–11	82
13:29	102	24:10	109
14:1–2	102	24:11	110
14:5	6–7	24:12	82, 228
14:28–30	3	24:13–35	101–2, 177
15:3–7	68, 213	24:15	174
15:8–10	213	24:15–16	102
16:19–31	104, 224	24:23	110
17:22	175	24:24	173
18:10–14	224	24:26	ix, 102, 105
19:1–10	70, 102–3	24:30	102–3
19:5	70	24:31	102, 174, 176
19:7	66, 70–71	24:33	82
22:7–13	70	24:34	ix, 73, 76–77, 79, 81–83, 87, 104, 115, 165–67, 170, 172–73, 225–26, 228, 236, 249–50
22:8–12	67		
22:10	55		
22:11	ix, 64, 67, 71		
22:12	71		
22:14–23	99	24:35	102–3
22:15–20	71	24:36	174
22:19	72, 102	24:36–43	101–2, 104
22:29–30	177	24:36–49	95, 115
22:30	103	24:39	99, 173
22:31–32	73, 75, 77–79, 83, 104	24:42	103–4
		24:42–43	ix, 94, 96–97, 99, 102–3, 105, 203
22:31–34	228		
22:32	82, 87, 236	24:43	94–95, 99, 101–2, 231
22:43	168, 171, 249		
22:61	89, 104	24:44–47	102
22:61–62	89	24:47–49	102
23:49	89, 104	24:49	48, 101
23:50–56	x, 33, 139, 142	24:50–51	101
23:53	63	24:52	66
23:55–56	141		
23:56b—24:53	108	JOHN	
24	102, 234	1:1	120
24:1–11	84	1:1–18	123
24:4	66	1:3–4	121

Biblical Index

1:4–9	121	5:19	120
1:7	133	5:19–47	128
1:8	133	5:20	240
1:14	120, 132–33	5:24	120
1:15	133	5:25	120
1:16	132	5:37	251
1:18	251	6	240–41
1:19	123	6:1	129
1:19–36	133	6:1–15	126, 128, 240
1:19—2:12	239	6:4–13	129
1:31	123, 239	6:8	127
1:35–40	132	6:8–11	129
1:35–42	122	6:9	126
1:38	120, 125	6:11	240
1:42	131	6:12–13	127
1:43	124	6:13	121, 129
1:45–46	124	6:19	239
1:45–51	124	6:22–59	128, 134
1:49	124	6:22–61	121
1:50	134, 239	6:22–71	130
1:51	120, 239	6:27	129
2:1–11	124, 240	6:35	129
2:3–4	130	6:44	127
2:11	123, 239	6:46	251
3:3	120	6:51	129
3:4	132	6:60–65	132
3:5	120	6:66–71	122, 129
3:11	120	6:67	125
3:16	126	6:67–68	131
3:16–17	128	7:4	123
3:29	124	7:5	80
3:35	240	7:6	123
4:31–38	128, 135	8:14	133
4:32	129	8:31	120
4:34	129	8:32	133
4:35–38	129	8:51	120
4:38	129	9:1–39	121
4:50	120	9:5	121
5:6–9	128	9:6–7	128

9:39—10:18	128	14:23	240
10:1–8	131	14:24	120
10:3	110	14:28	240
10:10	121	14:31	240
10:11	69	15:4–5	123, 134
10:11–15	131	15:5	128
10:11–18	121	15:8	132
10:14	69	15:9	240
10:16	128	15:10	240
10:16–17	128	15:12	240
10:17	240	15:12–17	125
10:17–18	131	15:13	240
11:3	240	15:14	240
11:5	125, 240	15:15	240
11:25	121	15:16	122
11:35	127	15:17	240
11:50	125	15:19	240
11:51	125	15:27	133
11:52	128	16:2–3	122
12:1–11	130	16:27	240
12:4–8	130	17:1	132
12:28	132	17:5	132
12:32	127	17:6	239
13—17	126	17:18	129
13:1	240	17:18–23	122
13:12	125	17:19	132
13:21–30	130	17:23	240
13:23	125, 132, 240	17:24	240
13:31–32	132	17:26	240
13:33	126	18:10	127
13:34	126	18:15–18	122, 130
13:35	240	18:18	129
13:36	89, 131	18:25	129
13:36–38	122	18:25–27	122, 130
14:6	121, 133–34	19:25–27	130, 132
14:12	122, 128	19:31	144
14:15	125, 240	19:34–37	132
14:21	240	19:35	241

Biblical Index

19:38–42	139	21:1–23	95
20	x, 110–11, 116–17, 122	21:1–25	109
		21:2	124
20:1–2	84	21:3	122–23, 238
20:2	240	21:4	121, 133, 174
20: 2–10	130, 229	21:5	120, 123, 125–26, 128, 134–35
20:3–10	122, 228		
20:4–6	130	21:6	121, 127
20:6–8	126	21:7	126, 130
20:10	110	21:8	121, 127
20:11–18	75, 83–85, 106, 108, 123	21:9	127, 129
		21:9–14	94
20:11–29	239	21:10	129
20:12	173	21:10–11	127
20:14	175	21:11	121
20:14–18	235	21:12	175
20:16	175	21:13	95, 100, 129
20:18	86, 115, 172–73, 175, 178	21:14	123, 174, 239
		21:15	126, 241
20:19	122, 174	21:15–17	73, 77–79, 83, 89, 91, 125, 129, 131, 241
20:19–29	95		
20:21	129		
20:21–22	122	21:15–18	75
20:22–23	100	21:15–19	126, 128, 227
20:24–25	100	21:16	120, 126
20:24–29	122	21:17	120, 126
20:24, 26	174	21:18	120, 133
20:27	175	21:18–19	89, 91, 120, 131, 230
20:28	238		
20:29	173	21:19	131
20:31	242	21:20	129
21	x, 83, 119–21, 123–24, 127–35, 228, 236–42	21:20–24	133
		21:20–25	126, 132
21:1	123, 129, 174, 239	21:22	131
		21:22–23	132
21:1–3	122	21:23–25	132
21:1–14	83, 105, 134, 236	21:24	132–33

Acts		8:23	179
1:1–2	100	8:29	48
1:3	174	9:7	83
1:4	94–95, 97, 101–3	9:10–16	48
		9:17	172–73, 249
1:4–5	101	9:27	172
1:6–11	101	9:32–42	87
1:8	101	10:1—11:18	87
1:13	87	10:19	48
1:15–26	87	10:30	212
1:21	102	10:40	169, 174, 249
2	101	10:40–41	94
2:1–4	100	10:41	94–95, 97, 101–3
2:1–13	178	13	x
2:3	167	13:2–3	212
2:8–11	93	13:16b–41	139
2:14	87, 143	13:27–31	139, 141, 144
2:23–24	143	13:28–31	x, 139, 141–43
2:24–32	141	13:31	165–66, 172–73, 249–50
2:25–32	143		
2:32	87	14:23	212
2:33	48, 176	15:1–29	87
3:1	224	16:6	48
3:1–10	87	16:7	48
3:11	224	16:9	172
3:13–15	88, 144	18:9–10	48
4:3	224	19:1–7	20
4:10	88	19:22	12, 172, 232
4:24	54	22:9	83
4:32–35	104	22:17–21	48
5:15–16	87	26:13	83
5:30–32	88	26:16	172–73, 249
7:2	172, 249	26:19	253
7:26	171, 249	27:9	212
7:30	171, 249	28:11–31	89
7:35	171		
7:55–56	50	Romans	
8:14	224	1:1	56
8:14–17	87	5:1	245

Biblical Index

5:5	100	12	188
5:8	158	12:1–13	178
5:8–11	x, 149, 153, 244	12:9	256–57
5:10	245	13	xi, 160
6:1–23	15	13:1–13	159
6:3–4	15	13:4	161, 247
8:26–27	49	13:4–8a	x, 159–60, 63–64, 247
8:34	49, 53	14:1–40	178
10:9	165, 169	15	81, 85, 166–69, 178, 248–49
11:15	153, 156–57, 244–45	15:1–11	227
12:9	160	15:3–5	26, 40, 80–81, 115, 144, 167
12:9–21	xi, 163–64	15:3–8	116
13:10	160	15:4a	26
15:21	179	15:4	165, 168–69
15:25	12	15:4–5	82
16:1–16	85	15:5	75–77, 82–83, 111, 115, 165, 169, 225–26, 248
1 CORINTHIANS		15:5–7	85, 95, 100
1:8	254	15:5–8	ix, xi, 80, 85, 111, 165–70, 172–74, 177, 203, 249–50
1:12	81	15:6	169–70, 178, 248
1:24	185	15:7	111, 176
1:25–27	188	15:8	83, 170, 177–78, 199, 250
1:25–28	188	15:11	81, 144
1:26–28	188	15:12–58	176
2:3–4	188–89	15:20	176, 252
3:22	81	15:23	176
4:7	254	15:35–54	95
6:7	254	15:42–44	252
6:12–13	95	15:43	184
6:13	96	15:44	175
7:11	151, 156	15:45–49	252
9:1	85, 116, 166, 170, 173–74, 177–78, 199, 250, 252		
9:5	81, 207		
9:25–27	212		
10:4	254		
10:10	254		
11:23–26	100, 199		

2 CORINTHIANS
3:3	209
4:1	185
4:6	250
4:7	188
4:7–12	188
4:7–15	195
4:8–12	185
4:12	188
5:12–13	186
5:18–21	x, 149, 153, 155
5:19	156–57, 245–46
5:21	245
6:4	209
6:4–10	185
6:5	212
10	186
10:4	186
11	186
11:8	209
11:23	209
11:23–33	185
11:27	212
11:30	190
12	186
12:1–4	171, 177, 252
12:1–7	186
12:1–10	187
12:4	37, 177
12:5	190
12:5–10	186
12:7	186, 194, 200
12:7–10	181, 189, 253
12:9–10	xi, 181–82, 189, 191, 195–96, 201, 255, 258
12:11	187
12:12	187
13:3–4	182
13:4	254

GALATIANS
1:12	169–70, 174, 178
1:15–16	165, 169, 197
1:16	170, 174–75, 178
2:1–2	170
2:10	185
2:11–21	91
4:6	178
4:14	172
5:6	160
5:22	160

EPHESIANS
1:19–20	49
1:21–22	49
2:20	90
3:4	46
6:5	40

PHILIPPIANS
2:6–11	159
2:12	40
2:25	85
3:2—4:1	171
3:8	171, 175
3:10	171, 175
3:11	175
3:20	175
3:21	175
4:18	85

COLOSSIANS
1:15	251
1:15–20	158–59
1:19–20	157
1:20	157, 246

Biblical Index

3:1	50	1 Peter	
3:4	50	1:3	227
		1:8	173
1 Thessalonians		1:21	227
1:10	165	2:4–8	89
		3:21	227
1 Timothy		3:22	49–50
1:17	251	5:1	227
3:16	165–66, 172–73, 249	5:1–4	227
6:16	251	2 Peter	
		1:16–18	227
Hebrews			
1:13	48	1 John	
2:3–4	51	3:10	179
2:8	179	4:12	251
7:25	53		
8:1	50	3 John	
9:28	175	11	179–80
10:12	50		
11:27	251	Revelation	
		1:13	50
James		11:19	171
2:24	179	12:1–3	171
		14:14	50